Christ the One and Only

A Global Affirmation of the Uniqueness of Jesus Christ

Edited by

Sung Wook Chung

Foreword by

Alister E. McGrath

PATERNOSTER

Baker Academic
Grand Rapids, Michigan

First published in 2005 by Paternoster Press in the UK and
Baker Academic in the USA

11 10 09 08 07 06 05   7 6 5 4 3 2 1

Paternoster Press is an imprint of Authentic Media,
9 Holdom Avenue, Bletchley, Milton Keynes, MK1 1QR, UK
www.authenticmedia.co.uk/paternoster
Baker Academic is a division of Baker Publishing Group,
PO Box 6287, Grand Rapids, MI 49516-6287
www.bakeracademic.com

British Library Cataloguing in Publication Data
A catalogue record for this book is available from the British Library

ISBN 1-84227-344-26

Library of Congress Cataloging-in-Publication Data
Library of Congress Cataloging-in-Publication Data is on file at the
Library of Congress, Washington, DC

ISBN 0-8010-2854-X

Cover Design by fourninezero
Typeset by GCS, Leighton Buzzard, Beds.
Print Management by Adare Carwin
Printed and Bound in the US by Dickinson Press

"What does it mean to affirm Jesus Christ as the only Lord and Saviour in our globalizing and pluralistic world? A distinguished team of international scholars provides thoughtful reflection on complex issues, thereby enriching a Christian theology of religions. Theologians and missiologists alike will profit from these stimulating essays."

Harold Netland, Professor of Philosophy of Religion and Intercultural Studies, Trinity Evangelical Divinity School

"This collection of essays covers the full spectrum of evangelical responses to the challenges raised by our contemporary experience of religious pluralism. And the breadth of this spectrum should not be underestimated, as alongside the expected evangelistic and apologetic approaches are dialogical engagements with other religious traditions that do not deny the uniqueness of Christ, but take the other faith perspectives seriously on their own terms. Make no mistake: the three essays on the Jewish-Christian relations, on the Buddhist-Christian dialogue, and on the Confucian-Christian encounter (by Ellen Charry, Paul Chung, and K.K. Yeo respectively) are resolutely evangelical but yet mark significant developments in evangelical theology today insofar as they insist on engaging the other side at its points of strength."

Amos Yong, Associate Research Professor of Theology, Regent University School of Theology

"A powerful exposition of biblical Christianity in the face of the challenges of syncretism and pluralism."

Donald G. Bloesch, Emeritus Professor of Theology, University of Dubuque Theological Seminary

"*Christ the One and Only* is for those of us who embrace missional dialogue as the most effective means to discuss the uniqueness of Christ with those of other religious traditions. The book provides numerous practical examples of how we can find common ground that will result in fertile soil for our confession of Christ."

Craig Williford, President, Denver Seminary

"A valuable collection of essays on one of the most important theological issues of our day. By parsing the life, work and teachings of Jesus into separable 'uniquenesses', the full meaning and importance the uniqueness of Jesus Christ gains clarity, richness and depth. By identifying the most important social touch points of Christ's uniqueness – with Judaism, Buddhism, Confucianism – the unavoidable centrality of this Christian doctrine becomes manifest. Yet all done with the love and grace that Jesus' uniqueness teaches. A book for today."

Terry C. Muck, Professor of Mission and World Religion, Asbury Theological Seminary

"All these essays are competent, some are outstanding, and between them they cover most of today's convoluted waterfront of debate about who and what Jesus of Nazareth was and where authentic Christianity stands among the religions. The symposium is a significant and successful counter to relativistic diminishings of Christ."

J.I. Packer, Professor of Theology, Regent College, Vancouver

Contents

Preface

Sung Wook Chung

Christian faith is grounded upon a confession that Jesus Christ is the Son of God and the only Savior of humanity. Christianity has been affirming the absolute uniqueness and majesty of Jesus Christ and this affirmation has distinguished Christian faith from other religious and philosophical traditions. Christian faith uncompromisingly affirms the uniqueness of the person and work of Jesus Christ manifest in his birth, life, miracles, teachings, sufferings, death, resurrection and ascension. The confession of the incomparable uniqueness of Jesus Christ is closely connected with the very identity of Christianity.

We are living in an age of a great change. Many religious sociologists and cultural critics have recently argued that Christianity is now a post-Western religion and Western society is a post-Christian society. On account of the rapid and drastic secularization, Christianity has been declining in continental Europe ever since the end of the Second World War. For example, although the United Kingdom has been regarded as a Christian nation for many years, only less than ten percent of the total population of Britain is currently attending churches regularly on Sundays. In contrast, Islam and Hinduism are growing rapidly in Britain, Spain, and France. In the continent of North America, the USA is rapidly becoming a melting pot in terms of race as well as religion. We have about one million Muslims, three million Jews, three million Mormons, more than one million Buddhists, more than one million Hindus and many other adherents to various religious traditions other than Christianity in America. Therefore, America cannot be called a Christian nation any longer in any sense.

Along with the process of multiplication of religions in the West, the centers of Christianity have been moving from the first world to the third world, including Asia, Africa, and Latin America. For example, Christianity in South Korea has been growing rapidly. South Korea now has the largest churches in the world, the largest Pentecostal church, the largest Presbyterian church, the largest Methodist church, and so on. Moreover, South Korea is currently sending more Christian missionaries than any other country all over the world. In China, we gain more than 30,000 new Christian converts per day and scholars estimate that China may currently have more than 100 million Christians. Christianity in Africa is also rapidly growing, especially in Nigeria. We have a similar story in Latin America. Brazil now has more than forty million Evangelical Christians besides 120 million Roman Catholic Christians, and Evangelical Christianity is enjoying a tremendous growth in Brazil and other Latin American countries. As a result, two-thirds of the total Christian population of the globe lives in the non-Western or the Two-Thirds World. Christianity is not a Western religion any longer; it is a world religion or a global religion.

In this context of the rapid globalization of Christianity, this book aims to reaffirm the absolute uniqueness of Jesus Christ as the only Lord and Savior of humanity. In doing so, this book intends to reconfirm the identity of Christian faith as a religion centered on the person and work of Jesus Christ. Furthermore, this book will demonstrate that Christians are ready to be engaged in dialogues with other religions without com-promising the absolute truth claims of Christianity. For Christians, interfaith dialogues provide excellent opportunities for missional engagement.

It is one of the outstanding features of this book that Christian theologians from various backgrounds not only denominationally but also ethnically make contributions to a global affirmation of the uniqueness of Christianity. Among the contributors, we have scholars who are working in Asia, Australia, Europe, North America and Latin America. I humbly hope that this book will become a useful reference for numerous Christians all over the world who want to celebrate and defend the uniqueness of Christian faith in the face of the challenge of religious pluralism and syncretism. Special thanks go to my wife, In-Kyung, who helped me with the editing of this book.

Sung Wook Chung

Contributors

Ellen T. Charry is Margaret W. Harmon Associate Professor of Systematic Theology, Princeton Theological Seminary, Princeton, New Jersey, USA. She received a BA degree from Barnard College and a doctor of philosophy degree from Temple University. She was formerly taught at Perkins School of Theology, Southern Methodist University, Dallas, Texas, USA. Her major publications are *By the Renewing of Your Mind: The Pastoral Function of Christian Doctrine* (New York: Oxford University Press, 1999) and *Inquiring after God: Classic and Contemporary Readings* (Oxford/Cambridge, MA: Blackwell, 2000).

Paul S. Chung is a native of South Korea and holds a doctorate in systematic theology at the University of Basel, Switzerland. His major publications include *Karl Barth und die Hegelsche Linke* (1994), *Spirituality and Social Ethics in John Calvin* (2000), *Martin Luther and Buddhism: aesthetics of suffering* (2002) and numerous professional articles. Currently he is teaching at Pacific Lutheran Theological Seminary, which is part of the Graduate Theological Union, in Berkeley, California, USA.

Sung Wook Chung is Assistant Professor of Theology in the Department of Bible and Religion at King College, Bristol, Tennessee, USA. A native of South Korea, he received his MDiv from Harvard University and DPhil from the University of Oxford. He is the author of numerous professional articles and academic books. He has recently published *Admiration and Challenge: Karl Barth's Theological Relationship with John Calvin* (New York: Peter Lang, 2002) and edited *Alister E. McGrath and Evangelical Theology: A Dynamic Engagement* (Carlisle/Grand Rapids, MI: Paternoster & Baker, 2003) and has served the Task

Force for the Doctrine of the Trinity in the Presbyterian Church (USA).

Elias Dantas has been Associate Professor of Mission at the Peeke School of Christian Mission, King College, Bristol, Tennessee, USA. A native of Brazil, he currently serves Douglasville First Presbyterian Church, at Douglasville, Georgia, USA as Mission Pastor. He received his DMiss and PhD from Fuller Theological Seminary, California. He is an author of numerous books and articles in English, Spanish, and Portuguese.

Gabriel Fackre is Abbot Professor of Christian Theology Emeritus at Andover Newton Theological School, Massachusetts, USA. He received his PhD from the University of Chicago and is an ordained minister in the United Church of Christ. He is past President of the American Theological Society and the author of numerous books and professional articles. Among his major publications are *The Doctrine of Revelation: A Narrative Interpretation* (Edinburgh/ Grand Rapids, MI: Edinburgh University Press/Eerdmans, 1997), *The Christian Story* (Grand Rapids, MI: Eerdmans, vol. 1, 1996[3]; vol. 2, 1987) and *Restoring the Center: Essays Evangelical & Ecumenical* (Downers Grove, IL: InterVarsity Press, 1998).

Veli-Matti Kärkkäinen is Associate Professor of Systematic Theology at Fuller Theological Seminary, Pasadena, California, USA and Dozent of Ecumenics at the University of Helsinki, Finland. A native of Finland, he received his MA from Fuller Theological Seminary, Ed.M from the University of Jyvaskyla and doctor of theology degree (Habil.) from the University of Helsinki. He has recently published *An Introduction to the Theology of Religions. Biblical, Historical, and Contemporary Perspectives* (Downers Grove, IL: InterVarsity Press, 2003), *Trinity and Religious Pluralism: The Doctrine of the Trinity in Christian Theology of Religions* (Aldershot: Ashgate, 2004), and *Doctrine of God. A Global Perspective* (Grand Rapids, MI: Baker, 2004).

Clark H. Pinnock is Professor of Theology Emeritus at McMaster Divinity College, Hamilton, Ontario, Canada. He received his PhD in New Testament studies, under F.F. Bruce, from the University of Manchester. His major publications include *A Wideness in God's Mercy: The Finality of Jesus Christ in a World of Religions* (Grand Rapids, Michigan: Zondervan, 1992), *Flame of Love: A Theology of the Holy Spirit* (Downers Grove, IL: InterVarsity Press, 1996) and *Most Moved Mover: A Theology of God's Openness* (Grand Rapids, MI/Carlisle: Baker/Paternoster, 2001).

Graham Tomlin is Vice Principal and tutor in Historical Theology and Evangelism at Wycliffe Hall, Oxford, UK. He is a member of the Theology Faculty of Oxford University, where he teaches on the Reformation (and in particular on Martin Luther) and on contemporary Mission. He holds the MA from Oxford University in both English and Theology, and a PhD from Exeter University (UK). He is the author of *The Power of the Cross: Theology and the Death of Christ in Paul, Luther and Pascal* (Carlisle: Paternoster, 1999), *Walking in His Steps: A Guide to Exploring the Land of the Bible* (London: Harper Collins, 2001), *The Provocative Church* (London: SPCK, 2002) and *Luther and his World* (Oxford: Lion, 2002).

Mark D. Thompson is Academic Dean and Senior Lecturer in Theology at Moore College, Sydney, Australia. He has degrees from Macquarie University and Moore College and his DPhil is from the University of Oxford for work on Martin Luther. He is the author of *A Sure Ground on Which to Stand: The Relation of Authority and Interpretive Method in Luther's Approach to Scripture* (Carlisle: Paternoster, 2004) and joint editor of *The Gospel to the Nations: Essays in Honour of Peter T. O'Brien* (Leicester: Inter-Varsity Press, 2000).

Ng Kam Weng, is Research Director and Resident Scholar at Kairos Research Centre in Malaysia. He is a Malaysian Chinese and received his PhD degree from Cambridge University, UK. Among his most recent publications are *Modernity in Malaysia: Christian Perspectives*, ed. Ng Kam Weng, Kairos Theological

Readings and Resources vol. 1 (Kairos, 1998), and *From Christ to Social Practice: Christological Foundations for Social Practice in the Theologies of Albrecht Ritschl, Karl Barth, Juergen Moltmann* (Hong Kong: Alliance BS, 1996).

KK Yeo, a Malaysian Chinese, is Harry R. Kendall Associate Professor of New Testament at Garrett-Evangelical Theological Seminary and Graduate Faculty advisory member at Northwestern University, Evanston, Illinois, USA. He holds an MDiv degree from Garrett-Evangelical Seminary and a PhD degree from Northwestern University. He is a visiting professor at major universities in China and has published in both English and Chinese on cross-cultural biblical interpretation. He has recently published *What Has Jerusalem to Do with Beijing? Biblical Interpretation from a Chinese Perspective* (Harrisburg, PA: Trinity Press International, 1998), and *Chairman Mau Meets the Apostle Paul: Christianity, Communism, and the Hope of China* (Grand Rapids, MI: Brazos Press, 2002).

Foreword

Alister E. McGrath

It is not the easiest of times to proclaim the traditional Christian belief in the uniqueness of Jesus Christ or the Christian gospel. The notion that any religion, philosophy or worldview – the relation between these being at present somewhat fluid and contested – can have a monopoly on the truth is vigorously contested in many quarters. Postmodernity excoriates such claims to uniqueness, seeing them as thinly disguised claims to power and the right to control. Some committed to inter-religious dialogue regard such claims as prejudicial to dialogue, and thus either refuse to allow such claims to be represented in discussion on account of their potential to disturb, or offer revisionist readings of religious traditions – in particular, Christianity and Islam – which eliminate or downplay distinctives. The outcome of such dialogue is, it need hardly be said, of questionable value.

This collection of essays considers how Christianity can and must be true to itself in its engagement with the world around it. Contributors from a wide range of backgrounds set out an impressive case for maintaining the uniqueness of the Christian vision of reality as a matter of intellectual integrity. Christianity must be allowed to be what it really is, rather than being forced to conform to what the "spirit of our age" regards as acceptable. As an historical theologian, I am uncomfortably aware of how the settled cultural wisdom of an age is often overturned, and occasionally inverted, within a generation. These essays represent a significant protest against cultural accommodation-ism which robs the gospel of its distinctive voice, and relegates it to the sidelines by making it merely echo the many voices of our complex and shifting culture.

This volume will be of fundamental interest to all those concerned with systematic theology, apologetics, and the mission of the church. It is to be commended warmly for its vision and its boldness, and the challenge to be attentive to the distinctive and identity-bestowing themes of the gospel. I hope it is widely read, and even more widely discussed.

Alister McGrath
Oxford University

1

The Incarnation of Christ and its Implications to the Ministry and Mission of the Church

Elias Dantas

1. Introduction

Contemporary theologian J. I. Packer writes: "Here are two mysteries for the price of one – the plurality of persons within the unity of God, and the union of Godhead and manhood in the person of Jesus ... Nothing in fiction is so fantastic as is this truth of the Incarnation."[1] What is the incarnation? It is simply what Packer refers to here as "the union of Godhead and manhood in the person of Jesus." It is, I would venture to say, the greatest and most stunning miracle that has ever been or ever will be. It is also the answer to the most important and relevant question in the universe: "Who is Jesus Christ?" The answer revealed by the truth of the incarnation is: Jesus Christ is fully God and fully man in one person. In other words, he is God incarnate.

2. The Fact

"Born of the Virgin Mary"

> This is how the birth of Jesus Christ came about: His mother Mary was pledged to be married to Joseph, but before they

came together, she was found to be with child through the Holy
Spirit

(Matt. 1:18)

When the fullness of the time came, God sent his Son born of a
woman ...

(Gal. 4:4)

A few years ago Joan Osborne, a secular singer, wrote and sang
a popular song, "One of Us," which asked the question, "What
if God were one of us?" I found this song riveting. Although the
theology was way off, a plea was made, seeking to know why
we exist. Where is God in this life, and what if he lived my life?
That is what the incarnation is all about. The incarnation simply
means God came to be a man. He was fully man while
remaining fully God. That way he could identify with our
plight in life. As he lived a normal human existence for over
thirty years, he experienced all that we experience, including
emotions, relationships, and temptations.

He drove nails as he worked with his earthly father. He
obeyed his earthly mother when she asked him to take out the
trash. He played, he worked, and he lived the life of a man, a
human being, with all that we have in our human makeup. He
went to sleep at night, and awoke to a normal life with all of the
stresses and opportunities a human could have in the first
century.

The how of the birth becomes believable when the who of the
birth is taken into account. What does the term, virgin birth,
mean? Jesus was born by the result of what we call the
miraculous conception. His mother, Mary, who did not have
sexual relations with his earthly stepfather, Joseph, conceived
our Lord in her womb by the power of the Holy Spirit. Then
Mary gave birth to Jesus without a biological father.

The virgin birth does not imply that Jesus was born in a
manner different from any other child. He was born in exactly
the same way as you and I. Nor does it suggest that there was
merely a miraculous conception as in the case of Sara or
Elizabeth who were past age. Mary was a young woman,
perhaps in her late teens, as was the custom then. It does not

mean immaculate conception as taught by the Roman Catholic Church, for that dogma asserts that Mary was also conceived and born without original sin, a claim for which there is not a scintilla of biblical evidence! Jesus came into this world as a baby, with all of the human weaknesses, needs and desires. He had to be fed, changed, cared for, nurtured, educated, protected and loved, just as one of us. Yet, it was a virgin conception, an event entirely without parallel! Yet, he was still fully God, Creator and Sustainer of all things.

Modern science with test-tube babies, artificial fertilization, and insemination still requires the seed of a man and the egg of a woman. Even in the case of cloning, the building blocks of the human genes are already in place, for God created them. Science does nothing but rearrange the "ego blocks" that God created. Contrary to the course of nature, Jesus was miraculously conceived in the womb of Mary. She was the host or segregate, as the Spirit overshadowed her. Which percentage of Mary's DNA did God use, 100, 50, 10, or 0? We do not know. So, our Lord and Savior could not only be identified as humanity's own, as one of us, but also be able to save us.

The normal process of original sin was short circuited so he could be the Adam who did not sin, take our place in life and in death, live for us in the perfection that we could not, and take for us the punishment of God's wrath that he did not deserve! All this was possible because of the virgin birth. The transmission of humanity's sinful nature and heritage was interrupted by this miraculous conception. Yes, Christ was one of us, he was fully human, born without corruption, and yet, he was also, and still is, and forever will be, fully God. Was he still able to sin? Yes. Although this may be debated theologically, the biblical evidence is that he was able to fall, but he did not! That was what his temptation in the wilderness was all about; yet he remained steadfast as our Protector and Savior.

It is argued by people of liberal thought that the Bible does not insist on our believing in the virgin birth as a requirement for salvation. It is further argued that the virgin birth did not even take place, but that believers added it later. Many pastors and denominations dismiss the supernatural aspects of the Bible and cut the virgin birth from their beliefs.

However, the Bible plainly teaches the fact of the virgin birth. If you believe the Bible to be true, then the virgin birth must be true also.

Let us consider the alternatives, and ask if this doctrine is fact or fiction. If the virgin birth did not happen, then:

1. The New Testament narratives are proven false and the Bible's authority is raided. Thus, it is also inaccurate in other matters.
2. Mary, instead of being blessed among women, is a fornicator, an adulteress, and must be branded as unchaste, for Joseph asserted that Jesus was not his son.
3. Jesus becomes the ordinary child of sinful parents with the corruption of original sin, and is not the result of incarnation. Thus, his pre-existence did not happen, and not only is he not God, but, he is also not able to redeem us, and is not worthy of our worship and adoration.
4. We no longer have a sufficient explanation of his unique character, if he had one. Thus, he did not have a sinless life, and was unable to take our place in living the sinless life that we could not live. He was unable to pay the price of our sin and appease God's wrath for us.
5. He was begotten of a human father. This could be the only alternative to the virgin birth. If he was just a man, a good teacher, and maybe a prophet, Jesus Christ could not be the second person of the Trinity as he claimed, and therefore could have no power to forgive our sin.
6. The miracle of miraculous conception is refuted and nullified. We no longer have a Savior, thus there is no need to "do" church.
7. Logically, we should deny all miracles, as they do not or cannot happen. The question we should be asking and seeking is, are we willing to accept the super-naturalistic claims of Scripture or not? The virgin birth is the starting point of knowing who Christ is. It points to his humanity, as he became one of us, and his Godhood, as the one who came to save us. When we deny this essential doctrine, we deny Scripture. We set ourselves up, as fallen humans, to be the ultimate authority. We say in essence that God is irrelevant

and perhaps even non-existent in our lives. We say there is no sin, which even the daily newspapers testify to be a false statement. We make the claim for ourselves that we have no need to be saved. What extreme arrogance and hopelessness we would have if we believed this.

The full meaning of the incarnation is tied to the virgin birth of Christ. "It is important to understand the doctrine of the Virgin Birth safeguards and communicates the significance of the event of the incarnation."[2] It does not prove the incarnation but serves to convey the reality of the incarnation from one generation to another.

The birth stories of Jesus emphasize the Christian belief that "God with us" (Matt. 1:23) is not just a beautiful idea or an abstract theological truth. It happened! John also tells us that it happened when he says that the "Word became flesh and made his dwelling among us" (John 1:14). But Matthew and Luke tell us more specifically that it happened at a particular time, in a particular place, in connection with a particular mother: "during the time of King Herod" (Matt. 2:1; Luke 1:5), "when Quirinius was governor of Syria" (Luke 2:2), in Bethlehem, of Mary. When we speak about God's presence and activity in the world, in a man dwelling among us, we are not talking only about a "spiritual presence" or a "feeling" of God's nearness or God "in our hearts." We are talking about geography: he was born in Palestine. We are talking about politics: he was born when a census was being taken, when there was danger of political revolution, and he himself was expected to be a political revolutionary (Matt. 2:3–5, 16; Luke 1:51–53). In short, we are not just talking about religious ideas and doctrines; we are talking about history.

The birth story is anything but the sentimental, harmless, once-a-year occasion for a "Christmas spirit" that lasts only a few days before we return to the facts of the real world. It is instead the story of a radical invasion of God into the kind of real world where we live all year long – a world where there is political unrest and injustice, poverty, hatred, jealousy, and both the fear and the longing that things could be different. John tells us that when Jesus comes "the light shines in the darkness" (John 1:5). Matthew and Luke tell us just what the darkness is into which the light shines. It is the same darkness in which we live. John tells us that the "Word became flesh" (John 1:14). Matthew and Luke emphasize that as the same flesh we know – that of a man who came into the world the same way and lived under the same threatening conditions we do. John says it happened. Matthew and Luke say that not only did it happen in sermons or in Christmas plays at church, but also outside the church, in the world.

The question we have to ask now is, "Can we still believe in the virgin conception?" The virgin birth of Christ itself is not the central mystery of faith, but like the empty tomb it is a sign that serves to communicate this mystery. It is not itself the stumbling block, but it is a potent witness to the real stumbling block of faith – the Son of God becoming man and taking upon himself the sin and guilt of humankind.

3. Alternative Christological Views to the Traditional Understanding of the Person of Christ and the Incarnation

Many Christian scholars throughout the history of the church have expressed alternative views for the understanding of the person of Christ. As we will see, these approaches are generally focused in one of the two main trends of alternative Christology.

One approach is a theocentric Christology. This paradigm emphasizes the divinity of Christ nearly to the dismissal of his humanity. Such a view is unwilling to hold in tension a person both fully human and fully divine. Theocentric Christology runs the risk of negating the truth and reality of the incarnation.

Another approach is that of an anthropocentric Christology. Just as a theocentric Christology overemphasizes the divinity of Christ, so this view overemphasizes the humanity of Christ.

These two separate approaches to the person of Christ have resulted in several controversial theories about his being. Some of the most important are:

3.1 Ebionism

The earliest heretical view concerning the person of Christ was that known as Ebionism. "In the interests of a supposedly pure monotheism, the Ebionites denied the Deity of Christ and held that He was merely a man on whom the Spirit of God rested in its fullness."[3] God and man were regarded as always external to each other. It denied the possibility of a union between the divine and human nature and so ruled out the doctrine of the incarnation. Some believed Jesus was virgin born, but none affirmed his pre-existence. "They were ascetics who camped on Jesus' teaching regarding the poor in spirit and continued to strictly adhere to the Law and circumcision."[4] They believed that Jesus was selected by God as the Anointed One because he perfectly kept the Law. For this reason, this group is sometimes associated with the Judaizers that Paul wrote against in some of his epistles (most notably, Galatians).

3.2 Docetism

Chronologically, the next important error to develop concerning the person of Christ was Docetism. This approach, "which is probably best regarded as a tendency within theology rather than a definite theological position,"[5] gave voice to an understanding among some in the early church who regarded the humanity of Christ as apparent rather than historically real. This term was derived from the Greek word *dokeo*, meaning to "seem," or to "appear." While the Ebionites believed that Christ had only a human nature, the Docetists held precisely the opposite error, asserting that he had only a divine nature and that his appearance in this world was only an illusion, or, more correctly, a theophany. There is slight evidence of this tendency in late portions of the New Testament (e.g. 1 John 4:1–3; 2 John 7) and evidence that it exercised some appeal among early Christians. This impulse came to fullest expression among Christians influenced by Gnosticism.

3.3 Gnosticism

Gnosticism is a highly variegated religious movement holding that spirit is imprisoned in matter and can be liberated through the application of secret teachings. A syncretistic congeries of myths, beliefs, and practices, Gnosticism was shaped by streams of thought from Egyptian, Syrian, Babylonian, Jewish, Neoplatonic, and Christian sources. Gnosticism in turn influenced aspects of orthodox Christian thought during the early centuries of the Christian era, although early Christians generally regarded the movement as a whole as antagonistic to Christianity. Basic to most Gnosticism was the conviction that the spirit of life is imprisoned in evil matter and that an escape from matter can only be accomplished with the help of secret teachings mediated by a teacher standing in the succession of those who possess this secret knowledge or *gnosis*. Some Gnostics believed that a divine deliverer would come to provide beings enslaved to matter with this knowledge and thus guide them back to the kingdom of light. Valentinus of Rome (second century) and Basilides of Alexandria (second century) were among the theologians most strongly influenced by Gnosticism. Followers of both formed sects that claimed to be Christian.

3.4 Arianism

Arius (A.D. 250–336) was a presbyter of one of the churches of Alexandria in Egypt. His doctrinal disputes with Alexander, the bishop of Alexandria, beginning about A.D. 320, grew into a much wider controversy which remained a problem in the church for the next two or three hundred years. The Arians misinterpreted certain Scripture statements relating to Christ's state of humiliation and assumed that temporary sub-ordination to the Father meant original and permanent inequality. Arius taught that Christ was the first and highest of God's creatures. As such, Jesus did not share in the divine essence but, like all of God's creatures, was made out of nothing. However, because of his moral integrity Jesus was adopted by God as his Son, and it was through him that God made the world. Arius was willing to concede that Christ was God in some sense, but he was only an inferior, secondary God. Christ was neither wholly God nor wholly man, but a third party between God and man. In the incarnation Christ had entered a human body, taking the place of the human spirit and reasoning.

Alexander, the Bishop of Alexandria, strenuously disagreed with these views, teaching that Christ was co-eternal with the Father, one in essence with the Father, and wholly uncreated. The controversy led an Alexandrian synod to condemn Arius, and he sought refuge among those sympathetic to his views.

Because of the widespread difference of opinion concerning the person of Christ an ecumenical council was called by Constantine, the first Christian Emperor, for the purpose of formulating a general doctrine which should be accepted by the whole church. Constantine, the Roman Emperor in Constantinople, felt the unity of his empire was greatly threatened by this controversy. Failing to achieve peace by mere counseling, he convened the first general council at Nicea in A.D. 325. There a creed was adopted which asserted that Christ was one in essence with the Father. The Arian idea that Christ was a created being and that there was a time when he did not exist was rejected. Constantine banished those who opposed this creed, including Arius.

3.5 Apollinarianism

This system denied the completeness of his human nature. It acknowledged his true Deity, and also that he possessed a real body and a soul which would continue after death; but it denied that he had a truly human mind, i.e. a reasoning mind that reached conclusions through mental processes as do ours. It asserted in effect that he was simply God masquerading in human flesh, and that ignorance, weakness, obedience, worship, suffering, etc., were to be predicated of the Logos, that is, of the deity or divine nature as such.

This teaching originated with Apollinarius of Laodicea (ca. A.D. 310 – ca. A.D. 390), a defender of Nicene orthodoxy concerning the Trinity. Apollinarius was concerned to explain the unity of Christ's person and argued in effect that Christ had a human body and divine mind. This teaching was rejected particularly by Antiochene theologians who argued that it did not sufficiently respect the humanity of Christ.

In Christology the principal emphasis is on the complete humanity of Christ which is sharply distinguished from his divine nature. Antiochene theologians strongly defended the *homoousios* in order to protect and exhibit both the divinity and humanity of Christ. *Homoousios*, or "of the same substance", was the term used to settle controversy over the place of Jesus Christ in the Trinity at the Council of Nicea I (A.D. 325). Exegetes of the Antiochene school emphasized a literal and historical interpretation of the Bible. Theodore of Mopsuestia (ca. A.D. 350–428) is a representative theologian.

Apollinarianism was rejected at the Council of Constantinople I (A.D. 381). Apollinarianism is also one of the alternatives rejected in the "Definition of Faith" adopted at the Council of Chalcedon (A.D. 451).

3.6 Nestorianism

Nestorianism was an early heresy concerning the person of Christ, maintaining that in Christ there were two distinct natures and two distinct persons.

This teaching originated with Nestorius (d. ca. A.D. 451), patriarch of Constantinople and representative of Antiochene theology. Nestorius emphasized both the complete humanity and divinity of Christ. He was concerned about maintaining the distinction between the two natures of Christ and argued that the divinity of Christ not be allowed to overwhelm his humanity in the eyes of the church. This teaching was rejected particularly by Alexandrian theologians who argued that Nestorius had divided Christ into two beings. Nestorianism was rejected at the Council of Ephesus (A.D. 431), one of the seven ecumenical councils. Nestorianism is also one of the alternatives rejected in the "Definition of Faith" adopted at the Council of Chalcedon to settle the early Christological con- troversies. Some Christians in Persia and Syria continue to hold the Nestorian position to the present.

3.7 Eutycheanism or Monophysitism

Eutycheanism or Monophysitism was an early heresy concerning the person of Christ, maintaining that Christ is of one substance with the Father but not of one substance with humankind. In other words, he had only one nature, rather than two – divine and human.

> Strict Monophysitism, or Eutychianism, explains the one nature in Christ in one of four ways: the human nature is absorbed by the divine; the divine Word (Logos) disappears in the humanity of Christ; a unique third nature is created from the combination of the divine and human natures; or there is a composition (a natural whole) of humanity and divinity, without confusion.[6]

This teaching was urged by Eutyches (ca. A.D. 378–454), a monk from Constantinople. This doctrine was rejected particularly by Antiochene theologians who argued that it did not sufficiently respect the humanity of Christ and that it promoted Docetism. The Council of Chalcedon also rejected this early Christological heresy in its "Definition of Faith." However, the Council's decision did not represent the end of this line of thought.

A more moderate Monophysitism was put forward by Severus (ca. A.D. 465–538), patriarch of Antioch. It was less rigid and in many ways differed only nominally from the doctrines of the Council of Chalcedon. Nonetheless, all Monophysites rejected the dogmatic formulas of Chalcedon, and efforts to reach an acceptable compromise failed. By the sixth century Monophysitism had a strong institutional basis in three churches: the Armenian Church, the Coptic Church, and the Jacobite Church, all of which remain nominally Monophysite today.

4. The Incarnated Christ as Defined by the Church Councils and Confessions

4.1 The Council of Nicea – A.D. 325

The Council of Nicea was an ecumenical gathering of the universal church which addressed the situation of the church after the persecutions and attempted to settle the Arian controversy. Constituted primarily by bishops from the East along with a few from the West, this council was summoned and presided over by the Emperor Constantine. It thus established a precedent for the subordination of the church to the state in the East. The council established regulations for the life of the church following the cessation of persecution. It also rejected Arianism when it condemned the teaching that the Word of God or Son of God was a creature or any less divine than the Father. It declared that Christ was of one substance (*homoousios*) with God the Father. This statement became a crucial element of the Nicene Creed and a hallmark of Nicene orthodoxy in both East and West.

4.2 The Council of Constantinople – A.D. 381

This council reaffirmed the decision of the Council of Nicea (A.D. 325) which taught that Christ was of the same substance as the Father. Apollinarianism was condemned and the humanity and divinity of Christ were correspondingly asserted. The so-called Nicene Creed stems from this council but was later expanded and approved.

4.3 The Council of Chalcedon – A.D. 451

This council attempted to settle early controversies concerning the person of Christ. It produced a "Definition of Faith" which declared that in Christ there are "two natures in one person." This echoed the earlier teaching of Tertullian and was compatible with the trinitarian affirmations of Tome of Leo. This statement did not seek to define precisely how the two natures are united in one person, but rejected heretical explanations that had early troubled the church. Apollinarianism, Nestorianism, and Monophysitism were among the rejected teachings. The "Definition of Faith" issued at Chalcedon became the standard of orthodox Christology in the West, although it remained highly controversial in the East.

4.4 The Reformation and the incarnation

As we saw before, Gnosticism flourished as a way of denying the incarnation (literally meaning, "in-fleshing") while sounding spiritual and very religious to those who sought some connection to the divine within themselves. By following Jesus, one could become truly enlightened and eventually rise from the crude, earthly existence into which he had fallen to the higher life of the spirit.

While this synthesis of pagan mysticism and Christianity was officially eschewed, it has always had its adherents throughout church history, especially in the mystical traditions. During the late Middle Ages, an Italian mystic by the name of Joachim of Fiore created a scheme in which "history was divided into the Age of the Father, the Age of the Son, and the Age of the Spirit."[7] The Old Testament, corresponding to this first age, is distinguished by its cruel, harsh deity who ordered the slaughters of entire people groups. We know the Age of the Son as the period in which the "good God," Jesus Christ, softened the harsher features of the Jewish deity. In the appearance of Christ, we learned about grace for the first time, and the church was founded, with its "material" way of worshipping God through sacraments (bread, wine, water) and words (Scripture). But an even greater stage of historical development yet awaited: the Age of the Spirit, when the institutional church would be eclipsed by the universal brotherhood of man and the word and sacraments would be rendered unnecessary by the intuitive life of the Spirit.

Joachim's commentary on the book of Revelation was quite popular, especially among the Spiritual Franciscans, a group that was convinced that the institutional Church of Rome had become so worldly and corrupt that even the monastic orders (including the world-denying followers of Francis of Assisi) were synagogues of Satan.[8]

While officially condemned, Joachim's teachings nevertheless gained wider popularity during the Renaissance, as great humanists such as Petrarch detected the Greek, Platonic mysticism inherent in the system and heartily approved its emphasis on "spirituality" rather than dogma, creed, and

history. Petrarch envisioned the Renaissance as the Age of the
Spirit, when the divinity in every person would realize a
universal religion of spiritual peace and harmony.

Ironically, the period of the Reformation, far from squelching
this reasoning, accelerated its prominence. The Reformers
themselves opposed the "Manichaeans" (i.e. another name for
"Gnostics") in the form of the Anabaptists. These heirs of the
medieval sects often argued that the word and sacraments
had been superseded by the Spirit. Dubbed the "Radical
Reformation," leaders of this movement, such as Menno
Simons (namesake of the Mennonites) were refuted by Calvin
for the former's doctrine of the "heavenly body" of Jesus.[9]
Arguing that the Virgin Mary was merely a "channel" or
"conduit" through which God came to earth, Menno denied the
reality of the virgin birth and, therefore, the true humanity of
Christ. Against the Polish Reformer, John Lasco, Menno
asserted, "that there is not a letter to be found in all the
Scriptures that the Word assumed our flesh; or that the divine
nature miraculously united itself with our human nature."[10]

Calvin replied to the Anabaptist revival of Gnosticism or
Manichaeanism by walking through the scores of biblical
passages which describe the humanity of Christ. He begins
with the Old Testament history: "For the blessing is promised
neither in heavenly seed nor in the phantom of a man, but in the
seed of Abraham and Jacob. Nor is an eternal throne promised
to a man of air, but to the Son of David and the fruit of his
loins."[11] Calvin emphasizes the historical genealogies and the
Jewishness of the Son of Man to defend Christ's human descent.
Further, Jesus was "subject to hunger, thirst, cold, and other
infirmities of our nature." He "expiated in our flesh" the debt
we owed. "And Matthew does not here describe the virgin as a
channel through which Christ flowed." By assuming our
humanity, Christ dignified our humanity and proved that there
is nothing wrong with matter or human nature in itself, as God
created it, but that evil and sinfulness are to be ascribed to the
perverse will and desire of the creature.

Calvin was always very clear on his position about the
incarnation of Christ and his divine and human natures. All the
subsequent Reformed Creeds and Confessions bring a clear

reaffirmation of the Nicene and Chalcedon affirmations of the Incarnation of the Divine Word.[12]

5. Implications of the Doctrine of the Incarnation for the Ministry and Mission of the Church

The question we need to address in the last part of this chapter is related to the implication of the doctrine of the incarnation to the ministry and mission of the church. How can we understand the ministry and mission of the church in the light of the incarnated Christ?

First, the incarnation makes God tangible. What does the incarnation tell us about the God and Father of our Lord Jesus Christ? Perhaps, most obviously, "it tells us that the God with whom we are dealing is no distant ruler who remains aloof from the affairs of his creatures, but one who is passionately concerned with them to the extent that he takes the initiative in coming to them."[13] God does not just reveal things about himself – he reveals himself in Jesus Christ.

God takes the initiative in approaching us, in disclosing to us that he wants us to know him. God reveals himself to human beings, and by revealing himself, discloses his love for us, and his desire to enter into a relationship with us. Just as the waiting father encountered the returning prodigal son, so God encounters us.

Second, God is made tangible through the embodiment of Jesus' message and life in his church. This affirmation has several consequences for the communication of the message of Jesus Christ in our contemporary world, and especially among its poverty-stricken, oppressed, and powerless majority. Indeed, it was out of the mystery of the incarnation, to which Jesus' resurrection and death bear witness that the early Christian community began to understand its mission as participation in the continuing mission of Jesus Christ. The church is to follow the pattern of the incarnation because it is the body of Christ indwelled by his Spirit.

One of the consequences is, in the words of Orlando Costas, "the need to experience the incarnation in contemporary history."[14]

The incarnation bears witness not only to the fact that God has become part of history in the man Jesus, but also to the fact that this man reveals authentic humanity. This fact led Barth to state that "since God Himself became man, humanity has become the measure of all things."[15] In the incarnation not only has God's true self been revealed, but also the true identity of women and men. This means that humankind discovers its authentic identity in Jesus Christ and comes to know the true God through him. The incarnation turns theology proper and anthropology into a Christological issue. It also makes contextualization an inevitable and indispensable process for a proper understanding and communication of the Christian faith.

Contextualization and incarnation are basic to the mission and ministry of the church. God is made tangible not only in Jesus Christ, but through the effective and humble witness of his church. The tangibility of God in the incarnated Christ through the ministry of his church, in the context of our racist, sexist, colonialist, profit and warmongering, success-crazy, manipulative, and poverty-stricken world will enable Christians today to share Christ anew.

"The Christ propagated by the oppressive powers of this world is not the true Christ. It is, rather, the Antichrist of whom the New Testament speaks."[16] It is imperative, therefore, that Christians learn to differentiate the true incarnate Lord from the false lords of this world.

As Costas says, "This differentiation can be done only when we discover Christ's real identity in our historical situations."[17] Without such a discovery, it is possible neither to verify our knowledge of the biblical Christ nor communicate the message of God in a tangible and relevant way to our oppressed world. Since Christ is the heart of the gospel, it follows that effective ministry is not possible where his liberating presence is not being experienced and his true identity is being distorted. In order to communicate him effectively to the world, we need to know experientially who he really is, where we may find him, and on what basis we can be related to him.

Third, we have to ask ourselves how we can make God tangible in our pluralistic world. How then do we bear witness to the lordship of the incarnated Christ from this new social reality? We are increasingly a minority faith, relegated to the sidelines of many public debates. Our confession of the universal lordship of the incarnated Christ seems to many quaint at best, and at worst a threat to the pluralistic fabric of our society. Some Christians, particularly in the Western World, respond to this situation by longing for and working for a reassertion of Christendom, where the church works hand in hand with government to influence public life. If we can only again seize the reins of power, they argue, we can reassert our nation's historic Christian identity and re-establish the credibility of the church's witness to the lordship of Christ. Yet thoughtful Christians are increasingly questioning this approach:

The rise of religious pluralism and the peripheral position of the church in our culture as a whole need not be seen only as a failure and a loss. In many respects, it can be seen as a fresh opportunity for the church. We may be in a situation today that is closer to that of the New Testament church than ever before. As we are freed from the false security of being an established religion and forced to compete in a wide-open marketplace of ideas and perspectives, the Holy Spirit may be opening an opportunity for renewal and transformation in the church, leading us into a fresh and deeper witness to the world, a witness undergirded not by the status and prestige of the institutional church, not by smarter politics, better marketing, or more money, but by the quality and character of our lives. Christians all over the world have been living and thriving as minority faiths in such pluralistic contexts, and they have much to teach us.

Even in a pluralistic world, the reality that no one can deny is the transformation of human lives into the image of Christ. Perhaps more than ever before, the church is called to witness to the gracious and transforming lordship of the incarnated Christ through a blended witness of word and deed. If our faith does not transform our lives to reflect Jesus Christ, no one will listen to us. If we do not find creative ways both to point to and to exhibit the radical, shocking, and subversive love of Christ, no one will pay any attention to us at all. But once we gain their attention, if we do not tell them the story of Jesus and challenge them to faith and discipleship, our witness will not bear fruit.[18]

6. Conclusion

In this chapter we focused on the incarnation of Christ. The great introductory message of the gospel is, "Emanuel, God with us!" Our God is not too good, too holy or too proud to "lower" himself to humanity's level to participate in earthly human life. He does not sacrifice but exercises his divine power, goodness and holiness by doing so. The incarnation means that unlike all false gods, the true God is not the prisoner of his own spirituality, unable to be God in the human realm. It means that unlike all false gods, the true God can accomplish his will in weakness as well as in strength, by sacrificing himself as well as asserting himself, in the non-religious as well as the religious sphere. It means that to identify himself with sinful man in a sinful world does not compromise goodness and holiness. For he is the God who gives himself to be known in the man Jesus, who was born in a stable, tried and condemned in a courtroom, and executed at public execution grounds. If you want to know what it means to be a human being and to stand for the humanity of man, look at Jesus Christ. If you want to know God, look at Jesus Christ.

Let me conclude by quoting the declaration of the Reformed Church in America about Confessing the Uniqueness of Christ in a Pluralistic Society. The document says:

> The great drama of history is not how humans will find God; it is rather when and how an active, seeking God will finally get through to a resistant humanity. When Jesus declared that the Reign of God was at hand ... he was claiming that God was blazing a new path to us in Jesus ... Christian faith is incompatible with a general affirmation of all religions because of a fundamental difference in understanding what religion is. For Christians, it is not our quest for God, but our response to God's quest for us in Christ.
>
> Nowhere is this more clearly seen than in the cross of Christ. Here is the moment where God meets us in all our rebellion,

resistance, idolatry, and violence. At precisely the point where humanity is most resistant to God, the love of God shines most brightly, overcoming our rebellion, forgiving our violence, and inviting us into a new way of living. Christianity's distinguishing mark is not that we are seekers who have found God; we are sinners – enemies of God whom God has loved and forgiven. Christianity is about grace, from beginning to end.

Consequently, Christians do not so much claim to have discovered the truth as to have been apprehended by the truth. Their great joy comes not so much from what they have found, but from the fact that they have been found by God. Their concern is not so much with the wisdom they have acquired, but with the Wise One who has drawn them to himself. If all Christians had to offer was another spirituality, another ethic, another path to fulfillment, Christianity would indeed be just one of many religions. But this is not the heart of the gospel. The gospel affirms that at the center of reality is the incarnation, life and resurrection of Jesus Christ, and his work in the world through the Holy Spirit; everything else flows from this living person who has gripped the hearts and minds of those who call themselves Christian.[19]

Notes

[1] James I. Packer, *Knowing God* (Downers Grove, IL: InterVarsity Press, 1993), p. 53.

[2] Donald G. Bloesch, *Essentials of Evangelical Theology: God, Authority, & Salvation, Volume 1*, (Peabody, MA: Prince Press, 1998), p. 130.

[3] Loraine Boettner, *Studies in Theology* (Washington, DC: P&R Publishing, 1974), p. 259.

[4] Walter A. Elwell, *Evangelical Dictionary of Theology* (Grand Rapids, MI: Baker Book House, 1984), p. 339.

[5] Alister McGrath, *An Introduction to Christianity* (Malden, MA: Blackwells, 1997), p. 135.

[6] Barry White, *The Catholic Encyclopedia*, Vol. I (Boston, MA: Robert Appleton Co., 1911; edition copyright © 2003 by K. Knight), p. 197.

[7] Dennis Ngien, *Apologetics for Filioque in Medieval Theology* (Carlisle: Paternoster, 1999), p. 302.

[8] Michael Morton, *The Incarnation of Jesus Christ* (Theological Journal, Fides Reformata; translated from the Brazilian edition by Elias Dantas; Sao Paulo: Brazil, 2002), pp. 13–22.

[9] Abraham Kuyper, *Calvinism and The Radical Reformation of Menno* (Amsterdam, 1957), p. 138.

[10] Iohannes Neumann, "The Annabaptist Movement in Muenster" (Ph.D. diss., Fuller Theological Seminary, 1979), p. 137.

[11] John Calvin, *Institutes*, *IV:XX–30–31* (ed. John T. McNeill; trans. Ford Lewis Battles; Philadelphia: Westminster Press, 1960).

[12] See the Heidelberg Catechism, the Belgium Confession, the Westminster Confession of Faith, the Westminster Short Catechism, and other documents of the Reformed Faith.

[13] Alister McGrath, *Studies in Doctrine* (Grand Rapids, MI: Zondervan, 1997), p. 76.

[14] Orlando Costas, *Christ Outside the Gate* (Maryknoll, NY: Orbis, 1984), p. 12.

[15] Karl Barth, *Against the Stream: Shorter Post-War Writings 1946–52* (New York: Philosophical Library, 1954), p. 35.

[16] René Padilla, *Cristo y anticristo en la proclamación* (Mexico: Fraternidad Teológica LatinoAmericana, 1981), p. 219.

[17] Costas, *Christ Outside the Gate*, p. 15.

[18] Reformed Church in America, *The Crucified Christ: Confessing the Uniqueness of Christ in a Pluralistic Society* (Orange City, Iowa, 1996).

[19] Reformed Church in America, *Crucified Christ*.

2

The Uniqueness of the Life and Teachings of Christ

Clark H. Pinnock

Christianity is the most significant and long-lasting influence to have shaped the culture of Western civilization over the past two millennia and, with the coming of global Christianity in the twenty-first century, its influence is only greater than ever and truly universal.[1] One wonders how this happened? Who was this Jesus of Nazareth from whom this huge influence has emanated? We too must face the ancient question: "Who do you say that I am?" (Matt. 16:15) And when we attempt to reply, one thing will become apparent – Jesus is not exactly like anyone else and the truth of his life does not lie on the surface and is not revealed by any slogan. A mystery runs through it and the truth of it is only gradually revealed to those able to receive it. Like John the Baptist in Matthew 11:3, we may also find ourselves asking Jesus: "Are you the one who is to come or are we to wait for another?"

"Ecce homo!" These words echo down the centuries: "Behold the man!" The phrase was uttered by the Roman procurator of Judea, Pontius Pilate, when he brought Jesus out to face the howling mob. (Rendered "Ecce Homo" in the Latin Vulgate translation of John 19:5.) He spoke much better than he knew – for what an extraordinary man he had in custody. Jaroslav Pelikan writes: "Regardless of what anyone may personally think or believe about him, Jesus of Nazareth has been the dominant figure in the history of Western culture for twenty centuries."[2] He was and is a figure of world-historical importance whose appearance among us has given rise to a series of events which has changed the world.[3] Atheist and heresiarch Friedrich Nietzsche appropriated the phrase to himself – for the sake of his own self-proclamation and will to power. But what a contrast exists between the whining philosopher, musing on his cleverness and wisdom and Jesus who stands among us as one who serves. What a very different "homo" is Jesus as compared to Nietzsche, the self-styled anti-Christ and antithesis of all that Jesus stood for.[4]

1. Ecce Homo

A gap exists in the Apostles' Creed which needs to be addressed in this chapter. The reader may recall how the text of the confession leaps from Jesus' birth all the way to his sufferings and death. It declares Jesus to be "born of the virgin Mary, suffered under Pontius Pilate" (*natus ex Maria virgine, passus sub Pontio Pilato*). Astonishingly, the text says nothing about the life which transpired between these two points. We cannot leave this unaddressed.

The gap cannot be left unbridged. We must say something about Jesus' history on earth. Otherwise, to say no more, how are we to follow him? How are we to heed what God says about him: "This is my Son, the Beloved; Listen to him" (Mark 9:7). We want to know more. Indeed, we must know more. We want to know everything we possibly can about him because we are his disciples and he is for us the very embodiment and self-revelation of God.[5]

Christians are sometimes called people of the book. But we are not actually people of the book, at least not in the way that Muslims are. At the center of our faith stands Jesus Christ, not the Bible.[6] We are a people of the incarnate Word and are Christocentric, not bibliocentric. This truth is often obscured by a too defensive concentration on the Bible.[7] Therefore, with Paul, we proclaim: "(we) want to know him" (Phil. 3:10), and with James Dunn, we declare that we want to "remember" him.[8] Jesus opens up for us the very mind and heart of God.[9]

He is not just a revelation *from God* but the revelation *of God*. For us he is the radiance of God's glory and the true image of the invisible God (Heb. 1:3; Col. 1:15). Islam has its Qur'an and Judaism has its law, but Christianity has Jesus, a living person, in John Stott's words "the incomparable Christ."[10] In Christianity, God's word is not primarily written revelation, but a human life. Therefore, we celebrate the revelatory significance of Jesus, a particular revelation with a universal validity, in whom God gives himself to the whole human race.

He is not only the revelation of God and the basis of salvation – he embodies the contours of redeemed life. He presents us with the true form of human existence. Therefore we look to him for inspiration and orientation, because he is the new "man from above" and author of a new humanity.[11] (Jesus has a mimetic as well as a revelatory significance.) Therefore, our goal is to be conformed to his image and to become imitators of Jesus. For this reason we simply must get in touch and stay in touch with the truth of Jesus which is manifested in his historical embodiment. Abstractions will not do – we must have the real Christ. A mythical figure will not do. We do not want or need a reflection of our own humanity in its brokenness. We do not need something that we dreamed up ourselves. We want to know the Jesus who was born on this earth in a specific location and at a particular time in human history, because knowing him will make possible that new form of human existence which is both instantiated by Jesus in his life and can be evoked in us through regeneration as we are conformed to his image.

But to be in touch with this reality means that we have to engage in historical inquiry and have to investigate historical questions. We want to know what happened and why it happened. (This can be true whether we are his disciples or not, as witness the huge interest in Jesus generally.) Granted, this involves historical judgments in which case we will have to be content with probabilities. History can deliver only so much proof and complete objectivity is surely an illusion. But this need not frustrate us – since no one lives by convictions that are wholly demonstrable. The most important things in life always involve trust and the decision to trust or not to trust. We have to decide what makes better sense out of different possibilities. There is no getting around it. There is no person who does not work with assumptions. Neither belief or unbelief can be completely proven. One has to decide about reality. This is the way it works especially when one is dealing with questions of God. Belief is possible but so is unbelief. One can open oneself to a reality which beckons or one can close oneself to it.[12]

2. The Circumstances of Jesus' Birth

The circumstances of Jesus' birth and the particularities of his upbringing, if not beyond historical reach, are at least less clearly established, as compared (for example) with the kind of evidence which supports the narrative which begins with John the Baptist. When it comes to Jesus' birth, we are on less solid ground. Only two of the New Testament witnesses mention it and the two stories differ significantly from one another. Though there is an important common core (Jesus being born of God's Spirit in a special way), we cannot be as confident about other issues (such as the visit of the magi). Without thinking of these events as contrived, we do admit that they are not very well established as facts, which is not to say they are not of value (at least) theologically.[13]

As a human being, Jesus must have had a historical beginning and one can fairly say that he was humbly born, likely in the small and unremarkable town of Bethlehem in Judea just south of Jerusalem, whose importance for the history of Israel had long since faded. A mighty leader was expected to come from there but he was not expected to be born there (Mic. 5:2). No one seemed to have been thinking of it as the birth place of the messiah at the time of Jesus. It is likely that his parents were there in connection with a census as people were required to return to their place of origin and be enrolled. After a brief stay in Egypt, perhaps in Alexandria, Jesus spent his youth in a small town in Galilee and thus became known as "Jesus of Nazareth." It was not until he moved to Capernaum that he emerged from the shadows and set out upon the mission which he believed he had been given from God and which God confirmed at his baptism by John. The fact that his origins were humble makes his enduring significance all the more remarkable.[14]

Both birth narratives offer a genealogy. Family trees were important in Jesus' time. Since the return from Babylonian exile, one had to prove that there were no mixed marriages in one's ancestry in order to enjoy rights as a citizen. Exactly how these two genealogies worked to establish Davidic descent, we cannot be sure – the genealogy in Matthew traces Jesus' lineage back to Abraham, while Luke traces it back to Adam and (finally) to God. Matthew wants to connect Jesus with God's previous activity in the history of the Jewish people. He looks to Israel's history for an appreciation of who Jesus is. He sees God's hand at work in the call to Abraham and in the covenant with David. He even mentions four women, each of whom had Gentile connections and scandalous sexual unions. I think he wants to tell us that the grace of God works through the likes of Gentile prostitutes and adulterers patiently redeeming human life in unexpected ways.

The mystery (or perhaps the scandal?) surrounding his birth is well-known. The evangelists agree that he was conceived by a young woman who had not had sexual relations. A degree of uncertainty existed surrounding his paternity. Why is he called "Mary's son" not "Joseph's son" (Mark 6:3)? And whence the rumor that he was illegitimate (John 8:41)? Even without Matthew and Luke to go by, there was some question about paternity. The birth was shrouded in mystery and was enigmatic from the start. Did a woman conceive a child without the aid of a man? The virginal conception cannot be proved or disproved. But for those who do not reject the possibility of miracle, belief in it is compatible with what can be known from history. And given what happens later before many witnesses (his resurrection), one is inclined to accept it as a sign from God.

Admittedly, the stories which indicate that Jesus was born without sexual intercourse could be understood as expressing in parable or legend something important. But there is a quality of eyewitness in them, if not in every detail. There is no suggestion that God required a virgin birth in order to implement the incarnation, for example, in order to shield the child from the influence of inborn sin. But the miracle may have played a performative role indicating that the child is special and perhaps more than human. It could be a case of an act of a God who controls nature, setting aside the laws of nature to produce a child in this way as a way of showing how special it is. Though it would be at the same time a private matter which very few would know about. So there is reason to think that God might have done this. One may regret, however, the way the virgin birth has become overly important and gotten confused with ideas of sexual impurity.[15]

3. Jesus' Public Ministry

Jesus came to the attention of the general public through his association with John the Baptist. He worked in the wilderness area close to where the river Jordan flows into the north end of the Dead Sea. Well-known to the Jewish historian Josephus, John saw himself as the voice crying in the wilderness, preparing the way of the Lord, in the spirit of Isaiah 40. He warned about the coming of God's judgment and called upon people to repent. He also announced the advent of a mysterious person "greater than he" who would play a decisive role in God's redemptive purposes. When Jesus came to him, John said: "This is the one of whom I spoke" (Mark 1:7–8). Since Jesus also made many references to John as "more than a prophet," it may well be that it was through John's mediation that Jesus perceived the nearness of the kingdom and his own role in relation to its coming. Jesus said that of those born of women there was no one greater than John (Matt. 11:11). While the two were close though, Jesus regarded John as belonging to a different age, the age preparatory of the gospel (Luke 16:16). We need not be surprised that John sent messengers from prison asking whether Jesus really was the one that should come (Matt. 11:3). He wanted to know how Jesus fitted into his own perceptions and expectations as we all do.

There were other differences between the two men. John was an ascetic, while Jesus was not. John remained in the wilderness, while Jesus traveled freely. For John, the kingdom was still in the future, while for Jesus it was already present. John preached judgment, while Jesus' message included the good news of God's love. For John, a right way of living would open the gates of heaven, while according to Jesus we depend on God's grace even with our best performance. But they agreed on some decisive points. Both were dissatisfied with the current situation, both had eschatological expectations, and both were convinced that people needed to surrender their lives to God. Like John, Jesus was concerned by the fact that the present situation of the people of God was a far cry from what God wanted and both believed that the time was right for the coming of the king. Take the Temple, for example. What was to have been a place of prayer had become corrupt and deserving of divine judgment. Jesus' cleansing of the Temple symbolized its coming destruction and God's judgment over this whole present evil age. He expected it to inaugurate God's kingdom and bring about a new order. Destroy this temple, Jesus said, and God will raise it up in a new form, the temple of his body (John 2:19–21).

4. Jesus' Place in Society

As for his place in society, Jesus did not fit an existing category. He did not belong to the ecclesiastical or social establishment – he was and remained an outsider. He certainly did not belong to the ruling classes. They quickly became his enemies. He was not a priest or a theologian. He was neither a Sadducee nor a conservative. He struck them as a kind of revolutionary figure. But Jesus did not fit that category very well either. Though he spoke of liberation, he was not what one might call a social revolutionary. He had no plan to set up a theocracy. He did not advocate rising up against the Romans. He did not proclaim war of liberation. He did not tell people to refuse to pay taxes. Besides, he advocated love of enemies, not their destruction, and forgiveness, not retaliation. He embodied a readiness to suffer rather than the use of force. Far from inciting violence he blessed the peacemakers. But then neither did he advise emigration or retreat from the world. He was not a monk and did not preach isolation from the world. He was not an ascetic. He did not follow the way of the Pharisees either which took the path of compromise. The four options in Jesus' day – establishment, revolution, emigration and compromise – he rejected them all. He did not fit in anywhere – neither with the rulers, nor with the rebels, neither with the moralizers, nor with the ascetics. He was provocative on every side. He could not and cannot be fitted in anywhere. Backed by no party and challenging all sides, the man fits no formula.[16]

Jesus' public ministry began after John met his death. He conducted his ministry in areas where Jews had settled and did not go out of his way to contact other groups. He had a calling (he said) to the lost sheep of Israel (Mark 7:27). He even distinguished himself from those who cross land and sea to make converts (Matt. 23:15). Like the scribes, Jesus was addressed as teacher and had a circle of followers called disciples. He also spoke in the style of scribes through dialogues and coined sayings and parables that could be easily remembered. Though his contemporaries realized that he was not just a scribe since "he taught them as one having authority" (Mark 1:22). He enjoyed a different line of authority, more like a prophet (Mark 8:27), and accompanied his teachings with miracles. "The things about Jesus Nazareth, who was a prophet mighty in deed and word before God and all the people" (Luke 24:19). He taught authoritatively in reference to the kingdom and he performed miracles. He healed the sick and cast out demons. He saw them as signs of the coming kingdom.[17]

One surprising even shocking thing about Jesus was his behavior. His association with sinners and the ritually unclean in table fellowship scandalized people. So too his apparent breaking of the sabbath commandments and regulations on purity. It even led to a jingle about him – "this man is a glutton and a drunkard, a friend of tax collectors and sinners" (Matt. 11:19). His behavior drew attention and aroused hostility. But he did not make trouble for the sake of making trouble. Behind it all lay his conviction that God's love was for everyone, which led him to act inclusively. But his openness made him seem like a false prophet, the penalty for which was death. In a curious way his violent end was written into the logic of his life.

5. Proclamation of the Kingdom

What was Jesus' cause and center? He did not proclaim himself or thrust himself forward. His cause was the coming of the kingdom of God into the world.[18] This he presented in a variety of ways without really defining it. He presented it in parables, in symbolic actions, and in figures of speech. The kingdom was central but also metaphorical such that it could not be described or pinned down. It was a feast and a harvest. It was present and yet future. One thing is sure – he did not have in mind God's rule from the beginning of time but was thinking of God's coming reign. It would not be a regime set up by force but a realm of love and forgiveness. It would be a kingdom where, in accordance with Jesus' own prayer, God's name is truly hallowed and his will done. It will be a context in which human needs are met, sins are forgiven, and evil is overcome. It will be a place where, in accordance with Jesus' promises, the poor, the hungry, those who weep and those who are downtrodden will come into their own – where pain, suffering and death will have an end. Such a kingdom cannot be described but it can be made known in metaphors – as a banquet, a new covenant, a seed springing up, a ripe harvest. It will be a kingdom, as the prophets foretold, of righteousness, love, freedom, reconciliation and peace. It will be a time of salvation, fulfillment, and consummation.[19]

Jesus put God and God's will at the center of everything. He had a vision of how things should be and could be and he wanted to see it happening now. He could not proclaim good news to the poor and liberty to captives and not start applying his vision to the present situation. Jesus was wholly and entirely concerned with God's cause and therefore with man's cause and welfare. He was interested in God's coming reign of love. He did not want a theocracy established by force. He did not want a kingdom constructed by women and men. He wanted God's kingdom where God's name will be truly hallowed and his will done on earth, and where humankind is blessed, their sins forgiven and evil overcome.[20]

Jesus emphasized the coming of the kingdom as the gift of God and something which is near at hand (Mark 1:15). He envisaged a new order, a new start, and the fulfillment of man's fundamental hopes. He preached the kingdom of God and God's lordship which brings salvation. This is the God and father of the prodigal son and of all the lost. Not God of the hereafter at the expense of humanity in the here and now. However vague the timetable, however light on detail, the hope of God's reign was the centerpiece of Jesus' message and integrates all he said and did. The God of Jesus was the God of compassion. This is why he criticized those who did not act compassionately, even in their scriptural interpretation. His faith in the God of love sustained his hope. It was the basis of his life of trust. What we see in Jesus is a theocentric style of life in which God's reign is what matters most. A God who is primarily compassionate and concerned with human well-being. A God who gives priority to the ethical above the cultic. When this God comes to reign, the poor and hungry will no longer be forgotten and there will be a new kind of human life in community.[21] And in this context, Jesus expects a new man, a changed awareness, a different attitude, a new orientation in thought and action. He wants practical and concrete love. Love even of enemies. Forgiveness without limit. Renunciation of rights because God puts grace before law and so must we. Small wonder there were people who wanted him put out of the way.[22]

6. Jesus and the Law

Central to Jesus' proclamation of the kingdom was his under-standing of the will of God which he proclaimed with great boldness as if he stood in God's place. Without abolishing any commandment, he pointed to what stood behind the law, namely, God's will for the enhancement of life. Thus Jesus challenged rabbinic interpretations of the law, interpretations which obscured its real meaning. For him, people's welfare matters most, not blind obedience to laws.[23]

Jesus' teaching lifted the interpretation of the law to a higher plane and gave the Decalogue new meaning by emphasizing that we should:

- have no other gods besides God, but must also love him with our whole heart, our whole soul and our whole mind.
- love our neighbor, but should also love our enemy, as ourselves.
- avoid using God's name pointlessly, and that we ought not even swear by him.
- keep the sabbath by resting, but must also be active in doing good on that day.
- honor our father and mother in order to have a long life on earth, but must also – for the sake of the true life – show them respect even by leaving them.
- not kill, but must also refrain even from angry thoughts and words.
- not commit adultery, but must also avoid even adulterous intentions.
- not steal, but must also renounce the right to reparation for the wrong we have suffered.
- not bear false witness, but must also be so absolutely truthful that our "Yes" means "Yes" and our "No" "No."
- not covet our neighbor's house, but must also put up with evil.
- not covet our neighbor's wife, but must also refrain from seeking a "legal" divorce.

Jesus interpreted God's law as if people mattered. God's will did not consist of flawless performance but human welfare. God's compassion is central. On the other hand, his opponents showed little flexibility. For them, the commandments are eternally valid and unchanging and must be obeyed without question to the smallest detail. Jesus, in contrast, places God and God's mercy at the center. The commandments are expressions of God's will but they serve God's unchanging love which may require us to go beyond them and even depart from their literal demands. His opponents set store on the letter but Jesus set store on the spirit in which they were given. They put what is written at the heart of things – Jesus put God at the heart of things. For the one, the laws themselves matter most. For the other, it is people who matter most because they matter most to God. One way brings death, the other way brings life. For Jesus, people matter most, not laws. He was willing to cross boundaries for the sake of people in need. Like when he healed people on the sabbath day because (he said) the sabbath was made for people, not people for the sabbath. This is what matters most. You can keep the rules and miss the whole point. Thus Jesus respected laws but approached them differently on the basis of a theology which understands that God is gracious. On this basis, he could set priorities that affected how laws are to be applied in everyday life. Rules are subordinated to God's overriding compassion for people. Jesus did not set the Scriptures aside but put them into perspective. It meant that, on the one hand, he expounded God's will in a way that went beyond the commandments. It meant, on the other hand, that he rejected the fundamentalism of his day which was obsessed with literal fulfillment.[24]

7. Pinning Jesus Down

It was not easy to pin Jesus down when it came to his identity. A number of people had hoped that he would play the role of a royal messiah, while others saw him as a prophet, an exorcist, and/or a teacher. But Jesus showed little interest in titles as such. It was not part of his mission to make very specific claims for himself. "Son of Man" comes closest, but it only proves the point by being ambiguous. When he did allude to his own role it would come out as a by-product of his preaching of the kingdom rather than an assertion of his own status. Evidently, it was his proclamation that was most important and not the exact identity of the proclaimer. What is clear (I think) is that Jesus was remembered as one who took on the role of God's eschatological agent and spokesman and, in that context, the agent of God's purposes, the beloved son of God who will play a decisive role in bringing the kingdom to fulfillment.[25]

Thus in subtle ways Jesus did make claims and did assert a uniqueness: in announcing the coming kingdom of God, in interpreting the law in an authoritative manner, in being conscious of the surpassing importance of his mission, indicating a pivotal turning point in history that involves a new conception of humanity's relationship with God. He was convinced that a turning point in the history of humankind was taking place and that he would occupy a strategic place in it as far as the relationship between God and man is concerned. What is important is not simply having faith in God but receiving the message of the coming of the kingdom which calls for a right relationship with Jesus. Because he is central to what God is doing he needs to be confessed and followed. He is the one who will sit upon the throne of God's glory and judge the world (Luke 22:69).

Jesus' claim was subtle and often hidden. His distaste for honorific titles was not because they were too lofty but because Jesus was something more and something different than they could express. In him, the disciples encountered God's grace and judgment. In him they met the Word of God and God's love in person, a reality greater and more exalted than any title. Jesus' reluctance to accept any such titles was not that he claimed to be less, but because he was more than they could express. In Jesus there are no signs of worldly greatness, none of the trappings that we associate with power and influence. Jesus was poor and homeless. He was among his disciples as one who serves. At the same time, his role was pivotal to the return from exile of the ancient people of God. He embodied what he had announced.[26]

In all of this Jesus was a very different kind of "messiah." Much more than a rabbi or a scribe, even the title of prophet does not do justice to him. He was conscious that his preaching and activities were to have ultimate significance and that he was the one bringing salvation. The overall impression that he left was of one who had assumed an authority unlike anyone before him. He considered himself empowered to go beyond the law and point to its real meaning. He claimed to stand in God's place as one who conveys God and God's will to people. He claimed that God would exalt him as judge and savior of all. The impression that Jesus left was of one who assumed an authority unlike anyone before him and one who felt empowered to go beyond the letter of the law and point to its true meaning. He claimed to stand in God's place as one who can convey God's will to the people. He believed that God would exalt him as judge and savior. Even his closest disciples did not grasp his true significance.

James Dunn writes:

> Jesus made no attempt to claim any title as such. It would appear that he saw it as no part of his mission to make specific claims for his own status. Allusion to his own role comes out more as a by-product of his proclamation of God's kingdom. His role was in relation to that rather than an assertion of his own status as such. Evidently, it was his proclamation of the kingdom which was important – the identity of the proclaimer was a secondary matter. Our review of the data has underlined the foolishness of pitching the discussion in terms of clear-cut titles. The discussion should rather be pitched in terms of more amorphous concepts, of embryonic insights, of roles taken on rather than titles claimed. The indications are more of a man who read the Scriptures with eschatological overtones and saw there possibilities and patterns which broke through the more established and traditional categories. We can begin to speak more firmly of a man who was remembered as one who above all took on the role of eschatological spokesman for God. And from this we can deduce without strain, something of Jesus' own self-understanding regarding that role – his conviction of being God's eschatological agent at the climax of God's purposes for Israel, his sense of intimate sonship before God and of the dependence of his disciples on him, and his strong hope for final acknowledgment as the man who was playing the decisive role in bringing the kingdom to fulfillment and consummation.[27]

8. Why was Jesus put to Death?

A striking feature of the story of Jesus is how it ends. How it differs from the fate of other great founders of religious traditions – Moses, Buddha and Mohammed, who all die in honored old age, surrounded by their followers who are resolved to carry on their work. But Jesus dies in mid-life, deserted by his followers and subject to a painful and a shameful death. Why would anyone want to kill such a good teacher? Why did he die with the cry on his lips: "My God, my God" (Mark 15:43)? On the face of it, it looks like defeat and the end of everything. What a tragic story!

In some ways Jesus brought it on himself by provoking conflict. Take, for example, his entry into Jerusalem, his cleansing of the Temple, and his prophecy of its downfall. His demeanor in these incidents had messianic overtones though without expectations. In a sense his death was the logical conclusion of his proclamation and activities. Jesus did not merely endure death – he provoked it. This man offended against almost everything that was sacred to this society and its people. What teacher sets himself against God's law? What prophet would claim to be above Moses? Is he not a fanatic and a heretic and (as such) supremely dangerous? Disturbing the existing order, stirring up unrest, seducing the people – these are serious infractions. He knew what was coming. He knew that he would be put to death. If nothing else, he knew what happens to faithful prophets like John the Baptist. He had to go to Jerusalem – the question had to be put. But he knew what would happen if he went. He was not naive. Nevertheless, he found meaning in the suffering.

Why was Jesus executed? The Romans had their reasons. Crucifixions send a powerful signal about who is in charge here. This is what happens to rebels. Cross us and we can do what we like with you. If you even look like a rebel against Rome you had better be careful. The Empire was familiar with failed messiahs and knew how to deal with them. Though in this case they knew Jesus was not a revolutionary and in killing him (ironically) they broke their own laws. The Jews too had reasons for wanting Jesus dead. They worried that, even though he did not pose a big threat, what if the people believe in him and the Romans come and destroy our holy place and our nation? (John 11:47) The leaders felt that Jesus was a trouble maker and presented him to Pilate in these terms. But they knew that Jesus was not a would-be messiah like Judas the Galilean. If he were, they would have had to arrest his followers as well. They knew that he posed no political threat. But he was leading the people astray. He was verging on blasphemy. And if the people follow him our national life could be at risk. It was not very difficult to make Jesus, whom they regarded as a false prophet, look like a seditious fellow in Pilate's eyes.

Understandably, the Romans and the Jews wanted him dead but why did Jesus seem to will his own death? Why did he submit so passively to it? The answer is found in the Last Supper. Being in some sense a Passover meal, Jesus' use of it recalled the divine victory over death and announced a new exodus and a new covenant. By means of his death, Jesus believed, along the lines of Isaiah 53 evil will be dealt with and a new order will dawn. Jesus celebrated a final meal with his disciples on the night before his death in the context of Passover in order to announce the strange victory of God through his death. He believed he would be the means in his death of the radical defeat of evil.

9. Jesus our Future and Hope

Had Jesus' life ceased at Calvary we never would have heard of him. He would have disappeared from history as many other religious claimants have. That we have heard of him is significant then. After his death there was a new beginning in spite of this disastrous end. How did this happen? The one who was crucified was not kept captive by death. God raised him up and assumed him into the life of God. God himself resolved the dilemma.[28] In Bach's B Minor Mass the solemn, slow-moving chorus *Crucifixus* is followed at once by the joyous allegro, *Et Resurrexit*. And so it should be, not just liturgically but historically. Based on the empty tomb and the appearances of the risen Lord, the disciples realized that resurrection is not just a future hope for all humankind at the end of history. It was an act of God in the midst of history which established Jesus as Lord. God had raised him up and therefore what he said before is true and we can go on taking him seriously. Without the resurrection, Jesus is an enigma – a wonderful teacher, a great leader, a wise man – but in the end a total failure. But with it he stands at the turning point of history and points to his victory over sin and death.

With the resurrection of Jesus, the
appearance. Snatched from death, he
existence no longer subject to the
Resurrection was not his private priv
universal significance for all who follo
prefigured in Jesus, will extend to the
day of the Lord finally comes, wher
world becomes the first and everlastir
Thus we have been given a living and ₁
been proleptically anticipated in the resurrection of Jesus.

Jesus' resurrection was an act of divine power. Being
raised up and exalted, Jesus lives forever with God. He has
become the first fruits of those who have fallen asleep which
promises the fulfillment of humankind in its wholeness. It
prefigures that toward which the whole creation looks (Rom.
8:19). Jesus is our future and our hope. The reality of
resurrection changes the objective situation of all men and
women and makes it possible for them to enter the new reality
by faith and baptism. Jesus' new redemptive presence among
his disciples not only establishes hope and freedom but gathers
a body of disciples around the Lord who is present in a new
way among them.

After the resurrection and the appearances, the Gospels and
Acts tell us that the glorified Christ was taken away into
heaven, God having given the seal of approval to Christ's
sacrifice and demonstrated to us the hope of everlasting life. It
marked the end of his incarnate life on earth and his
(re)entrance into glory. It was another of God's symbolic
actions. And like the birth, the ascension was not so much a
proof as an indication. And like it also, a mystery.

10. Conclusion

With the whole church, we confess of Jesus: "From his fullness
have we all received, grace upon grace" (John 1:16 NRSV). And
thanks to the historical traditions recorded in the New
Testament we, his disciples of today, encounter Jesus as he
preaches and debates, shares table-fellowship and heals the

...en to the texts, we sit with the early disciples as ...eir memories of Jesus, nurture their identity as his ..., equip themselves for witness and controversy, ...te and learn new lessons for life. Through the Jesus ...ition it is still possible for anyone to encounter the Jesus ...om whom Christianity stems. Dunn concludes:

> As Jesus himself lived in the light of the coming kingdom, so the Jesus tradition continues to serve as a resource and inspiration for all caring and concerned living. Not as a blueprint for such a life, nor as an instruction manual for a complete social ethic or politically mature society but as a witness indicating the character of the deep personal relations and priorities, values, and motivations without which any social structure or political manifesto will fail to realize its best ambitions. The Jesus tradition heard responsively could and can still function as a test of the caring community, as a rebuke and challenge to any self-indulgent society, arrogant in maintaining its own prerogatives and careless of the needs of others.[29]

For Christians, Jesus is the focus of attention because God's word is not first of all a written document but a human life. We have a relational revelation, not of a timeless man, not of a heavenly figure, but of a first-century Jew. The coming to be of persons was a significant event in cosmic history and thus the category of the personal is of great importance in our understanding of reality. If the world has its origins in the will of a personal God, then we may expect the personal to be the prime vehicle for the creator's interaction with us. It leads us to expect that the self-revealing of God will be focused in a particular person acting on the stage of history, playing his role in the drama of salvation being staged by the God of Israel. Jesus is the one through whom God's purposes for Israel and the world are coming to pass. It was he who announced the long-awaited kingdom and he celebrated it with all who welcomed the proclamation, sharing table-fellowship and assuring sinners that they are forgiven. Though the kingdom was not exactly what they expected it did not take the form of a war of liberation against Rome). It involved Jesus taking center stage, entering Jerusalem, cleansing the Temple, and promising a new covenant. He would be the one through whom Israel's destiny would be realized. God's Temple might be destroyed but Jesus was vindicated. Though it would call down on his head the wrath of his enemies and he would have to suffer as many had suffered before him. Yet, conscious of his vocation, he would enact the great symbol of a new exodus shown in the Passover meal eaten with his disciples. Evil would be defeated and the purposes of God for the world would be realized. In Jesus, God himself would come to reign. And he would be raised up, not at the end of history, but in the midst of history. Jesus' vocation was to bring Israel's history to a climax and he succeeded in his aim.

Notes

[1] Philip Jenkins, *The Next Christendom: The Coming of Global Christianity* (Oxford: Oxford University Press, 2002).

[2] Jaroslav Pelikan, *Jesus Through the Centuries* (New Haven: Yale University Press, 1985), p. 1.

[3] Consider J. R. Seeley, *Ecce Homo: A Survey of the Life and Work of Jesus Christ* (London: J. M. Dent, 1908).

[4] Compare Nietzsche's *Ecce Homo: How One Becomes What One Is* (New York: Penguin Books, 1979). For more on Nietzsche see Hans Küng, *Does God Exist? An Answer for Today* (New York: Doubleday, 1978), pp. 343–424.

[5] His significance is captured by N. T. Wright in a telling phrase: (he is) "God with a Human Face," in *The Original Jesus: The Life and Vision of a Revolutionary* (Grand Rapids, MI: Eerdmans, 1996), ch. 7.

[6] The truth of this is nicely expressed by Alister McGrath, "The Uniqueness of Jesus Christ," in *A Passion for Truth: The Intellectual Coherence of Evangelicalism* (Downers Grove, IL: InterVarsity Press, 1996), ch. 1.

[7] Consider again McGrath, "The Authority of Scripture," in *A Passion for Truth*, ch. 2.

[8] James D. G. Dunn, *Jesus Remembered* (Grand Rapids, MI: Eerdmans, 2003).

[9] William Temple, *Christ's Revelation of God* (London: SCM, 1925).

[10] John R. W. Stott, *The Incomparable Christ* (Downers Grove, IL: InterVarsity Press, 2001).

[11] See Wolfhart Pannenberg, "Anthropology and Christology," in *Systematic Theology*, Vol. 2 (trans. G. W. Bromiley; 3 vols.; Grand Rapids, MI: Eerdmans, 1994), ch. 9.

[12] On such epistemological matters, see Dunn, *Jesus Remembered*, ch. 6 and Küng, *Does God Exist?*, pp. 425–583.

[13] James Dunn (for example) does not believe we can begin the history of Jesus with his birth in Bethlehem: *Remembering Jesus*, pp. 340–48. For details, see Raymond E. Brown, *The Birth of the Messiah: A Commentary on the Infancy Narratives in Matthew and Luke* (updated ed.; London: Chapman, 1993).

[14] Markus Bockmuehl, "Where did Jesus come from?" in *This Jesus: Martyr, Lord, Messiah* (Downers Grove, IL: InterVarsity Press, 1994), ch. 1.

[15] Richard Swinburne, *The Christian God* (Oxford: Clarendon Press, 1994), pp. 233–35.

[16] Hans Küng, "The Social Context," in *On Being a Christian* (London: Collins, 1974), pp. 175–213.

[17] N. T. Wright, "Jesus' Career in Outline," in *Jesus and the Victory of God* (Christian origins and the question of God, vol. 2; London/Minneapolis: SPCK/Augsburg-Fortress, 1996), pp. 147–50.

[18] N. T. Wright, "Kingdom of God in Early Christian Literature," in *Victory of God*, 663–70; George E. Ladd, *Jesus and the Kingdom: The Eschatology of Biblical Realism* (New York: Harper & Row, 1964).

[19] Walter Kasper, "Jesus' Message – the Kingdom of God," in *Jesus the Christ* (New York: Paulist Press, 1976), pp. 72–88.

[20] William Loader, *Jesus and the Fundamentalism of his Day* (Grand Rapids, MI: Eerdmans, 2001), pp. 64–66.

[21] Küng, "The God of Jesus Christ," in *Does God Exist*, pp. 667–77.

[22] Hans Schwarz, "Announcing the Kingdom," in *Christology* (Grand Rapids, MI: Eerdmans, 1998), pp. 102–105.

[23] Donald A. Hagner, "Jesus Relation to the Law," in *The Jewish Reclamation of Jesus* (Grand Rapids, MI: Zondervan, 1984), ch. 3.

[24] W. R. G. Loader, *Jesus' Attitude Towards the Law: A Study of the Gospels* (Grand Rapids, MI: Eerdmans, 1997).

[25] James D. G. Dunn, "How did Jesus see his own Role?" in *Jesus Remembered*, ch. 16.

[26] Wright, *Victory of God*, pp. 538–39.

[27] Dunn, *Remembering Jesus*, pp. 761–62.

[28] Pannenberg, "The Justification of Jesus by the Father in his Resurrection," in *Systematic Theology*, Vol. 2, pp. 343–63.

[29] Dunn, *Remembering Jesus*, pp. 892–93.

3

The Uniqueness of Christ's Suffering and Death on the Cross

Graham Tomlin

In 2004, a film took the Western world by surprise. It contained hardly any well-known actors, the screenplay was delivered in an ancient language virtually unspoken in the world today, and contained some of the most graphic scenes of violence moviegoers could remember. Despite all this, it soon became the seventh highest box-office success in US film-making history, after taking a total of $370m (£200m) in its first five months. It was of course Mel Gibson's *The Passion of the Christ*. The impact made by the film and the controversy it aroused was an indication of how the death of Jesus of Nazareth can stir the blood more than almost any other. Two thousand years after the event, the death of this particular enigmatic Jewish rabbi, executed under Roman government in Palestine in around A.D. 30, and of course the manner of the death itself, still has the power to provoke, to shock and to evoke feelings of outrage, sympathy and suspicion in equal measure.

As much as it was loved by evangelical Christians (perhaps ironic given that it was made by the deeply traditional Roman Catholic Mel Gibson), the film was hated by many of the liberal intelligentsia. The controversy it raised drew attention to continuing controversy which the death of Jesus tends to evoke in the minds of many educated people today. It is perhaps as offensive to sensitive ears today as it was in its own time. However, this does mean that if we are to speak of the uniqueness of the cross of Christ, we will need to address the particular ways in which that claim is challenged and confronted *today*. The crucial task is to address not so much the challenges raised by other eras, but the points where the cross of Christ directly cuts across the assumptions and concerns of contemporary societies. Those turning to this chapter to seek an exposition of models of the atonement will be disappointed. Then again, there is no shortage of books and articles which do just that, and I recommend they look to those places for answers to those questions. Those who objected to *The Passion of the Christ* did not do so primarily because they rejected a particular view of the atonement. Their difficulties took other forms, and it is those problems that this chapter will try to address. However, first, we do need to do some historical work to locate the cross firmly in its own context. It was a historical, not an idealized metaphysical event, and so to history we must first turn.

1. The Cross in Historical Context

In one sense, the death of Jesus of Nazareth was far from unique. Many criminals, escaped slaves and failed revolutionaries were executed in this barbaric and public manner by the Roman imperial machine in the first-century A.D. This was the "supreme Roman penalty" reserved for slaves, violent criminals and rebellious foreigners kept in use because of its effectiveness as public shaming and its deterrent value.[1] Jesus took his place among many unknown others who suffered this extreme form of tortured death under the police state that was Roman Palestine.

Yet from the very beginning, the earliest Christians saw his death as in some way different from all these other politically inspired executions. The Gospels contain little explicit reflection on the saving significance of the death of Jesus, with the exceptions of Mark's well-known inclusion of the phrase "to give his life as a ransom for many" (Mark 10:45), and the Last Supper narratives, which contain clear links between Jesus' forthcoming death and the forgiveness of sins and the coming of the kingdom.[2] The evangelistic sermons in Acts, probably written in their current form some years after our extant Pauline letters, also do not tend to focus a great deal on the atoning significance of the death of Jesus, normally referring to it with such a phrase as "Jesus Christ of Nazareth, whom you crucified …" (Acts 4:10).

However, if we consider the earliest documents of the New Testament, it is striking that around twenty years after the event, Paul was writing about how this death was "for our sins according to the Scriptures" (1 Cor. 15:3; cf. Gal. 1:4), and a little later of how it was "a sacrifice of atonement" (Rom. 3:25).[3] He and his followers repeatedly use the formula that Jesus was "given up" or "gave himself up" to death on a cross, indicating time and again that this was in some sense "for us."[4] And even if the Gospels do not offer lengthy reflection on the meaning of Jesus' death, they do dwell in considerable detail on the manner and fact of it. It did not take long for the followers of Jesus to realize and start believing that this was no ordinary death.

The reason why Jesus' death was transformed from the execution of yet another failed messiah to an event of epochal significance is simple: it came about because of the resurrection. The story that this Jesus had been raised from death in a completely unexpected anticipation of the resurrection of the just at the last day, could not but lead these Jewish friends of Jesus to a complete re-evaluation of his death. There is a strong case to be made that even Jesus himself understood his own death as more than just the tragic unwanted consequence of confronting the Jewish and Roman authorities, or the sad outcome of a risky political and religious strategy at a time of great national tension. Although this is not the place to develop the argument, he does seem to have foreseen his own death at the hands of the Romans as his own vocation, to die on behalf of the people, in some way to take on himself the fate of God's people, to act out the sin-bearing role of Israel in his own person.[5]

So, belief in the unique significance of Jesus' death was there at the very beginning of the new movement he initiated. It was there most probably in the mind of Jesus, among his earliest followers and it was there in the early writing of Paul. The death of Jesus can even have been said to have affected the way the early Christians thought about God himself. At a very early stage, it seems to have begun to subtly nuance Jewish monotheism into a form which included the crucified Jesus within the unique identity of God.[6] The claim therefore stands from earliest Christian times that despite its commonness as a means of execution, the cross of Jesus is absolutely unique as the way in which atonement is made for the people, and reconciliation is effected between humanity and God.[7] Out of all the deaths which occurred on Roman crosses in the first-century A.D. God chose to vindicate this particular one.

2. The Cross in Contemporary Context

Yet in the contemporary world, the uniqueness of the cross is radically questioned. It still stands as one of the most powerful symbols in the world today, an instantly recognizable corporate logo which hangs around necks, is tattooed onto arms, stands on the top of spires and adorns communion tables across the planet. And yet as such a symbol, it takes its place alongside many others: the Islamic Crescent, the Star of David, the Hindu Lotus, the Sikh sword, and even historical political symbols such as the hammer and sickle, or even the swastika, as a sign recognizable for a movement. In a consumerist, brand-conscious world, the cross represents just one sign among many. More than that, it now carries with it a great deal of historical baggage, accumulated over centuries of use.

For Muslims, it still recalls the red sign imprinted on the banners of the Crusaders who killed their ancestors, and in the light of recent events, it represents Western (and hence "Christian") aggression against the Muslims of Iraq, Palestine or Bosnia. For many feminists, the cross is just as compromised. The feminist critique argues that Jesus' willing acceptance of death has led to a glorification of suffering within the Christian tradition, justifying the oppression of minorities such as women, or at least recommending passive acceptance of suffering inflicted by others.[8] For Jews, the cross is even more offensive. *The Passion of the Christ* served to re-ignite old tensions about whether the Romans or the Jews bore responsibility for the death of Jesus, and highlighted the controversial nature of Matthew's narrative (upon whose account the film was based), with its apparent ascription of at least some of the blame not only to Jews in the first century, but to their descendants as well (Matt. 27:25). Not only that, but of course it was in the name of and under the symbol of the cross that pogroms against the Jews were launched, in medieval Europe, nineteenth-century Russia and countless other places.

The charge stands again, that the cross is in fact far from unique. It is yet another oppressive symbol used by the powerful (typically male, white, Western agents of historic Christendom) to oppress and hold in subjugation the power-less, whether the poor, women, Jews, Muslims or any other minority group. A culture which sometimes calls itself post-modern is deeply conscious of the way in which power relates to truth. In the words of Michel Foucault, power produces truth and truth produces power.[9] Discourses which claim to be "true" in an ultimate sense have a habit of producing mechanisms which protect and promote their claim to truth. In turn, those in power tend to produce ideologies which legitimate their hold on power. It is not that this is deliberate or devious, just unavoidable and inherent in any set of human relations. Hence, all we can do is maintain a kind of continuous suspicion of the way power operates in societies such as ours. The "word of the cross" is just such another discourse which both serves and is served by the interests of power. As such, it has no more claim to ultimate truth than any other.

Can the cross be rescued from such a critique? As the symbol of Christianity, it holds a central place within the faith it represents, but is it fundamentally compromised within a pluralist world deeply conscious of issues of power and abuse? As a way of finding an answer, we will take a look at just a few key theologians of the Christian tradition who have focused on the cross as a key central theme, and (to anticipate the argument) have shown how the word of the cross is a very different kind of discourse to all others, precisely because it contains within it a revolution in the way power is exercised and operates.[10]

3. Paul and the Cross in Corinth

As we have seen already, one of the first Christian theologians to explore a theology of the cross was Paul. His correspondence with the church in Corinth is particularly important in this respect. To understand how this theology of the cross works in relation to power in the context of Corinthian Christianity requires a stab at the difficult task of reconstructing the situation in the church, and the contentions present in it.

Paul's relationships with the church in Corinth were unpredictable. Although the problems have often been thought to be primarily doctrinal in character, research over the past few decades has highlighted some persistent socio-economic factors in the disputes.[11] This social analysis has been complemented by greater understanding of the role played by rhetoric in the city, both the interest shown by the Corinthian Christians in *sofia logou*, and in Paul's own use of rhetoric.[12] Whether it concerns the way in which the Eucharist was conducted (cf. 1 Cor. 11:22), the tendency to seek justice in secular litigation (only the rich could afford to go to court),[13] or food offered to idols,[14] there is clearly a social and economic dimension to the issues the church is struggling with, and hence the issue of power, and how it operates and is used is never far away. Of course, the church itself was socially quite varied (1 Cor. 1:26), which brought additional tensions to the task of making it work, especially in such a class-conscious society as Corinth.

Having said all this, social factors do not explain everything in the Corinthian church. There are still some real ideological issues which divide the church from Paul, and, presumably, amongst themselves. Of the famous "parties" in Corinth, it seems that, despite what 1 Corinthians 1:12 would suggest, there are in fact two main sides involved.[15] Although some argue for a contentious division between Paul and Cephas, perhaps reflecting a Gentile-Jewish divide in the church,[16] the conclusion that Apollos is the main rival to Paul's authority and loyalty within the congregation is the more likely.[17] In particular, the interest in rhetoric and Apollos' skill at it, along with the Acts 18 evidence that he *had* visited Corinth, whereas it is at least uncertain whether Peter ever did, indicates that he is the focus of attention here. Peter virtually disappears from view after the brief mention in 1 Corinthians 1:12, and in chapters 3 and 4, it is Apollos who is discussed in detail. In addition, the absence from the letter of the normal contentious issues in Jewish-Gentile Christian relations, such as law, promise, circumcision and the like points to the likely conclusion that the main points of contention here are not between Jewish and non-Jewish believers but disputes between different groups of Gentile Christians.

Gerd Theissen's study showed how most of the people named in the letter were probably of high social status, and most probably supporters of Paul. The letter also suggests that 'some' within the church disdained Paul's ministry and reputation, perhaps because of his lack of rhetorical ability (as opposed to Apollos) and his artisan status (ch. 9), and at the same time, disparaged the poorer members of the church, as they "despise those who have nothing."[18] Perhaps this is the same group who claimed that "there is no resurrection from the dead" (1 Cor. 15:12–13), that "an idol is nothing at all in the world" (1 Cor. 8:4), argued for the right to eat in pagan temples, maybe even joining in the cultic meals in honor of idols (1 Cor. 8:1–13; 10:7–33), and displayed a strange mixture of sexual license (1 Cor. 5:1) and asceticism (1 Cor. 7:1).[19]

It is a fair guess that the church in Corinth was experiencing a power struggle between two groups of wealthy Christians. One, perhaps converted by Apollos' rhetorical skill and charismatic ability, had uncritically and maybe even unconsciously brought some of their pre-Christian ideas into their new faith to justify their behavior. In reaction, a number of those who had been in the church longer, originally converted by Paul, began to disapprove (maybe this group had already written to Paul to complain about those who associated too closely with "immoral people" – 1 Cor. 5:9?). This argument quickly degenerated into an argument about names and loyalties, one side disparaging the ministry and abilities of the other's "leader." The poor in the congregation, for example, Chloe's slaves (1 Cor. 1:11), saw just an argument over names. The rich took sides, some even staying aloof from the quarrel by claiming to follow the distant Peter. Paul, it seems, has to address two quite separate problems, *boasting* by those who followed Apollos and valued rhetoric, knowledge, wealth, status, and charismatic gifting, and therefore disparaged both the poor and Paul, and *quarrelling* between these and Christians who thought they were remaining loyal to Paul. Both of these attitudes, of course, touch on the use of power within the church.

As Paul responds, he chooses to do so by taking the church back to the cross of Christ, as the place where God has revealed his "wisdom," or his "characteristic way of working." As he begins a carefully argued reply in 1 Corinthians 1:18, he shows that the unity of this small group of Christians, so easily fractured, is found in the fact that Christ has died for them. Paul was not crucified for them, Christ was. They were baptized not into Paul's or Apollos' death, but Christ's.[20] Their dispute over who baptized whom would "empty the cross of its power" because it denies the reality of the unity which the cross achieved. The cross stands at the very center of the teaching which gave the church its original identity and unity (1 Cor. 15:3). It is what makes this group of people unique in the varied social and religious landscape of Corinth.

Furthermore, the cross answers not just Corinthian quarrelling, it also answers Corinthian arrogance. God's wisdom is exemplified in his scandalous choice of a crucified Messiah as the means of salvation, a relatively low-status group of people for the majority of his church in Corinth, and a weak, rhetorically unskilled, and spiritually exhausted apostle (1 Cor. 1:26–2:5). The cross gives value to the weaker, poorer brother, as one for whom Christ died (1 Cor. 8:11). Whereas these Corinthian Christians disdained the poor and Paul, *God has chosen them for his purposes*. The cross thus deconstructs both competitiveness and arrogance.

Beyond this still, the cross acts as a model of the use of power. Paul displays how the cross has worked out in his own life and ministry as a model for how power is to operate in this community. He appeals to them to imitate him (1 Cor. 4:16) in his role as servant/slave (1 Cor. 3:5; 4:1). As chapter 4 proceeds, the imagery of crucifixion creeps into the text, as Paul portrays the apostolic life as one of shame, suffering and degradation.

Paul's boast is that he "made himself a slave to all, that I might win the more" (1 Cor. 9:19), that by choosing the life of a common artisan, he became socially "weak, in order to win the weak" (1 Cor. 9:22). Paul's own life has taken on a cruciform shape, sacrificing his own social power and status for the sake of others. The true content of Christian wisdom is not "knowledge" but "love," in other words, self-giving towards one's fellow believers, and especially the poor. It is this pattern of life he recommends to these Christians, the way of servant-hood, the way of the cross. Theology which begins at the cross is for Paul the radical antidote to any religion which is only a thinly veiled copy of a power-seeking culture.

Paul points to the cross as the identifying mark of this particular group of Corinthians. The sign of the cross is to mark off their identity, not as a liturgical gesture, but in a cruciform life. In practical terms, this means quite a lot. Even though these rich Christians have a perfect right to dine at pagan dinner parties and eat meat offered to idols (after all, idols are nothing – 1 Cor. 8:4) Paul urges them to consider the good of their "weaker" brothers and sisters, and voluntarily surrender their rights, their freedom (1 Cor. 8:9) for the sake of their poorer fellow Christians who did not understand why their wealthier brothers and sisters were acting in such a way. To those members of the church eager to use their spiritual gifts, but doing so in a way that disparaged those who were less gifted, Paul recommends the way of love (chapter 13 follows directly after chapter 12!) which demands those gifts be used expressly to build up the church, not for private satisfaction.

In this local church setting, the cross functions as the controlling sign of their life together. It signifies the way in which God used his power to achieve the most difficult task of all – to reconcile the world to himself – and he does it through the powerlessness of a cross. This picture of utter helplessness, a man nailed to two roughly joined pieces of wood, unable to move, hardly able to breathe, is in fact the power and the wisdom of God – God redeeming the world – scandalous though it may be to think so. If this is so, then in Paul's mind it has clear implications for the way power operates in Christian communities. Power is to be exercised for the benefit of those who have no power; it is the ability to surrender rights and privileges; it is power exercised through love.

4. Martin Luther, the Cross and the Medieval Church

After Paul developed his *theologia crucis* in Corinth, the idea that the cross reveals something essential about God lay pretty well dormant for many years, at least in mainstream Western theology. Throughout the patristic and medieval periods, most theologians were wary of viewing the cross as directly revelatory of God and his ways. This was due partly to their reluctance to question the impassibility of God (too close an association between the cross and the being or action of God would seem to compromise this), and to two-natures Christology, which neatly enabled an ascription of suffering to the human rather than the divine nature of Christ. For example, although Tertullian is the first to coin the phrase "the crucified God," this seems little more than a rhetorical flourish for him: he is not really interested in developing a *theology* from this point. Despite his great theology of atonement, Anselm also fights shy of reading any implications for the doctrine of God from the cross. For Thomas Aquinas, the cross is a contingent, not necessary means of salvation. God could have chosen to save the world in another way, had he chosen to. So it is hard to see how the cross could have any great theological significance for him either.

When Martin Luther begins to outline his *theologia crucis* in the Heidelberg Disputation of 1518, he does so without the help of a long tradition of use within academic patristic or medieval theology. Where then did he get the idea? In part, he appears to get it from 1 Corinthians itself. Towards the end of his first set of Lectures on the Psalms (the *Dictata super Psalterium* of 1513–1515), and then during the period leading up to Heidelberg, 1 Corinthians 1–2 are quoted with remarkable frequency. As with Luther's other Reformation insights, however, it would not be true to say that he simply rediscovered this theology by sitting alone with Paul in his Wittenberg monastery. Luther gained his interest in the cross as the heart of Christian life and thought not so much from mainstream academic theology (which had largely forgotten this type of theology), but from popular traditions of practical spirituality and piety.

Contemplation of the sufferings of Christ lay at the heart of late medieval piety. Many popular works had appeared aimed to help the meditator to focus upon the sufferings of Christ, some reminding people of the efficacy of the sacraments, some aiming at a more affective individual response to Christ's sufferings.[21] At several points in his early writings, Luther shows himself to be distinctly aware of this practice of Passion meditation.[22] He particularly commends the more affective kind, whereby the sufferings of the cross are expected to have an emotional impact upon the meditator. However, he takes it further by insisting that meditation on the cross is not meant merely to evoke sentimental sorrow for Christ, but sorrow for one's own sins which put him there, and a sense of thankfulness for God's love and forgiveness.

Besides this tradition of popular passion piety, Luther seems to have learnt his *theologia crucis* from at least one other source as well. Bernard of Clairvaux's sermons on the Song of Songs, standard fare in the monastic circles in which Luther spent his early years, contain several themes which found their way into Luther's developing *theologia crucis*, for example, the importance of suffering for the Christian, the dialectic between God's proper and alien work, the insight that God reveals himself in Christ's lowliness and humility rather than his glory and power, and the idea suggested by Exodus 33 of God revealing his "back," taken up by Luther in the Heidelberg Disputation.

What Luther gained from late medieval monastic and popular Christian life was therefore not so much theology, but spirituality. In fact, much of the young Luther's problem is his experience of dissonance between this late medieval spiritual tradition and the semi-Pelagian theology of the *via moderna* which underpinned it.[23] On the one hand, this spirituality taught him to examine his sins, to despair of himself so that he would acquire humility, to value suffering as God's way of making him penitent. On the other hand, his nominalist theological training taught him to value works of contrition, penance, indulgences, masses, to nurture the growth of humility as a virtue, and to try to love God above all else *ex puris naturalibus*. Within the young Luther, therefore, a spirituality of self-accusation lived uncomfortably alongside a theology of self-justification. What his spirituality led him to accentuate (his own nothingness and worthlessness before God), his theology told him to deny. It was not just his individual experience, but also the spirituality which he had learnt, which was at odds with the prevailing theological resources available to interpret it. Due to this mismatch, theological concepts such as *iustitia dei,* and *poenitentia,* which were intended as consolatory, became terrifying. Luther found in them not peace of heart, but uncertainty and despair over his ultimate salvation, because they set before him a standard of holiness which his spirituality taught him he could never achieve. Luther found himself caught between a spirituality and a soteriology that he increasingly felt to be mutually incompatible.

Luther found the resolution of his dilemma in the cross of Christ. Following the advice of his mentor Johannes Staupitz, to "begin with the wounds of Christ," and with his mind full of the sufferings of Christ from his monastic background, Luther began to re-evaluate his experience in the light of the cross.

It seems that sometime towards the end of 1515,[24] Luther arrived at a realization that the cross was not just the way God chose to save the world, or the path to be trod if salvation was to be achieved, but that it reveals God's characteristic way of working in the world. God condemns before he saves. After all, that is what he did with Jesus. If God is to be able to save him, the sinner must be made passive, brought to a sense of his own powerlessness before his creator. He can only come with empty hands. God reveals this pattern in the cross, where Christ too is made passive before God, before he can be raised. On the cross, Christ seems to be suffering defeat, yet to the eye of faith, God is working out the salvation of the world. In this theology, therefore, like in that of Paul before him, revelation is back to front, hidden, and contrary to what is expected. Things are not what they seem and the sign and the thing signified are out of joint. What seems to be valuable (human piety, wisdom, philosophy) is in fact worthless, and what seems weak and negligible (the experience of suffering, temptation, awareness of sin and failure) is in fact God's precious work to humble and then save the sinner.

How then, did this new understanding of the cross help to resolve Luther's dilemma? All the contrition, self-accusation and awareness of sin which late medieval spirituality evoked in a monk like Luther, seemed to him a barrier to his acceptance by God. His spirituality taught him to magnify his own unworthiness, his distance from God. If he had nothing he could offer to God, how could it help him to be told that "to those who do what lies within them, God will assuredly give his grace"?[25] This new understanding of the cross as the revelation of God's ways with sinners taught him a new meaning to his experience of despair about himself. Far from a disqualification from grace, it became the only qualification for it. As Anders Nygren put it, for Luther we have "fellowship with God on the basis of sin."[26] God only saves sinners, only teaches the stupid, only enriches the poor, only raises the dead.[27] Therefore to be saved one must become sinful, foolish, poor, helpless, exactly what his spirituality had led Luther to acknowledge himself to be.

Another way of expressing this dissonance in Luther's experience is that revelation was divided from salvation. The way God had revealed himself in Christ bore no particular relation to the way he saved people in the present. Christ's life, death, suffering were past actions which could arouse emotional sympathy or validate the sacraments, but which were quite definitely *past*. Because Christ had suffered, there was no great need for the sinner now to suffer. God, it seemed had acted one way in Christ and another in Luther. For Christ, God was savior; for Luther, he was judge. Only a theology of the cross can overcome such a disastrous divide.

At the Heidelberg Disputation of 1518, Luther's theology centered upon two assertions: that God first condemns in order to save, and that he reveals himself at the cross. At the core of Luther's theology lies the connection he makes between these two insights. The way God saves people in the present, and the form in which he has revealed himself historically are joined at the cross. The vital clue for understanding the way God works is always the cross: God works and reveals himself in suffering and weakness, not strength and glory, whether in Christ or the Christian, in the first century or the sixteenth. God's activity in the present is always continuous with his revelation in history. Luther's *theologia crucis* is therefore an assertion of the unity and continuity of God's action in history and in the present, in revelation and in salvation. He is not one God in Christ and another God for us. This is why Luther insists that to know God is to know him in Christ alone, or in the words of the Heidelberg Disputation, "true theology and the knowledge of God are in the crucified Christ."[28] This theology of the cross roots God's present action in his revelation in history, and refuses to sever the two. It therefore asserts in the strongest possible way the faithfulness of God to his promise and his revelation.

This theology, fed by meditation upon the themes of 1 Corinthians 1–2 in the spirit of late medieval spirituality thus became for Luther the vantage point from which the Reformation began. In subsequent years he conducted a polemic against the scholastic theological hegemony which had become the monopoly of experts and remote from the realities of everyday Christian life, and the power, prestige and wealth of the papal church. In this church, the wise and the powerful fed off one another, and the Indulgence controversy of 1517 was a prime example of false theology being used to legitimate an oppressive practice which only served to increase papal wealth. If God's action in the present is continuous with his action in Christ, then the papacy and the church needed to model itself upon the weakness and poverty of the cross, rather than on images of imperial power. It needed to seek sufferings and the cross, not the false peace of Indulgences.[29] The papacy's failure to do that simply betrayed not just its moral deficiency, but its theological misunderstanding. As in Corinth, so in Wittenberg, theology which began at the cross had served to critique the abuse of power.

Luther came to believe that the papal church had rendered itself unaccountable to anyone, even God. As he pointed out in

"To the Christian Nobility of the German Nation" in 1520, the laity could not call the church to account because the "spiritual estate" was deemed higher than the "temporal," a Council could not do so because only a pope can call a Council; and Scripture cannot do it either, as only the pope can interpret Scripture. His critique of the church focused on the cross of Christ and its lack of conformity to its vision of the way in which God does his work. "No vicar's role can go beyond that of his lord ..." Luther writes of the pope, the "vicar of Christ" in 1520, "Moreover, he is not the vicar of Christ glorified but of Christ crucified ... Christ needs a vicar in the form of a servant, the form in which he went about on earth, working, preaching, suffering and dying."[30] The cross marks not just the way in which salvation was won, it is also the characteristic signature of God's work in the world, so the cross must always be the mark of the church's life. In this very symbol at the heart of the church lies this powerful antidote to delusions of power, worldly success, and grandeur. A church which lives by the cross can never become seduced by power.

5. Blaise Pascal, the Cross and the Politics of Power

Seventeenth-century France was also another place where theological controversy was closely intertwined with political power. Blaise Pascal's theological career saw him engaged in polemic on three fronts at once, against the confident dogmatism of Cartesian Rationalism, the skeptical tradition of Montaigne and Pyrrhonism, and on behalf of the Jansenists against their sworn enemies, the Society of Jesus. The place of the cross in Pascal's theology has seldom been noticed, in fact Pascal's significance as a theologian is not often recognized as much as it should be, perhaps in deference to his reputation as apologist, satirist and scientist.[31] Yet for Pascal, as it was for Paul and Luther, the cross was the decisive hallmark of Christian life and theology, a stone against which these contemporary trends, whether rationalist, skeptical or Jesuit, all stumbled.

Uniquely among "orthodox" Christian apologists of his day, Pascal had a great interest in the identity of God. Many seventeenth-century apologists such as Antoine Sirmond, Pierre Charron, Jean de Silhon and Yves de Paris had tried to prove the existence of God or the immortality of the soul.[32] The attempt had failed, Pascal thought, not so much because it chose the wrong methods, as because it aimed to prove the wrong God, a God susceptible to proof.

Especially after 23 November 1654, his "Night of Fire," commemorated in the famous *Mémorial*, sewn into his coat and found only after his death, Pascal identified the Christian God of the Augustinian tradition[33] represented in his own day by the movement associated with the Abbé de Saint-Cyran, the convent at Port-Royal outside Paris and in the Jansenist movement.[34] In one particularly important fragment of the *Pensées*, L449,[35] he argues that much of the contemporary polemic against Christianity does no harm at all to the Christian God, but merely undermines the God of Deism. Pascal is quite clear what Christianity is NOT. It is by no means "the adoration of a God considered great and powerful and eternal; that is really Deism, almost as far distant from true Christianity as atheism." Instead Pascal depicts the true God of the Christians, the God of the Bible. Using the motif of the God of the Patriarchs, as in the *Mémorial*, this God, far from merely the "author of geometrical truths and of the order of the elements," is one who fills the soul and heart, directly invading the interior emotional life of believers to bring about a sense both of their own *misère* and his mercy, who desires intimacy with them at the deepest level of the soul, a jealous God who instills in those whom he possesses an insatiable and exclusive desire for himself. In place of the impersonal creative force of Deism, or even of Cartesianism,[36] Pascal evokes an intensely personal, passionate God. Pascal's God is not object but subject; he is the Augustinian God of love and consolation. This passage points to the "God perceived by the heart, not by the reason" (L424), a God apprehended in an entirely different way from the God of the Deists, pagans or Epicureans, and at an entirely different level of human cognition. God is known in this radically different way because he is a radically different kind of God.

This God can be only approached by love, not speculation, through moral reorientation, not rational deduction. In a characteristically Augustinian way, God can only be known by the person who has learnt to love him. This God therefore hides himself from human attempts to find him through objective observation. Pascal's famous theme of the Hidden God is a direct result of his belief in Jansenist theology.[37] Pascal's world is not the neat Thomist world where God gives clear indications of his existence and nature, but the deeply ambiguous fallen Augustinian world which speaks simultaneously of God's presence and absence. For human creatures to know this hidden God will involve a much more radical solution than contemplating obvious proofs in nature. It will involve an engagement with God not as object but an encounter with him as subject.

At the heart of Pascal's discussion of these questions lies the symbol of the cross, again, strongly colored by the themes of 1 Corinthians 1–2. First, for Pascal, in one range of fragments of the *Pensées*,[38] the cross *hides* God from unbelievers. God "hides himself from those who tempt him but reveals himself to those who seek him" (L444). From the perspective of indifferent unbelief, God's revelation seems foolish and obscure, far from compelling and sure. From this angle the only face of God to appear is the crucified Christ, which by definition seems so complete a picture of degradation and failure that to those who view it critically and objectively, faith seems nonsensical. Thus the cross closes the door to an abstract, speculative knowledge of God.

Yet, on the other hand, the cross also has the ability to *reveal* God to those whose hearts have been moved to find him.[39] For Pascal, the cross represents the dialectic of fall and redemption. It indicates that there is a Creator, yet humanity is fallen so that it no longer recognizes him clearly in his creation. The cross also indicates the place where this creator acts to redeem humanity (L427, 431). Once Christ and the cross, the act of reconciliation between man and God, are understood, both God and human wretchedness, both human *grandeur* and *misère* are understood. When this duality is grasped, with all that it implies about both the reality of God, and yet human inability to see him, the reason for the obscurity of God behind creation is understood: we do not see him because we are blind to him. In the light of Christ (and this principle of creation and fall understood within him), everything in creation now "bursts forth with proofs of these two truths." Without him, all remains confusing. To grasp that Christ was crucified for the sins of the world is to confess one's own fallenness and epistemological weakness, the obscurity in one's own mind. It is to understand that we fail to see God clearly in creation not because he is not there, but because of human blindness which can only partially glimpse truth. Christ crucified therefore becomes the key which unlocks the mysterious ambiguity of nature, and reveals God to the seeker.

Yet another set of fragments shows how for Pascal the cross represents the pattern of the Christian life, and the way in which the transition is made between unbelief and faith, namely through the denial and death of obstinate self-will, and a willingness for moral and spiritual reorientation which is the evidence of God's touch of grace.[40] The famous argument of the "Wager" is not intended to compel belief. It is in fact a device intended to show that the real reason why people do not believe is not the illogicality of faith (any gambler weighing the odds at face value would opt for belief over unbelief any day, owing to the huge amount potentially to be won by such a small stake), but that the unbeliever simply does not want to believe.[41] The obstacle to belief is not epistemological, but moral:

> if you are unable to believe, it is because of your passions, since reason impels you to believe, yet you cannot do so. Concentrate then not on convincing yourself by multiplying proofs of God's existence, but by diminishing your passions.
> (L418)

From these three insights, all focused on the cross, Pascal is able to address the three opponents of Augustinian theology in seventeenth-century France.

1. The followers of Descartes fail to take into account the cross as representing man's fall, his consequent epistemological

blindness, and need for grace. Those confident of their rational powers only see the apparent foolishness of Christianity, which bars the way to an objective, direct rational knowledge of God. God hides himself from these *dogmatistes,* and until they recognize their sin and their need for the sacrifice of the cross, they remain misguided, thinking they see while they are blind. Reason is always blinded by passion, and until the moral issue of desire is addressed, it is useless as a tool for discovering truth. They fail to understand the cross, the hiddenness of God.[42]

2. *Pyrrhonistes,* the spiritual descendants of the skeptical Montaigne, on the other hand propose universal doubt, where nothing can be known at all. For Pascal however, the revelation of God in Christ who was crucified is the perspective from which truth can be grasped, once the inner disposition to believe has been given. Knowledge is possible, to those who have grasped the fundamental principle which the cross contains: man's degradation and his potential. Truth is the sole possession of God, it rests not on this earth, but in his presence alone (L131), yet the cross is the sign (*chiffre*) which Paul gives, (L268) which enables us to begin to grasp it. The Pyrrhonists have failed to account for the way in which God does make knowledge possible, so that their reductionism, although true from the perspective of indifference, is not total, and is overcome from the perspective of faith. Pascal's qualification "having no certainty *outside of faith*" in L131 is highly significant. Outside Jesus Christ and the cross there can be no self-knowledge or knowledge of God, life or death (L416, 447, 449). Conversely, *in* Jesus Christ crucified there is true knowledge, which not even the acids of skepticism can destroy.

3. The *Jesuits,* who were dedicated to the elimination of the Jansenist movement, were known for their flexible approach to ethics, and accommodation of a wide variety of behavior within the church, brilliantly lampooned in Pascal's earlier *Lettres Provinciales.* For Pascal, such moral laxism suggested that it was possible to become a true Christian without the need for deep moral change. Jesuit moral theology allowed a

sinner to receive absolution, attend Mass, live with a clear conscience while remaining exactly as he is. When Pascal accuses them in both the *Pensées* and the *Lettres Provinciales* of preaching "Christ not crucified," of "suppressing the scandal of the cross,"[43] his charge is that they have neglected the third aspect of the cross which we noted in the *Pensées*, the cross as signifying the profound moral realignment that needs to take place if a person is to come to know and love God. When they "hide the mystery of the cross," they deny Pascal's (and Augustine's) fundamental insight that conversion, the change of perspective, takes place initially through moral and spiritual, not intellectual reorientation.

Towards the end of Pascal's short life, as the royal absolutism of the court of Louis XIV grew (and of course Jesuit confessors were regularly to be found among the great and the good of the time),[44] his stand against the Jesuits, his insistence on the importance of holding to the Augustinian God in opposition to trends in seventeenth-century French theology which were abandoning it, and his extreme self-denial and regard for the poor during his final months, should perhaps be read not purely as world-renouncing negativity, but as an eloquent form of dissent from the economically comfortable, morally lax and socially divisive theology of his day, which took little notice of the poor, and suggested that conversion to Christ made few demands for moral and economic change. For Pascal, a theology centered upon the cross was the only kind which could stand against the sell-out of the French church to political or intellectual power.

6. Conclusion

Is the cross unique? Is it just another oppressive truth claim in world which has seen far too many of these already? In the ideas of these three very different theologians, in very different times, we have seen how the "word of the cross," a type of theology not always prominent in the history of the church, has stood as an eloquent protest against the abuse of power, and the tendency of the church, like any human organization, to use ideology to legitimate its claims to power. Whether it faces the rich aristocrats of Corinth, the overblown papal church of late medieval Europe or the slippery pretensions of seventeenth-century Cartesians and Jesuits, the cross of Christ represents a theology which subverts the will to power and replaces it with a will to love. God is seen to do his work characteristically through the cross. And with that simple and fundamental insight, all normal perceptions of power and how it operates are turned upside down. True power becomes the ability (or power) to give up rights for the sake of another. It is handled best by those who have already had the experience of being humbled and made powerless, realizing their own creature-liness and sinfulness before God. Truth is found not in brilliant rhetoric and convincing proofs but by learning to love God.

To offer one simple example of the uniqueness of the cross: Jesus and Muhammad share a common experience. Both knew the struggle of being a persecuted and misunderstood prophet, one in Jerusalem, the other in Mecca. Yet they react in very different ways. In 622, Muhammad migrates to Medina, in what later became known as the "Hijra," a crucial moment which marks the official beginning of Islamic history, to set up a new kind of kingdom, with a new role as military and religious leader there. Jesus takes a diametrically opposite path. Instead of migrating to Rome or Alexandria, or even back to Galilee, to set up a new movement to take the Roman Empire by storm, he takes the road to Golgotha, to a willingly undertaken death. Much of the differences between the two faiths they brought into being can be traced back to these seminal decisions.

The word of the cross is unique in the modern or postmodern world, as a discourse or metanarrative unlike any other. It will not allow Christians to impose their faith forcibly on others, instead waiting patiently for its truth to be recognized, suffering misunderstanding and disdain before it will retaliate or compel. It is a metanarrative, a Truth with a capital "T," but a humble, patient one. In a world justifiably nervous that absolute truths are inherently violent and oppressive, a cross-centered Christianity offers an absolute Truth which by its very nature denies coercion as a way to assert itself. Instead, it offers and forms a community dedicated to learning ways of love for enemies, forgiveness and hospitality to the "other" which promises a way forward for a fragmented and frightened world.

Notes

[1] See Martin Hengel, *Crucifixion* (trans. John Bowden; London: SCM Press, 1977).

[2] Matthew 26:27–29; Mark 14:22–25; Luke 22:16–20.

[3] Martin Hengel, *The Atonement: A Study of the Origins of the Doctrine in the New Testament* (trans. John Bowden; London: SCM Press, 1981), argues that from the very beginning of the church's life, Jesus' death was considered as salvatory and hence unique.

[4] E.g. Romans 4:25; 8:32; Galatians 1:4, 2:20; Ephesians 5:2, 25; 1 Timothy 2:6; Titus 2:14.

[5] For an exposition of this kind of view, see N.T. Wright, *Jesus and the Victory of God* (Christian origins and the question of God, vol. 2; London/Minneapolis: SPCK/Augsburg-Fortress, 1996), pp. 540–611.

[6] See Richard Bauckham, *God Crucified: Monotheism & Christology in the New Testament* (Didsbury Lectures 1996; Carlisle: Paternoster, 1998).

[7] This of course begs the question of what particular model, or perhaps preferably, metaphor of the atonement is to be preferred. I would take the view that the New Testament offers us a rich variety of metaphors for the underlying reality of salvation. For an exposition of such a view, see Joel B. Green, and Mark D. Baker, *Recovering the Scandal of the Cross* (Downers Grove, IL: InterVarsity Press, 2000).

[8] See, for example, the essays in Joanne Carlson Brown and Carole R. Bohn, *Christianity, Patriarchy and Abuse* (New York: Pilgrim, 1989).

[9] See Colin Gordon, ed., *Power/Knowledge: Selected Interviews and Other Writings by Michel Foucault 1972–1977* (New York: Harvester Wheatsheaf, 1980); Paul Rabinow, ed., *The Foucault Reader: An Introduction to Foucault's Thought* (London: Penguin 1984) for a taste of Foucault's thought on these themes.

[10] For a fuller exploration of the themes of this chapter see Graham Tomlin, *The Power of the Cross: Theology and the Death of Christ in Paul, Luther and Pascal* (Carlisle: Paternoster, 1999).

11 For example, see the contributions of Andrew D. Clarke, *Secular and Christian Leadership in Corinth: A Socio-Historical and Exegetical Study of 1 Corinthians 1–6* (Leiden: Brill, 1993); David G. Horrell, *The Social Ethos of the Corinthian Correspondence* (Edinburgh: T&T Clark, 1996); Peter Marshall, *Enmity in Corinth: Social Conventions in Paul's Relations with the Corinthians* (Tübingen: Mohr/Siebeck, 1987); Gerd Theissen, *The Social Setting of Pauline Christianity*, ed. John Riches, *Studies of the New Testament and Its World* (Edinburgh: T&T Clark, 1982).

12 See Duane Litfin, *St Paul's Theology of Proclamation: 1 Corinthians 1–4 and Greco-Roman Rhetoric* (Cambridge: Cambridge University Press, 1994); M. Mitchell, *Paul and the Rhetoric of Reconciliation: An Exegetical Investigation of the Language and Composition of 1 Corinthians* (Tübingen: Mohr/Siebeck, 1991); Stephen M. Pogoloff, *Logos and Sophia: The Rhetorical Situation of 1 Corinthians* (Atlanta: Scholars Press, 1992); Ben Witherington, *Conflict and Community in Corinth* (Grand Rapids, MI: Eerdmans, 1995).

13 Bruce W. Winter, "Civil Litigation in Corinth: The Forensic Background to 1 Cor. 6.1–8," *New Testament Studies* 37 (1991), pp. 559–72.

14 Theissen, *Social Setting*, pp. 121–43.

15 N. A. Dahl, "Paul and the Church at Corinth According to 1 Corinthians 1.10–4.21," in *Christian History and Interpretation: Studies Presented to John Knox* (eds. W. R. Farmer, C. F. D. Moule and R. R. Niebuhr; Cambridge: Cambridge University Press, 1967).

16 Michael D. Goulder, "'Sofia' in 1 Corinthians," *New Testament Studies* 37 (1991), pp. 516–34; Gerd Lüdemann, *Opposition to Paul in Jewish Christianity* (Minneapolis: Fortress, 1989).

17 E.g., see Witherington, *Conflict and Community*, pp. 83–87.

18 "Some" are arrogant, thinking Paul will not return (1 Cor. 4:18); "some" of the congregation "say that there is no resurrection of the dead" (1 Cor. 15:12); there are "those" who want to judge Paul (1 Cor. 9:3). One group of people eat food offered to idols, leaving others (1 Cor. 8:7) defiled. Paul addresses the man who has knowledge (*gnosko*), who eats with a clear conscience at a pagan table, asking him to consider the "weak man ... the brother for whom Christ died" (1 Cor. 8:11). Some separate themselves from the rest of the congregation at the communal meal (1 Cor. 11:17–22). Some feel themselves to be self-sufficient in the realm of spiritual gifts, having no need of others (1 Cor. 12:21). Others are made to doubt their value to the body because they lack certain gifts (perhaps the *sofia* and *gnosko* mentioned in 1 Cor. 12:8) (1 Cor. 12:15,

16). One group separate themselves because they feel their spiritual gifting is superior, another group feel they do not belong because they do not come up to scratch.

[19] It is even possible to suggest ideological settings in first century Corinth which would explain the origin of some of these ideas and practices. For example, local Epicureans, as explored in Graham Tomlin, "Christians and Epicureans in 1 Corinthians," *Journal for the Study of the New Testament* 68 (1997), pp. 51–72.

[20] 1 Corinthians 12:13; cf. Romans 6:4; Galatians 3:27f.

[21] See Martin Elze, "Das Verständnis Der Passion Jesu Im Ausgehenden Mittelalter Und Bei Luther," in *Geist Und Geschichte Der Reformation: Festgabe H. Rückert* (ed. H. Scholder and K. Liebling; Berlin: Walter de Gruyter, 1966); Martin Elze, "Züge Spätmittelalterlicher Frömmigkeit in Luthers Theologie," *Zeitschrift für Theologie and Kirche* 62 (1965), pp. 382–402; M. Nicol, *Meditation Bei Luther* (Göttingen: Vandenhoeck & Ruprecht, 1984); Kurt Ruh, "Zur Theologie des mittelalterlichen Passionstraktats," *Theologische Zeitschrift* 6 (1950), pp. 17–39; Graham S. Tomlin, "The Medieval Origins of Luther's Theology of the Cross," *Archiv für Reformationsgeschichte* 89 (1998), pp. 22–40.

[22] Especially in Luther's Hebrews commentary – LW 29.210 (WA 57–3.209.16–21) – written in early 1518, the Good Friday sermons of the same year, and his *Sermon von der Betrachtung des Heyligen leyden Christi*, published in 1519.

[23] On several occasions he even describes this sense of being at war within himself, for example, in the Romans commentary, while discussing his former difficulties with scholastic theology: "I could not understand in which way I should regard myself as a sinner like other men and thus prefer myself to no-one, even though I was contrite and made confession … Thus I was at war with myself." LW 25.261 (WA 56.274.2–11).

[24] This conclusion is suggested by an analysis of Luther's exposition of Psalm 4, a passage he reworked in late 1515 in the light of his new understanding "according to the cross of Christ."

[25] This is of course the phrase frequently found in contemporary theological literature, especially that of the *via moderna*: *facienti quod in se est infallibilite Deus infundit gratiam*.

[26] Quoted in B. A. Gerrish, *Grace and Reason: A Study in the Theology of Luther*, *Midway Reprint* (Chicago/London: University of Chicago Press, 1979), pp. 114.

[27] From Luther's Romans Commentary – LW 25.418 (WA 56.427.3–4).

[28] Thesis 20, LW 31.53 (WA 1.362.18–9).

[29] See Theses 93–5 of the 95 Theses of 1517. See also Gordon Rupp, "Luther's 95 Theses and the Theology of the Cross," in *Luther for an Ecumenical Age Essays in Commemoration of the 450th Anniversary of the Reformation* (ed. C. S. Meyer; St Louis: Concordia, 1967), pp. 67–81.

[30] LW 140, 165.

[31] Although see, for example, Jan Miel, *Pascal and Theology* (Baltimore: John Hopkins, 1969).

[32] For the works concerned and more extensive lists of contemporary apologists see J. E. d'Angers, *L'apologetique En France De 1580 À 1670: Pascal Et Ses Précurseurs* (Paris: Nouvelles Editions Latines, 1954), pp. 35–46.

[33] For Pascal's relation to Augustine, see P. Sellier, *Pascal Et Saint Augustin* (Paris: Armand Colin, 1970).

[34] For introductions to Jansenism and Port-Royal, see L. Cognet, *Le Jansénisme* (Paris: Presses Universitaires de France, 1961); F. Hildesheimer, *Le Jansénisme En France Aux Xviie Et Xviiie Siècles* (Paris: Publisud, 1991); R. Taveneaux, *Jansénisme Et Réforme Catholique* (Nancy: Presses Universitaires, 1992).

[35] This way of numbering the fragments of the *Pensées* is taken from the Lafuma edition in *Blaise Pascal, Ouvres Complètes* (ed. Louis Lafuma; Paris: Editions de Seuil, 1963). The same numbering is used by A. Krailsheimer in the Penguin Classics edition of the *Pensées*: Blaise Pascal, *Pensées* (trans. Alban J. Krailsheimer; Penguin Classics; Harmondsworth: Penguin, 1966).

[36] Pascal thought Descartes' view of God was inadequate. According to Pascal, Descartes imagines God using a *chiquenaude* (a "flick of the fingers") to start the world off. Pascal places Cartesianism under the same critique as he applies to Deism (L1001).

[37] Cf. Lucien Goldmann, *The Hidden God: A Study of Tragic Vision in the Pensées of Pascal and the Tragedies of Racine* (London: Routledge and Kegan Paul, 1964). Goldmann's understanding of the Hidden God as a "Tragic Vision" implies an inevitability about human separation from God, whereas for Pascal it might rather be called a comic (or perhaps tragi-comic) vision, implying a serious condition but one which is not inevitable, and from which there is the possibility of a joyful outcome, through the certainty of faith.

[38] E.g. L241, 253, 268, 964.

[39] See e.g. L291, 808, 834, 842.

[40] E.g. L271, 964. Also see Pascal's letter to his sister: Pascal, *Ouvres* (Paris: Editions de Seuil, 1963), p. 278.

[41] See B. Howells, "The Interpretation of Pascal's *Pari*," *Modern Languages Review* 79 (1984), pp. 45–63.

[42] See Sara Melzer, *Discourses of the Fall: A Study of Pascal's Pensées* (Berkeley: University of California, 1986), for a fascinating study of this aspect of Pascal's thought.

[43] See the fifth *Lettre, Œuvres*, p. 388, and L834. Richard Parish, *Pascal's Lettres Provinciales: A Study in Polemic* (Oxford: Clarendon, 1989), argues that the two works share a fundamental unity of purpose and perspective. On this particular point, see pp. 82–83: "the burden of the refutation in the *Lettres Provinciales* is identical to that in the *Pensées*: the Society of Jesus, by its suppression of the 'scandale de la Croix' and all that follows from it ... does not just offend the sacred truth; it also, it is asserted – in paradoxically, the very act of proselytizing – makes the claims of Christianity inefficacious and so, ultimately, unbelievable."

[44] See M. Foss, *The Founding of the Jesuits* (London: Hamilton, 1969).

4

The Resurrection and the Uniqueness of Jesus Christ

Gabriel Fackre

"Why Not Stop Here?" James Dunn poses that question after probing the meaning of the cross in his magisterial study of New Testament scholarship, *Jesus Remembered*. His answer is that it cannot be done. The reason is in the title of his chapter taken from the Apostles' Creed and the allegro of Bach's B Minor Mass, *Et Resurrexit*,

> What Christians have always (from the first) believed was the most remarkable thing about Jesus – his resurrection from the dead. That belief seems to have been not only fundamental for Christianity as far back as we can trace, but also presuppositional and foundational.[1]

The resurrection is "presuppositional and foundational" for the Christian faith. Pannenberg puts it in the strongest of terms in his objection to views that trace the singularity of Jesus to his teaching and its sequel, the cross:

> … without the Easter event, this interpretation of the crucifixion is absurd … the biblical testimony presents the Easter event as the basis of the faith of the disciples.[2]
>
> In what did this "Easter event" consist? The New Testament describes it as encounter with an embodied Christ. Reach out your hand and put it in my side … (John 20:27). The bold physicality

makes us wince. "My Lord and my God!" (John 20:28) ... But, but ... The accounts of the risen Jesus are strange indeed: a body that dines but "vanishes" (Luke 24:30–31); one that can be touched, but not "held on to" (John 20:17) ... He rose again, fully but differently, "the first born from the dead" (Col 1:18). And, so shall we.[3]

These assertions are vigorously disputed by not a few in both academia and the church who urge us to "stop here." Or, better: go way back to the Galilean Jesus. So the vocal "Jesus Seminar" whose leader wants us to be *Honest to Jesus*,[4] and the indefatigable bishop, John Spong, eager to have us know that he does "not see God as a being" and that the resurrection of Jesus' body is "not just naive but eminently rejectable."[5]

While a corps of critics of this sort may act like a new magisterium, prompting us to smile at their pontifications, there is a place for tough academic inquiry into this matter. Indeed, James Dunn, in his study, has reviewed the range of scholarly dismissals of the New Testament witness to the resurrection of Jesus, and found them suspect on their own grounds. He argues that historical investigation must grant that the only evidence with which it can work is "the impact made by Jesus as it has impressed itself into the tradition."[6] That tradition has two foci, the empty tomb and the resurrection appearances. A careful examination of all the New Testament data on these subjects discloses the physical resurrection of Jesus to be a "core belief" from the beginning, one that did not correspond to any then-current paradigm – from hallucination through apocalyptic vision to resuscitation.[7] Even given the diversity of reports of the risen Jesus,

> It is in the end of the day the tradition itself which pushes us to the conclusion that it was something perceived as having happened to *Jesus* (resurrection evidenced in empty tomb and resurrection appearances) and not just something which happened to the *disciples* (Easter faith) which provides the more plausible explanation for the origin and core content of the tradition itself.[8]

While it is interesting to learn that plausibility now seems to lie with historical investigations that make room for, if not support, classical Christian teaching, Hans Schwarz rightly observes that "the resurrection of Jesus cannot be fathomed by purely historical research."[9] It has to do with trust in the Word that speaks to us through Scripture as it is read Christologically in the church immersed in the world.[10] That final authority is the premise of this chapter. As Carl Braaten, after a comparable review of alternative construals of the resurrection that look to extra-biblical norms, rightly asserts: "There can be no authentic Christianity without belief in the resurrection of Jesus," adding, as it relates to our subject of the uniqueness of Christ,

> If Jesus is the risen Lord, that makes him different from all other putative messiahs, prophets and religious founders. There is no need to be mission-minded if we do not believe that Jesus' resurrection is God's unique way of reclaiming the whole world for himself, and that he is the one and only way of salvation for Christians and people of other religions and no religion alike.[11]

Thus, the resurrection as foundation and basis of the Christian faith includes its role in establishing the uniqueness of Jesus Christ vis-à-vis world religions. What follows is a commentary on that affirmation.

1. A Three-Dimensional Singularity

The Christian faith makes three claims about the uniqueness of Jesus Christ. They are summarized tersely in John 14:6: Jesus Christ is "the way," "the truth" and "the life." To translate these biblical assertions into historic theological terms: Jesus Christ is the "way" (path/*hodos*) God makes into the world to effect *reconciliation* with the world, the "truth" of *revelation* about God and the world, the "life" of *redemption* from the death consequent upon alienation between God and the world.[12] The resurrection is the validation, the announcement and the application of these Christian assertions about the uniqueness of Jesus Christ.

In John 14:6 "truth" and "life" are epexegetical of the primary predicate "way."[13] When God in Jesus Christ makes the one reconciling way into the world to overcome sin, attendant are revealing truth and redeeming life. Easter is more than mortality overcome, a near universal hope in the world's religions. In the Christian story, the triumph over physical death is the sign of the conquest of *eternal* death as estrangement from God and thus reconciliation accomplished, the bringing of "eternal life." Paul puts it this way in a letter to Timothy as he distinguishes "life" so understood from "immortality" and gathers up all three of the Johannine threads in describing how reconciliation has now been revealed through the appearing of our Savior Christ Jesus, who abolished death and brought life and immortality to light through the gospel (2 Tim. 1:10).

To grasp the inter-relationships of way, truth and life, we shall explore their uniqueness in the framework of the over-arching biblical story.

2. The Grand Narrative

The Christian account of the world differs from all others, religious or secular.[14] The difference is based on its premise about the seriousness of the world's plight. Not ignorance, not suffering, not physical death, the issues that come to the fore in alternative religions and philosophies. These problematics are also within the Christian judgment about the world's present state, but are situated in a deeper context. That abyss is the alienation of "the made" from its Maker because of *sin*. Christians measure the full meaning of sin by our response to the coming of the Son among us: hanging him on a cross, and thus "crucifying God." The state of the world is disclosed in all its horror on Golgotha. Our exposure there as the enemy of God is the framework for the Christian reading of the Old Testament report of a tree's enticements. Our radical estrangement requires a deed of God in kind, and thus the singularity of the primary Johannine predicate of Jesus Christ, "the way" of radical reconciliation with its accompanying gifts of truth and life. There's a story here. We move to it.

2.1 Prologue

The doing of God rises from the being of God. And who is God? As with the state of the world, so with the nature of deity, we look to the center of the Story for an understanding of its origins. To anticipate again, the only Son came from the Father by the Holy Spirit disclosing thereby the Author, as well as the chief Actor of this drama. As such, the authorial prologue is about a triune Life Together.

The unique source of this unique story is the one tripersonal God. Father, Son and Holy Spirit are Persons that indwell one another in such a manner that "They" are, in fact, a "Thou." While other religions may profess that God is loving, the Scriptures of this faith declare God *is* Love, the triune Life Together.

2.2 Chapter 1

"God calls the worlds into being ..." So says one church's narrative Statement of Faith.[15] To what end? By our trinitarian reckoning, the call is into the temporal "being" of a life together with the eternal triune Being. God's purpose for creation, and the covenant with creation to pursue that end to the End, mirrors the divine Life Together. The *perichoresis* of Father, Son and Holy Spirit is willed for the world, but only in derivative pointer form as there is no parallel in our sphere to the divine coinherence.

Who and what are called into this derived mutuality? In the canon, three candidates emerge: ourselves, our habitat, and the mysterious realm of "principalities and powers."[16] (As triplicity recurs in our account, do we have to do with Augustine's *vestigiae trinitatis,* the traces of the Trinity found everywhere?) We can describe these invited partners of God as nature, human nature and supernature. They are made for a life together, within their arena, among one another, and each and all with God, so portrayed in Revelation's vision of the goal toward which God moves the world (Rev. 21).

Special steward of God's creative bounty is the one made in the divine image. Within the call to, and covenant with, creation is the call to, and covenant with, the creature with the human face. In the Genesis account, our representative figures, Adam and Eve, are gifted and charged to image the divine mutuality (Gen. 2:26–27) in their response to God, care for one another and for the earth. As such, the future of creation is inextricable from their call and response.

2.3 Chapter 2

What response did and do we make to the divine beckoning? Not a Yes returned to God's Yes, but a stark No! The made seeks to usurp the place of the Maker, playing God (Gen. 3:5), turning away from the role chosen for us in the divine drama. Such idolatry – ourselves at center stage in the place of the chief Author and Actor – our Story names "sin." We have been in bondage to it since our beginnings.

"The wages of sin is death" (Rom. 6:23). Death, in this narrative, is the "life apart" juxtaposed to life together, the stumble and fall away from the reaching hand of God. This killing "fall" is the consequence of sin, and thus the alienation of humanity from deity, "eternal death." All creation is impacted by this posture, the inter-relationships of fallen humanity, fallen nature and fallen angels, asserted but never explained in our story.

How the fallen are raised up, how alienation can become reconciliation, how death can be overcome by life are varied ways in which creation's conundrum is posed by the unfolding Christian narrative. Chapter 3 tells of God's next move.

2.4 Chapter 3

2.4.1 Chapter 3, Part I
"God gave Noah the rainbow sign ..." So it is sung in an African-American spiritual. The implacable quest of the God of Scripture will not let us go our own way. Comes yet another promise: "I have set my bow in the clouds, and it shall be a sign of covenant between me and the earth" (Gen. 9:13). The covenant-making Creator moves back toward creation with the pledge to continue the story. Our No will not deter the divine Yes.

The Noachic covenant brings with it visible signs of God's patience. The multi-colored rainbow indicates the multiple mercies scattered across creation that sustain us in our journey toward another end than the death we have brought upon ourselves. They are glimpses of "truth, beauty and goodness" still discernible by our *imago Dei*, an image broken by the fall, but not destroyed. To the extent that it is intact, its preservation is by a "common grace." Commonality is an everywhereness of the divine generosity that makes possible intimations of truth and life and "orders of preservation" – family, nation, economy – that institutionally both set boundaries to our rampaging sin and reflect something of our intended life together. However identified, all of these are signs and supports of God's faithfulness.

Enter at this point in the story one interpretation of the place of the world's religions in the purposes of God, a view yet to be explored more fully. To follow the rainbow imagery and the promises of Noah's covenant: wherever "holiness" keeps company with truth, goodness and beauty, making human life livable in a fallen world, we have the work of a common grace. All such gifts have their source in the triune God, hence what is common is also Christological, the blessings of the Spirit of the Son of the Father. The varied colors of the bow in the sky suggest the manifold ways in which common grace is present in the world's high religions.[17]

As with every evidence of sustaining grace in a fallen world, so too that discernible in a world religion is measured by the gold standard of the gospel.[18] The source and norm of common grace can be only discerned and measured by "Jesus Christ, as attested by Scripture ... the one Word of God."[19] To that Word we listen in our Christian encounter with world religions. More to follow on this as we probe more deeply into the Work of the Word enfleshed.

2.4.2 Chapter 3. Part II

There is one "world religion" different in kind from all the others. The covenant promise to keep the Story moving forward moves from the universal to the particular. The rainbow ends at a point in time and settles at a point in space, resting on a chosen community: "I will take you as my people, and I will be your God" (Exod. 6:7).

In a broken world the promise of an unbreakable bond comes to a small Mediterranean tribe. The mystery of its election is an integral part of this epic. The importance of this special covenant is demonstrated by the two-thirds of the Christian Bible devoted to the chosen people's history.

Through all its ups and downs the story unfolds. The covenantal pledge and call to Abraham and his response in faith sets the stage. Times of testing come, and generations of heroes and villains pass before our eyes. Living in a land bridge between marching armies North and South, turmoil is a constant, finally turning to captivity. But then another turn in the tale, a baby rises from the reeds, grows to lead an escape from tyranny, a pilgrimage to a promised land, the reception of "the law" on the way, but a leader left at the boundary with others to take up the trail. Kings arise, David, Solomon, a temple is built and priests appear; wars rage, injustice is rife, nations rampage, prophets speak their words of protest and peace, exile intrudes and with it lamentations. But more – hope for redemption ahead, even apocalyptic assurances thereof, all grounded in the covenant promise of the faithful God.

Yes, there will be things to come in this story, chapters yet to be, hopes fulfilled. But after-the-fall covenants with Noah, Abraham, Moses and their heirs are not over and done with. Just as God never abandons his original covenant with creation itself, as manifest in this very story we are tracing, so the rainbow promise of a preserving grace can be counted on to the End, and God's promises to Israel will be kept. Paul reminds us of the first in his speech at Lystra, asserting that God "has not left himself without a witness in doing good ..." (Acts 14:17), and of the second in his letter to the Romans, the "gifts and the calling of God are irrevocable" (Rom. 11:29). The book of the people in this chapter is about the covenant faithfulness of God, and without it we would not have evidence of the divine patience and persistence that have brought us to this point.

And beyond this point? So many indicators in the chapter itself – the expectation of a "man of sorrows acquainted with grief" (Isa. 53:3 KJV) who will be "wounded for our transgressions, crushed for our iniquities" (Isa. 53:5). The establishment of offices – prophetic, priestly and royal – necessary for any exposure, expiation and triumph over what separates creation from its Creator. And on the boundary of this chapter and the next, one Jew who points to another and says, "Here is the Lamb of God who takes away the sin of the world!" (John 1:29)

2.5 Chapter 4

Now we are at the center of the story, its symbol, appropriately, a cross, the intersecting of vertical and horizontal lines. So God comes into our midst, as the visible One who all along has been the invisible Logos source of light and life in earlier anticipatory covenants. If the Noachic rainbow arced over the whole of the world, with an end reached in Israel, then it penetrated earth itself at Bethlehem.

How could "the sin of the world" that makes for a life sundered from God otherwise meet its match than by the presence of a Life Together in its midst? "And the Word became flesh and lived among us, ad we have seen his glory, the glory of a father's only son ..." (John 1:14). The Son is the perfect image of the Father, and so the second Person of the triune life together arrives among us to do battle against estrangement. Source of all the preserving and promising traces of the Trinity to date, here is now One "full of grace and truth ... From his fullness we have all received, grace upon grace" (John 1:14c, 16).

With Word among us, what does it take to rescue the world from alienation? Trajectories from Israel's irrevocable "gifts and calling" come now to their place in the central chapter, Jesus Christ in his prophetic, priestly and royal acts. Incarnation makes atonement possible, the at-one-ing Work of the divine-human Person.

Jesus Christ is the Prophet who discloses the purposes of God. In his life, preaching, teaching, praying, healing and miracle-working, he forth-tells who God is and what he does and what we are to be and do. These are signs of the kingdom of God coming now here among us. But Christ is the Prophet who exposes as well as discloses, lighting up the dark places in the human heart and history, foretelling as well as forth-telling the accountability to be, the tough as well as the tender love of God.

The supreme act of prophecy is at one and the same time the center of Christ's priestly work. On the cross, his death exposes the depths of human sin, so profound that it is willing to crucify God. Yet at the very bottom is to be found as well the love of God's broken heart that takes into itself the wrath we deserve. Here is fulfilled the other prophet's words that anticipate the one who will be "wounded for our transgressions, crushed for our iniquities" (Isa. 53:5).

Christ our Priest makes the supreme sacrifice. On Good Friday God proved his love for us that "while we were still sinners Christ died for us" (Rom. 5:8). Because of Bethlehem, the work of Christ transpired within the divine heart as well as on Calvary's hill. It was not just the human nature of Jesus that took away the sin of the world, for "... in Christ, *God* was reconciling the world to himself" (2 Cor. 5:19).

How do we know these things are so? Enter Easter. In this unfolding drama the resurrection of Jesus Christ confirms the work done in Galilee and on Golgotha, and declares it to all who have ears to hear. Easter is the *demonstration* of the victory of life over death, and its *proclamation*. Thus the royal office assures and announces the validity of the prophetic and priestly offices. Death, the consequence of the sin that separates has been undone and the life-in-communion that God is and wills for us is secured! On the matter of confirmation, Robert Jenson puts it this way:

> The message which Jesus' followers brought into the world was, in briefest statement, "Jesus is risen." The import of this statement depends of course on what "risen" means, and we can see in Luke's account of Paul's visit to Athens that this could be problematic. But precisely when "risen" is explained, whether the message is then good news or bad news or no news depends on who Jesus is, i.e. on how we should identify him ... the message "Stalin is risen" would be no gospel. Replace the proper names with identifying descriptions, "The unconditional friend of sinners and publicans is risen" is good news to anyone willing to be a

sinner or publican; "The chief keeper of the gulag is risen" would be good news to very few.[20]

The identity of Jesus is associated with what Jesus does: proclaims and manifests the coming of the realm of God in his Galilean ministry, and suffers and dies on Golgotha in our place for what we have done to thwart its arrival. The work of this Prophet and this Priest has been vindicated by this victorious King, the one and the same Person who thereby brings good news to we "sinners and publicans."

The good news is that the life apart that has marked this fallen world is now a life together that mirrors the divine Life Together. Whereas before, death was our destiny – estrangement from God – now its opposite is ours. The resurrection as the life that overcomes death removes the wages of sin. And the physical sign of that deeper death of estrangement – mortality – is also replaced by the One who brings *both* "life and immortality."

How could such good news not have breath-taking consequences? Those who saw the risen Lord could not still this story! This event "was basic to the faith of the disciples," and is "presuppositional and foundational" for the church's being ever since. Without the resurrection as announcement to those able to hear it, there is no continuation of the narrative in a community called to proclaim the gospel. More about that when we move to the next chapter. For now, attention is given to this second side of the empty tomb, its publication as well as its confirmation of the good news.

How then are the "three Rs" related to the fourth one focal to this chapter of the Great Story? And the Christian claim of uniqueness inseparable from John 14:6? If the prophetic office is the disclosure of who God definitely is, obscured from the world as a consequence of the fall, then here definitive *revelation* is given. If the priestly office delivers us from the sin that estranges us from God, then on the cross *reconciliation* is accomplished. If the royal office delivers us from death in all its dimensions then *redemption* is ours to have and hold. The life that resurrection brings is the confirmation of the revealed truth and the reconciled way. The singularity of Jesus Christ among the religions of the world is the reconciliation achieved, the revelation granted, and the redemption sealed.

All these things have to do with revelation, reconciliation and redemption accomplished at the *center* of the Story. But the narrative goes on. So too do the scandalous Christian claims of uniqueness. Revelation, reconciliation and redemption having been "accomplished," have yet to be "applied." Here, as well, the resurrection is key to this claim. The risen Jesus is a living Lord. His prophetic, priestly and royal ministries by the person and power of the Holy Spirit continue until the end of time.

2.6 Chapter 5

From the right hand of the Father, Jesus the Prophet discloses to us *now* who God is and what God does and wills. The prophetic office of Christ is exercised where Christ lives among us in his Body, the church. Here the Word – written, studied, preached, taught and shared – is his organ of communication, an office exercised in the ministries of both pastor and people.[21] From that same locale, Jesus the Priest sprinkles the waters of baptism on those brought to the Temple, nourishes them with his own body and blood received by a faith that ascends to his throne of grace, and lights the incense of worship directed to those heights.[22] Jesus the King rules from that same throne. Wherever death is defeated through the Word proclaimed and life triumphs through worship, water, bread and wine there the King rules. The Work of the Spirit of the Son thus calls, gathers, enlightens and sanctifies the church of Christ.

The church as the "ark of salvation," the steward of the means of saving grace deserves a chapter in itself. To it, the chapter on salvation, we shall presently turn. But, first, associated with this ecclesial chapter is the question, "What of the world beyond the church?"

In one sense, there is no "beyond' in the universal realm of Christ, for all are under the rule of the risen Lord. As such, there is prophetic, priestly and royal work in the wider world as well in the church. We have met it before in another chapter of the story, the covenant with Noah. Yet now in retrospect, after the resurrection, it is impossible to read any chapter without taking account of the resurrection of Christ and his rule, universal in time as well as space.

As he reigns everywhere through his threefold office, whatever things are found that are "true … honorable … just … pure … commendable" (Phil. 4:80), there his universal grace is present. Thus the Prophet speaks sustainingly in every truth, as that is discerned by the measure of the one Word spoken in Jesus then, and in the Word heard in the church now. And the Priest acts preservingly wherever egoity is acknowledged and suffering assuaged by the measure of Calvary's sacrifice. And the King acts with power to keep the story moving to its Center by life triumphing over death as it is measured by resurrection morning.[23]

As noted, the singularly enfleshed Word of 4 A.D., who lives on as the Head of the Body of Christ also rules the wider world and gives it the sustaining common grace. The Word we are granted in the church remains to the end of time always received under the conditions of finitude (Chapter 1) and sin (Chapter 2). As such, the definitive revelation given to us is "in a mirror, dimly" and only then "face to face" (1 Cor. 13:12). Yet the promise is for growth in understanding of the truth, even as there is the sanctifying growth in the Christian life, "more truth and light" to break forth from the Word.[24] Our Teacher in that learning can use any of his avenues of grace, and has. Could that universal range even include the wisdom of the world given to us to better understand Jesus Christ? And, by the same logic, could the wisdom of a world religion be a means of better grasping the Person and Work of Jesus Christ? Why not? asks evangelical Gerald McDermott.[25] Of course, only if such were measured by "Jesus Christ, as he is attested for us in Holy Scripture, is the one Word of God."[26] But the freedom of the risen Christ is such that he can exercise his prophetic office in Christian encounter with a world religion, drawing out as a fruit of such a meeting, aspects of truth, latent but not to that point patent in Christian faith itself.

2.7 Chapter 6

The intention of the tripersonal God is for a life together with persons. At the heart of the story is their sin that separates them from that communion with their Maker. As Christ has removed that barrier in his life, death and resurrection, a grateful faith is the response commensurate with such saving grace. Such justifying faith brings a person into union with Christ.[27] As a Person within the Life Together that God is, such an engrafting into Christ brings the believer into the divine Communion, a participation which some traditions name as "deification."[28]

Salvation by grace through faith that brings persons into the Community that God is means the gift of a special kind of life. Though originating at a point in time and therefore unlike the everlastingness of God, it is denominated by Scripture as "eternal life." The Father loved us so much "that he gave his only Son so that everyone who believes in him may not perish but have eternal life" (John 3:16).

To enter into union with Christ by faith is to begin in time participation in the eternity God always was and will be. Here is "life" in its meaning as "immortality." Physical death is not the last word for the believer. Nor is mortality the end for the unbeliever. But in this case immortality is conjoined to life-as-the-end-of-estrangement-from-God, and thus never-ending fellowship with the triune God.

This eternal life does not wait upon the moment of death. It begins now. So the letter of John: "I write these things to you who believe in the name of the Son of God so that you may know that you have eternal life" (1 John 5:13). For the believer the estrangement of God has ended and the promise of life with God is forever assured.

The victory over death in the eternal life of the faithful is the continuing work of the royal office. With it is the continuing work of the Prophet whose Word draws the believer into a "knowing" like no other. And the continuing work of Priest renders personal through saving faith the sacrifice made once and for all on Calvary.

The beneficence of the triune God wills mutuality not alone for persons in communion with deity, but also in human to human relationships. In this story there is no God without the kingdom of God, the hope for its final coming being at the center of Jesus' own message and its earnest in his very being among us. The ultimate community is one in which "the nations will walk by its light and the kings of the earth will bring their splendor into it" (Rev. 21:24).

Salvation is from suffering, misery, war, injustice, error in and among human beings as well as rescue from the sin that lies behind all the inglories of our fallen world. Believers look for that kind of ultimate life together. Indeed, they participate in its fragmentary life together here and now, as members of the body of Christ that exists as a sign and portent of the kingdom to come, albeit in the broken form of a community, like their own eternal life, *simul iustus et peccator*. And more, they can share in, and are called to be in solidarity with, yet other signs of the divine intention for the world walking together: the struggle for bread, justice and peace, the witness to God's will for our harmony with nature as well as neighbor. All these things will finally be in the Realm which has no end, and as such, are a lure and mandate for our participation in those dimensions of life together right now.

How are these penultimate signs of what is to come not also the portion of others who know no "union with Christ"? The generosity of the triune God is such that these penultimate portents of what is to be in and among persons, among nations and with nature are everywhere to be seen. Indeed, without them the story would close before its center and end. Thus we return to the rainbow light and life of God, the multiple gifts of a universal grace that preserves the fallen world. Here is Christ's general revelation spread in many and diverse ways across creation, in worlds religious and secular, wherever "human life is made and kept human,"[29] suffering and physical death assuaged, ignorance challenged, justice done, peace made in hearts, homes and on the battlefields of nations and nature. There the extra-ecclesial work of Prophet, Priest and King are done by the power of the Spirit according to the will of the Father. While not "life eternal," it is the good "life earthly," a broken mirror in a fallen world of the kingdom yet to come.

In this chapter we meet once again the uniqueness of Jesus Christ. The "foolishness" to the Greeks (1 Cor. 1:23) is unambiguously affirmed in the accent on *sola fide*. Only by faith in Jesus Christ does a person enter eternal life, being so brought into the divine Community. Graced faith saves from the ultimate estrangement.

At the same time, a generous universality is asserted in conjunction with the scandalous particularity. Christ does not abandon in this world those who do not hear and receive the Word. Temporal life – as the relief from suffering, release from the fears and pains of physical death, lightening the darkness of ignorance – is made possible through the many and varied streams of common grace, not the least being those at work in the world's religions. Such is also a work of worldly rescue done by the hidden Christ.[30]

2.8 Chapter 7

The final chapter in the Christian story has to do with "last things." In creedal summary they are: the return of Christ, the resurrection of the dead, final judgment and everlasting life.[31] "Christ will come again," as we confess in the liturgy, the dead will join the "quick" before Christ in the Great Assize, and for the faithful, life with God in the eternal realm will climax the purposes of the Creator for creation.

"What about those who have not heard?" asks a recent book.[32] So is raised the ultimate personal question about the relation of the uniqueness of Christ to the world religions. And more, to the billions of persons who have not heard the saving Word before Christ and beyond the church. And yet more, how the purposes of the all-loving and almighty God can be fulfilled while there are yet those who are consigned to eternal death rather than granted eternal life. To answer these questions, we must go first through a doorway into the last things, the "next-to-last things" – "the intermediate state" – the interim between our death and the fourfold End.

The resurrection means that Christ ranges over all creation, including the realm of the dead. Read Christologically, the Psalmist says,

Where can I flee from your presence?
If I go up to the heavens, you are there;
if I make my bed in the depths, you are there ...
(Ps. 139:7–8).

With that in mind, the Apostles' Creed has us declare that Christ "descended to the dead." Earlier generations of theologians took that to mean that believing Jews before Christ heard on Holy Saturday from the lips of the descended Christ about the triune Source of their own justifying faith, and hearing so confessed. Later Christian thinkers, who, from the missionary movements of their day, had their consciousness raised about the vast numbers not reached by the gospel, took yet another step. We take it with them.

Nineteenth-century missionaries to the Pacific's Sandwich Islands (now Hawaii) were asked by converts shaped by a deep reverence for their forebears, "What of my ancestors? Will they go to hell because they have not heard the gospel?" The question was passed on to the faculty of Andover Seminary in Massachusetts that had spawned the era's North America outreach overseas. To the creed they turned and to the New Testament texts behind it (eminently 1 Pet. 3:18–20; 4:11) and concluded that the divine perseverance could not be stopped by the gates of death. The Hound of Heaven breached them and pursued the last and the least. Thus Christ spoke the Word to those who had not heard, for "the gospel was proclaimed even to the dead" (1 Pet. 4:11).

When so understood, this passage opened one's eyes to the similar import of others (Matt. 8:11; 12:40; Luke 13:28–30; John 5:25–29; Acts 3:21, 25; Rom. 10:7; Eph. 1:9ff.; 4:8–9; Col. 1:20; Phil. 2:10f.; Heb. 9:15; 1 John 2:2; Rev. 1:18; 5:13; 21:25). Although it was articulated by earlier European nineteenth-century theologians,[33] it came to be called in America, "the Andover theory," or "postmortem evangelism" as it is sometimes described.[34] This view is now espoused by ecumenical as well as evangelical thinkers of the stature of Donald Bloesch and George Lindbeck.[35] Its strength has to do with an unswerving commitment to the uniqueness of Christ with special reference to Chapter 6 of the story – the New Testament association of salvation with the confession of Christ in numerous New Testament references,[36] along with the Christian story's overall trajectory that purposes the good news for all people. At the heart of this double accent is the resurrection of Jesus Christ. Only as a risen Lord carrying forth his threefold ministry can the prophetic Word be spoken to all, the priestly sacrifice be made available to all, and the royal power to breach the gates of death making possible the universal prophetic and priestly work.

If there is no one excluded from the good Word, why would its power not convict and convert every hearer? Is not the persevering love of God that universally seeks out the last and the least not of a piece with the persevering love of God that would seek as well "universal salvation?" The homecoming of all by the grace of God appears to be a logical partner to the pursuit of all by the grace of a God who will not stop short of the total life together intended for creation. Such has been argued by great minds of the church from yesterday's Origen to a company of today's ardent evangelicals.[37]

As Scripture is the source for our Story, does it speak of a universal homecoming? One reference to "all" does appear in Paul's searching inquiry into the destiny of the Jewish people. So the assertion that "all Israel will be saved" in his letter to the church at Rome (Rom. 11:26).[38] While, together with the affirmation that "the gifts and call" of the chosen are "irrevocable," an anti-supersessionist case can be made,[39] the exegetical complexities of that "all" are too many to build a case for the salvation of every Jewish believer on a single verse. And as for the whole of the human race, the New Testament message is clear that a double destination for the sheep and the wolves is integral to the End. And it is no less than Jesus Christ himself, the judge of the living and the dead, who will send each on their respective paths (Matt. 25:31–46).

Yet, it is fair to ask: how long the path? If the fires of hell are the fires of love – how can they be other than so purposed if their source is in the Christ of the divine Life Together? Then is the burning road lasting, or everlasting? Can fires be cleansing, and punishment rehabilitating? We put these as questions which do not lend themselves to clear biblical answers. *Apokatastasis* is not a teaching of Scripture and cannot be a doctrine of the Church. Yet the trajectory of the story we have been following is toward the fulfillment of God's purposes. And about a Lord persisting and a love persevering beyond the grave. But that all-seeking God as the all-loving One that will not let us go is by nature invitatory, working not by despotic force but by persuasion as the Fathers asserted ever and again. An eternal No is our option then as well as now.[40] Or if this C. S. Lewis-like judgment seems to grant too much to human choice, then let the modesty fall on the Calvinist side, and say, it is God's decision, not ours that will determine just how the divine intention for life together will be achieved. But surely we have to do, here in eternity as in time, with the paradox of grace, "I … yet not I" (1 Cor. 15:10).[41] On no basis, our choice or God's, or the more profound paradoxical both/and, can we forecast a universal homecoming. At best, as with Barth, it is an article of hope, not an article of faith.[42]

3. Conclusion

Our survey of the path God has taken to fulfill the divine purposes has been from its peak point in the resurrection of Jesus Christ. From this site, we see second hand what the disciples first viewed in the flesh. Discernment of the turn in the trail, yes. But more, for the risen Christ there defeated eternal death as well as disclosed its end. Thus a fourth "R" made possible the "3 Rs" that define the uniqueness of Jesus Christ. Resurrection is the guarantor of reconciliation, revelation and redemption. We have traversed in this narrative the journey of the One who is and wills communion with and for the world from creation through fall, through the covenant with Noah and its multi-colored preserving grace from which the world's religions are not excluded to the irrevocable special covenant with Israel, one that leads to the singular deed done in Christ, the birth of the church, the flow of salvation and the consummation of the divine plan. At its center, we find the only *way* God made into our midst to bring reconciliation out of alienation, and with it the definitive *truth* of revelation and the derivative *life* of our redemption. Both the pilgrimage over time, and its decisive center, is the Work of the second Person of the triune God, in response to the Father's will and by the power of the Holy Spirit. All along the storyline it has been, is, and will be, in church and world, the Prophet, Priest and King who brings the light and life of rainbow, pillar of fire, Easter sunrise, and the meridian yet to come. To God be all the glory.

Notes

[1] James D. G. Dunn, *Jesus Remembered* (Grand Rapids, MI: Eerdmans, 2003), p. 826.

[2] Wolfhart Pannenberg, *Systematic Theology,* Vol. 2 (trans. G. W. Bromiley; Grand Rapids, MI: Eerdmans, 1994), p. 286. So too a myriad of commentators as in A. M. Ramsay's small classic, *The Resurrection of Christ* (revd edn.; London: Collins, Fontana Books, 1961), p. 9: "For them [the first disciples] the Gospel without the Resurrection was not merely the Gospel without its final chapter: it was no Gospel at all." And in another landmark work, Oscar Cullmann's *Immortality of the Soul or Resurrection of the Body* (New York: Macmillan Co., 1953), p. 43: "Is *Easter* the starting point of the Christian Church, of its existence, life, and thought? If so, we are living in an interim time. In that case, the faith in resurrection of the New Testament becomes the cardinal point of Christian belief. Accordingly, the fact that there is a resurrection body – Christ's body – defines the first Christian's whole interpretation of time."

[3] Gabriel Fackre, "I Believe in the Resurrection of the Body," *Interpretation* 46.1 (January 1992), pp. 44, 45.

[4] Robert E. Funk, *Honest to Jesus* (New York: HarperCollins, 1996).

[5] John Shelby Spong, *A New Christianity for a New World: Why Traditional Faith is Dying and How New Faith is Being Born* (New York: HarperCollins, 2002). On the details of his criticism of the New Testament teaching about resurrection, see *Resurrection: Myth or Reality?* (New York: HarperCollins, 1995).

[6] Dunn, *Jesus Remembered,* p. 876.

[7] Dunn, *Jesus Remembered,* pp. 870–76.

[8] Dunn, *Jesus Remembered,* p. 876. Contra Edward Schillebeeckx, the theologian whose massive works, *Jesus and Christ* have been the most ambitious modern effort in systematic theology to relate Christology to historical-critical studies, given thereby pride of place to Easter experiences rather than to the New Testament witness to the resurrection of Jesus from the dead. See the writer's detailed examination of Schillebeeckx's writings on the subject, "Bones Strong and Weak in the Skeletal Structure of Schillebeeckx's Christology," *Journal of Ecumenical Studies* 21.2 (Spring 1984), pp. 248–77.

9. Hans Schwarz, *Christology* (Grand Rapids, MI: Eerdmans, 1998), p. 268. See also in this work Schwarz, "Critical review of current feminist and pluralist Christologies," in *Christology*, pp. 277–336.

10. So argued in Gabriel Fackre, *The Christian Story*, Vol. 2 *Scripture in the Church for the World* (Grand Rapids, MI: Eerdmans, 1987), *passim*.

11. Carl Braaten, "The Reality of the Resurrection," in *Nicene Christianity: the Future for a New Ecumenism* (ed. Christopher Seitz; Grand Rapids, MI: Brazos Press, 2001), pp. 116, 118.

12. See the writer's development of this trinity in "Claiming Jesus as Savior in a Pluralist World," *Alister McGrath and Evangelical Theology* (Carlisle: Paternoster Press, 2003), pp. 213–34.

13. Explored in my *Christian Story*, Vol. 2, pp. 254–340.

14. The history and faith of the Hebrew people as interpreted in the Christian Bible being the exception to be investigated in Chapter 4 of the Story.

15. The United Church of Christ Statement of Faith.

16. For an exploration of the latter see the writer's "Angels Heard and Demons Seen," *Theology Today* 51.3 (October 1994), pp. 345–58.

17. With a question raised to Gerald R. McDermott who in an otherwise splendid book assumes that common grace is monochromatic. See *Can Evangelicals Learn from World Religions? Jesus, Revelation and Religious Traditions* (Downers Grove, IL: Intervarsity, 2000), pp. 52–53, 113, *passim*.

18. See, interestingly, Karl Barth, *Church Dogmatics* IV/3.1 (Edinburgh: T&T Clark, 1961), pp. 114–37.

19. The Barmen Declaration, II, 1.

20. Robert Jenson, "Jesus' Identity as a Theological Problem" (unpublished paper, Center of Theological Inquiry, 2003), 3.

21. See the writer's "Christ Ministry and Ours" in *The Laity In Ministry: the Whole People of God for the Whole World* (eds. George Peck and John Hoffman; Valley Forge: Judson Press, 1984), pp. 109–26.

22. So John Nevin, *The Mystical Presence: A Vindication of the Reformed or Calvinistic Doctrine of the Holy Eucharist* (ed. O. P. Augustine Thompson; Eugene, OR: Wipf & Stock, 2000).

23. The various interpretations of the weight of Christ's work outside the range of Christ-church-salvation are taken up in the aforementioned essay cited in footnote 1, viz. as in Rahner's anonymous particularity, Barth's Christological particularity, etc. Currently receiving much attention is the "parallel particularity" developed in most detail by S. Mark Heim. He makes a case for describing these extra-ecclesial graces as "salvations" in *Salvations: Truth and Difference in Religion* (Maryknoll, NY: Orbis Books, 1995), and later,

declining to impose Christian categories on others, speaks of them as "religious ends" in *The Depths of the Riches: A Trinitarian Theology of Religious Ends* (Grand Rapids, MI: Eerdmans, 2001). While not reaching the fulfillment God intends in Christian faith, they can be seen as lesser realizations of the purposes of the triune God, made possible by the objective Work of Christ, with the hope that exposure to gospel, here or hereafter, the truth that is in them will lead their believers to confess Jesus Christ. In these works, Heim makes an admirable attempt to affirm, unambiguously, the scandal of particularity, even the urgency of evangelism, while at the same time, seeking to honor the universal reach of the triune God. The case for the role of other religions as gifts of the grace of preserving the world on its movement toward the Center is here strong. When a further step is taken to project their ends into the eternal purposes of God, and hence into forms of "eternal life," the biblical evidence is missing. Then can these eternal ends be viewed as "hell" rather than "heaven"? Heim chooses to leave the question open. But it must be asked: would God so order world religions as agents of damnation? The Dantean alternative to this would be a multi-tiered heaven, a view that is intimated in Heim's cordial exposition of Dante. However, again, the biblical warrants for such are not there. Understandably so, as the singularity of eternal life in and with the risen Christ is the clear New Testament vision of personal fulfillment.

24 The words are from the farewell sermon of Pastor John Robinson when he sent the Pilgrims on their way to new lands on 20 July 1620: "The Lord hath more truth and light yet to break forth out of his holy Word."

25 McDermott, *Can Evangelicals Learn from World Religions?*, passim.

26 Arthur C. Cochrane, *The Church's Confession Under Hitler* (Philadelphia: Westminster Press, 1962), p. 239.

27 P. Mark Achtemeier has shown the importance of the *Unio cum Christi* teaching in the Reformed tradition, beginning with Calvin, in "The Union with Christ Doctrine in Renewal Movements in the Presbyterian Church (USA)," in *Reformed Theology: Identity and Ecumenicity* (Grand Rapids, MI: Eerdmans, 2003), pp. 336–45.

28 Carl E. Braaten and Robert E. Jenson, eds., *Union With Christ: The New Finnish Interpretation of Luther* (Grand Rapids, MI: Eerdmans, 1998).

29 A formula widespread in the "secular mission" accents of the 1960s, as in Colin Williams, *Where in the World?* (New York: National Council of Churches, 1963).

30 Note the two means of "salvation" in Cruden's famous 1737 *Concordance*, salvation as "deliverance from sin and its

consequences" and also "preservation from trouble or danger." (561).

[31] For their exploration see Gabriel Fackre, *The Christian Story*, Vol. 1, *A Narrative Interpretation of Christian Doctrine* (3rd edn.; Grand Rapids, MI: Eerdmans, 1996), pp. 210–34.

[32] John Sanders, ed., *What About Those Who Have Never Heard?: Three Views on the Destiny of the Unevangelized* (Downer's Grove, IL: InterVarsity Press, 1995).

[33] As, for example, Isaac Dorner. See *Dorner on the Future State* (trans. with introduction and notes, Newman Smyth; New York: Charles Scribners Sons, 1883), pp. 91–112. For a review of the literature, see John Sanders, *No Other Name: An Investigation into the Destiny of the Unevangelized* (Grand Rapids, MI: Eerdmans, 1992), pp. 177–214.

[34] See Thomas P. Field, "The 'Andover Theory' of Future Probation," *The Andover Review* 7 (May 1887), pp. 461–75.

[35] George Lindbeck, *The Nature of Doctrine: Religion and Theology in a Postliberal Age* (Philadelphia: Westminster Press, 1984), pp. 57–63, and Donald Bloesch, *The Last Things: Resurrection, Judgment, Glory* (Downers Grove, IL: InterVarsity Press, 2004), pp. 44–47, 277–78.

[36] See Fackre, *Christian Story*, Vol. 1, pp. 219–20.

[37] See the evangelical pros and cons in Robin Parry and Christopher Partridge, eds., *Universal Salvation?: The Current Debate* (Carlisle: Paternoster Press, 2003).

[38] Of course, 1 Timothy 2:4 speaks of God "who desires everyone to be saved ..." short, however, of the unambiguous assertion of universal salvation.

[39] Investigated in my essay, "The Place of Israel in Christian Faith," in *Gott Lieben: Und Seine Geboten Halten* (eds. Markus Bochmuehl and Helmut Burkhardt; Giessen: Brunnen Verlag, 1991), pp. 21–38.

[40] C. S. Lewis, *The Great Divorce* (New York: Macmillan, 1946).

[41] For wise words of struggle on this perennial question see, Paul Jewett, *Election and Predestination* (Grand Rapids, MI: Eerdmans, 1985), pp. 106–15.

[42] See Barth: "If we are certainly forbidden to count on this as though we had a claim to it, as though it were not supremely a work of God to which man can have no possible claim, we are surely commanded the more definitely to hope and pray for it as we may do already on this side of this final possibility. I.e. to hope and pray cautiously and yet distinctly that, in spite of everything which may seem quite conclusively to proclaim the opposite, His compassion should not fail, and that in accordance with His mercy which is 'new every morning' He 'will not cast off forever' (La 33:22f.,31)" (Barth, *CD* IV/3.1, p. 478).

5

The Uniqueness of Christ as the Revealer of God

Mark D. Thompson

No one has ever seen God, but God the One and Only, who is at the Father's side, has made him known.
(John 1:18)

I am the way and the truth and the life. No one comes to the Father except through me.
(John 14:6)

It is scandalous in the current climate to claim that Jesus of Nazareth is the unique revealer of the living God. In an international interfaith environment the public opinion makers and even some denominational leaders prefer the illusion that Jesus is but one of many ways to a true knowledge of God. That this flies in the face of the explicit teaching of the New Testament has proved no difficulty – hermeneutical maneuvers have always been available for those who wished to evade the plain meaning of the biblical text. However, it is not always recognized just how much is at stake in this issue. As we shall see, the character of God is the ultimate casualty when we pursue the pluralist agenda. Though its advocates claim to be enlarging our picture of God, the result is almost invariably that our picture of the true and living God is diminished or even obscured entirely. What is needed urgently at this hour is the recovery of the biblical concept of idolatry.

In this paper I propose to examine the uniqueness of Christ as the revealer of God as it arises in the context of both testaments and then explore the theological necessity of this truth. If the biblical picture of God and his relationship to creation is true, if it is not merely a reflection of the religious convictions of the Jewish nation and the Christian communities of faith which emerged near the middle of the first century A.D. but is instead an ineradicable feature of reality in the universe, then do we have any clues as to why this must be so and why all other avenues remain closed? This exploration will lead us finally to a reconsideration of idolatry, an almost lost and certainly unfashionable category of biblical thinking.

1. The Uniqueness of Christ: An Exegetical Reality

The God of the Hebrew and Christian Scriptures is a God who must be known, can only be known, by revelation. He is not an object that can be studied without his consent, so to speak. The inescapably personal character of God means that, as is the case with all persons, he can only truly be known as he gives himself to be known. Furthermore, true knowledge of God as the Scriptures understand it can never be a disinterested or detached observation about God and his purposes. It is deeply experiential and relational, indeed at a number of points it is almost synonymous with salvation: "Now this is eternal life," Jesus said, "that they know you, the only true God, and Jesus Christ, whom you have sent" (John 17:3). Precisely because God is personal in his being and because true knowledge of God has this character of an intimate, saving relationship, this conviction that God can only be known as he gives himself to be known has long been a basic conviction of Christian theology. Hilary of Poitiers famously remarked, "For He whom we can know only through his own utterances is a fitting witness concerning himself."[1] Karl Barth concurred, "God is known through God and through God alone."[2] But what is the exegetical basis for such a claim?

1.1 The Old Testament backdrop

The uniqueness of Jesus Christ as the revealer of God fits within the larger biblical context of God's Lordship in his own self-revelation. From cover to cover the teaching of Scripture is that God is to be found, only to be truly known, when, where and how God wishes to be known. So, one of the critical lessons of the Eden narrative in Genesis 1–3 is that human beings are created to know God and his purposes in the context of creaturely dependence upon him. Indeed, the primal temptation was the opportunity "to be made wise," to take hold of a knowledge of how things are, of good and evil, in independence from God: "For God knows," the serpent told the woman, "that when you eat of it your eyes will be opened, and you will be like God, knowing good and evil" (Gen. 3:5). The serpent proposes an alternative route to knowledge about spiritual realities, the way things are. The man and the woman need not rely on God himself to interpret reality and especially his own character and will. The allure of autonomy, so evident in our own time and itself a major distraction for contemporary theology,[3] reaches back to the earliest stages of our history.

God's initiative is emphasized at each point in the biblical narrative where the knowledge of God and his purposes is advanced. Abram is not presented as an especially religious man, in fact little is known about his life prior to the call in Genesis 12. God takes the initiative and addresses Abram, establishing a relationship with this wandering Aramean and his descendants. There is no sense that Abram sought out the living God, nor that any of his descendants embarked on a similar quest. Rather, God chose to make himself known at particular times to particular people. Especially significant are the calling narratives of Moses (Exod. 3), Samuel (1 Sam. 3), David (1 Sam. 16), Solomon (1 Kgs. 3) and the prophets (e.g. Jer. 1). In each, God is the one who chooses to make himself known, in a particular way and at a particular time. God always remains the Lord, and no more so than in the matter of revelation.

Not only does God's sovereign will determine when, where, and to whom he will reveal himself, he also makes clear that he will not be found or known elsewhere. The instructions to the Israelites as they entered the Promised Land include warnings about seeking to know God or to serve him elsewhere than in the places and by the means he himself has provided:

> The LORD your God will cut off before you the nations you are about to invade and dispossess. But when you have driven them out and settled in their land, and after they have been destroyed before you, be careful not to be ensnared by inquiring about their gods, saying, "How do these nations serve their gods? We will do the same." You must not worship the LORD your God in their way, because in worshiping their gods, they do all kinds of detestable things the LORD hates. They even burn their sons and daughters in the fire as sacrifices to their gods. See that you do all I command you; do not add to it or take away from it.
> (Deut. 12:29–32)

The golden calf incident years earlier (Exod. 32) should have taught the Israelites the same lesson: God is known and served, not by the religious ingenuity of his people, but by close attention to the way he has chosen to make himself known. Aaron had given the people a visual representation, a tangible connection to the One who brought them up out of the land of Egypt (Exod. 32:4). He did not present the statue of the calf as the image of some new God; indeed, as he built an altar before it he proclaimed "Tomorrow there will be a festival to the LORD" (Exod. 32:5). Yet to look for the LORD elsewhere, to invent their own way of conceiving of him, was in reality to turn aside from the true and living God and to place themselves in great peril: "the LORD struck the people with a plague because of what they did with the calf Aaron had made" (Exod. 32:35).

The sanctuary or tabernacle, and in particular the Ark of the Covenant which was placed within, was identified by God himself as his exclusive meeting place with his people (Exod. 24:8). Of course God was not absent from his people when they were in other places, take as an example the battlefields on which the forces of Israel fought their enemies. Nevertheless, there was a unique sense in which God was heard and known only here. God spoke with Moses "from between the two cherubim above the atonement cover on the ark of the Testimony" (Num. 7:89). Indeed, it was this direct encounter with God himself, his hearing of the voice of God no less, that marks Moses out as unique and irreplaceable. Rebuking Miriam and Aaron after their rebellion against Moses, God speaks to them too from within the tent of meeting but distinguishes between them and his faithful servant:

> When a prophet of the LORD is among you,
> I reveal myself to him in visions, I speak to him in dreams.
> But this is not true of my servant Moses;
> he is faithful in all my house.
> With him I speak face to face,
> clearly and not in riddles;
> he sees the form of the LORD.
> (Num. 12:6–8)

In time the Temple would replace the tabernacle as the unique location of God's presence, just as Samuel (1 Sam. 3) and Nathan (2 Sam. 7; 12) would in turn become those who heard and spoke for God in a way reminiscent, at points, of Moses. Here was the one place in all the earth where the LORD would put his name. As the LORD said to Solomon,

> I have chosen and consecrated this temple so that my Name may be there forever. My eyes and my heart will always be there. (2 Chr. 7:16)

It was the shunning of this unique place of meeting with the LORD and the building of alternatives in Bethel and Dan – and in an astonishing refusal to learn from history, the construction of two golden calves as a focus for worship in each place – which represents the sin of Jeroboam, a sin which plagues the northern kingdom of Israel long after the division following Solomon's death (1 Kgs. 12:25–33). Jeroboam failed to take seriously the simple fact that it is God who determines where and how he will meet with his people. He determines where his name will dwell. He determines the means by which people will know him there. The LORD does not approve of human proposals which are in effect a refusal to be constrained by his word.

The prophetic call in the latter years of the kingdom, during the exile and beyond, was a call not to discover new pathways to God or new truths about him but rather to "look to the rock from which you were cut" (Isa. 51:1). The religions of the nations, those associated with the Canaanite local deities or the magnificent pantheons of the great empires of Assyria or Babylon, are never portrayed as alternative approaches to a genuine knowledge of God. They are not complementary perspectives on divine reality. Rather, they are false trails, illusions with no substance, the work of the deceiver. The confrontation between Elijah and the prophets of Baal was not a battle between two gods. The sarcasm of Elijah and the irony of the writer of 1 Kings is meant to drive home the absurdity of any alternative to the one true God: "But there was no response, no one answered, no one paid attention" (1 Kgs. 18:29). No true knowledge of God was to be obtained through the prophets of Baal. The almost relentless prophetic attack upon the idols of the nations makes the same point emphatically (Isa. 41:21–24; 44:6–20; 46; Jer. 10:1–5; 44; Ezek. 6; Dan. 3; Zech. 13:2 etc.).

Closely tied to the renunciation of the idols of the nations is the prophetic protest against the lies and empty imaginations of the false prophets (Is. 56:9–12; Jer. 14:13–16; 23:9–40; Ezek. 13:1–16; Zech. 13:2–6 etc.). The massive failure of the religious leadership of Israel and Judah consists in just this: that they withheld from God's people a true knowledge of God and his purposes and substituted for it an illusory mythology. They led the people of the covenant down a false path. They refused to remain under the word which the LORD had spoken. They spoke of peace when there was no peace (Jer. 6:13–15), they refused to be messengers of the LORD of hosts and instead provided an instruction of their own which caused many to stumble (Mal. 2:7–8), and they were complicit in the syncretism and idolatry that distorted rather than enriched the true knowledge of God (Hos. 10:1–6; Zech. 10:1–2; Mal. 2:10–12).

As the Old Testament closes, the failure of the post-exilic nation to learn from the exile and to live as those who had been rescued and claimed by the one true God is laid bare. Yet the nation had never ceased to be a religiously oriented one. The Temple and the altars remained in constant use. The tragedy lay in their history of failure to allow God to set the terms of their knowledge of him and in their fascination with the religious practices of their neighbors. Their social and moral failure arose from this basic repudiation of their rationale for existence: they had been called out to be the unique possession of the only living God in order to bring blessing to the nations (Exod. 19:3–6; Gen. 12:1–3). Their persistent failure to be constrained in their thinking about God and their response to him by the word which God himself had spoken is the reason why the judgments of the Assyrian dispersion and Babylonian exile cannot be seen as something entirely in the past as the Old Testament writings cease. As the so-called "four hundred years silence" begins, there was a sense in which the people and the land remained under judgment awaiting the only deliverance that could be effective: the personal appearance of the LORD himself to confront the apostasy of Israel (Mal. 3:1–4), to shepherd his people (Ezek. 34:7–16; Isa. 40:9–11), to deal decisively with sin (Jer. 31:31–34), and to put his Spirit in the hearts of those who are his (Ezek. 11:14–21). The living God will settle for all time the question of how he is to be known and by whom.

1.2 The explicit teaching of the New Testament

It is against this backdrop of God's Lordship in his own revelation and the promise of God's direct intervention in judgment and salvation that Jesus is presented in the Gospels as the unique revealer of God. Each of the Gospels begins by placing Jesus firmly in this context. After the genealogy which echoes the universal scope of the Abrahamic promises, Matthew's infancy narrative draws on the promise in Isaiah 7:14, identifying the child to be born as "'Immanuel' (which means God with us)" (Matt. 1:23–25). Matthew goes on to introduce Jesus' public ministry by highlighting John the Baptist's role as forerunner along the lines of Isaiah 40. A long-expected arrival is about to take place and its dimensions are nothing short of cosmic. This is the note on which Mark's

Gospel begins: the preaching and baptizing ministry of John the Baptist is focused on the one who comes after him, one who is much more than a prophet and who baptizes with the Holy Spirit (Mark 1:1–8). The Song of Zechariah performs a similar function in Luke's infancy narrative.

It is, of course, John's Gospel which takes us further in understanding the significance of the moment of Jesus' arrival at the Jordan to be baptized by John. The prologue of John's Gospel takes a cosmic perspective, identifying Jesus as the Word, one who was in the beginning with God and who cannot be separated from God. Alongside the great spiritual battle which is the proper context for Jesus' ministry (vv. 5, 9–11) and the salvation of believers which stands at its center (vv. 12–13), the prologue accents the revelatory dimensions of Jesus' life and work. It is not insignificant that he is identified here as the Word, the self-expression of God, and "the true light which enlightens everyone" (vv. 1–3, 9). Inextricable from his work of rescuing men and women from darkness and death is his work of truly and directly making God known. The evangelist goes further by speaking of Jesus' glory as "the glory of the One and Only [*monogenous*], who came from the Father" (v. 14). All that Jesus does in salvation and revelation is predicated on a unique relationship with the Father. This is emphatic in the last verse of the prologue:

> No one has ever seen God, but God the One and Only [*monogenēs theos*] who is at the Father's side, has made him known. (v. 18)

A clear distinction is made between the access Jesus has to the Father and that of every creature. The mention of Moses in the preceding verse enables the reader to recall the interchange between the LORD and this great Old Testament figure following the golden calf incident:

> Then Moses said, "Now show me your glory."
> And the LORD said, "I will cause all my goodness to pass in front of you, and I will proclaim my name, the LORD, in your presence. I will have mercy on whom I will have mercy, and I will have

compassion on whom I will have compassion. But," he said, "you cannot see my face, for no one may see me and live."

Then the LORD said, "There is a place near me where you may stand on a rock. When my glory passes by, I will put you in a cleft in the rock and cover you with my hand until I have passed by. Then I will remove my hand and you will see my back; but my face must not be seen."

(Exod. 33:18–23)

For all the greatness of Moses as a mediator between God and Israel, despite his role in conveying the word of God to God's people, Moses was not able to see God's face. There was a limit to his capacity to be an instrument of divine revelation. He remained one of those who "may not see me and live." It is precisely because he is not constrained in such a way, because his relationship to the Father is so different to that of Moses, indeed because he shares an intimacy with the Father that is naturally unknown to any other being, that Jesus Christ, "God the one and only," is able genuinely, personally and directly to make him known. In Jesus, God is making himself known. Amongst other things, the incarnation is the climactic expression of God's Lordship in his own revelation.

This is the context in which the claims of Jesus throughout John's Gospel are to be understood. For instance, at the conclusion of the Nicodemus incident reference is made to salvation through faith in the Son.[4] As elsewhere, though, this discussion of salvation cannot ultimately be disentangled from consideration of Jesus' role as the revealer of God. What is noteworthy for our purposes is that once again reference is made to "God's one and only Son [*tou monogenous uiou tou theou*]" (John 3:18). The argument of the prologue finds its echo in this conversation where the uniqueness of Jesus' relationship to the Father is once again the anchor for his exclusive claims.

In the midst of the Bread of Life discourse Jesus again echoes the words of the prologue:

It is written in the Prophets: "They will all be taught by God." Everyone who listens to the Father and learns from him comes to me. No one has seen the Father except the one who is from God;

only he has seen the Father. I tell you the truth, he who believes has
everlasting life. I am the bread of life.
(John 6:45–48)

The context is a rebuke of the Jews who were grumbling about
his claim to be the bread that came down from heaven (v. 41).
They thought they knew where Jesus had come from and
considered his claims to be outrageous. In response Jesus insists
that it is nonsense to pit the teaching of the Old Testament
Scriptures against him and the things he has been saying.
Indeed, those who have truly listened and understood what
those Scriptures made known of God and his purposes cannot
help but be drawn to Jesus and his message. His relation to the
Father is of a different order even from that of the great
prophets of old. He has seen what they could not have seen.
Precisely because of this unique relationship he is "the bread of
life."

The point is made again and again throughout the Gospel
(e.g. John 8:23–29, 42–47; 10:34–38). However, the best known of
the Johannine passages in this regard is the claim from the
Farewell Discourse:

I am the way and the truth and the life. No one comes to the Father
except through me.
(John 14:6)

The context is well-known, namely Thomas' misunderstanding
of Jesus' words "you know the way to the place where I am
going" (v. 4). Jesus responds with what some consider to be the
most scandalous of all the claims in the New Testament. He
excludes all other means of access to the Father, including those
Jewish structures such as priesthood and temple which, with
some legitimacy, could lay claim to root and precedent in the
Old Testament. Nevertheless, with Jesus' arrival the Old
Testament era has come to an end. In Jesus, God now directly
confronts the world. The truth about God can no longer
be considered apart from Jesus. Life from God is to be
sought nowhere else. All other purported ways to God are
closed.

Once again Jesus anchors this claim in a unique relationship with the Father: "Anyone who has seen me has seen the Father … Don't you believe that I am in the Father, and that the Father is in me?" (John 14:9, 10). From this point on the unique intimacy of the relationship between the Father and the Son will be a major theme of the Farewell Discourse. What is more, that which Jesus enjoys by nature he now invites his disciples to share through grace (v. 20). This unity between Father and Son is so profound that to see Jesus is to see the Father (v. 9), to be loved by Jesus is to be loved by the Father (v. 21), and to glorify Jesus is to glorify the Father (John 17:1; cf. 13:32). Indeed, all that belongs to the Father belongs to Jesus (John 16:15). There remains an order in this relationship; the Father and the Son are not strictly interchangeable (John 14:28). Nevertheless, the fundamental characteristic of this relationship is mutual love (John 15:9; 17:26). In the face of such a reality, to know Jesus is to know the Father. Here again the Gospel can be said to be unfolding the theology of its prologue.

It should not be thought that this emphasis on the uniqueness of Jesus as the revealer of God and his purposes is a peculiarity of John's Gospel, though it undoubtedly plays a larger part there than in the other Gospels. The most obvious example is Matthew 11:27 (with its parallel in Luke 10:22):

All things have been committed to me by my Father. No one knows who the Son is except the Father, and no one knows who the Father is except the Son and those to whom the Son chooses to reveal him.

Jesus' authority had been recognized even by those outside the immediate circle of his followers (Matt. 7:29; 8:9; 9:8; Mark 1:27). Yet Jesus himself made mention on a number of occasions of a unique authority which was his (e.g. the authority to forgive sins on the earth, Matt. 9:6) and both here and in the great commission which concludes Matthew's Gospel he speaks of a supreme authority given to him by his Father (cf. Matt. 28:18). What is of particular importance for our study is the way this is tied to the knowledge of God in Matthew 11. Here is a claim every bit as exclusive as John 14:6 and John 1:18.

Jesus determines who will truly know God. In the wake of his appearance and ministry, the knowledge of God cannot be separated from the person of Jesus.

These convictions about the uniqueness of Jesus in both salvation and revelation find expression in the apostolic ministry recorded for us in Acts. Best-known is the testimony of Peter and John before the gathering of Jewish religious leaders in Jerusalem: "Salvation is found in no one else, for there is no other name under heaven given to men by which we must be saved" (Acts 4:12). "No one else" (*allō oudeni*) and "no other name" (*oudev onoma eteron*) are distinct echoes of the exclusive claims of Jesus in the Gospels. The evangelistic mission of the early church finds a critical impetus here. Apart from hearing of Jesus, the nations are not only in the dark about God and his purposes but lost and facing judgment. Jesus must be proclaimed to the ends of the earth because without him there is no knowledge of God and no hope. Paul's commission at the time of his conversion is to carry Jesus' name "before the Gentiles and their kings and before the people of Israel" (Acts 9:15). The reason for this commission surfaces again and again in Paul's letters: outside of Jesus – without hearing the gospel of God's Son and responding to it in faith – men and women are "objects of wrath" and "without God in the world" (Eph. 2:3, 12).

A classic – and classically misunderstood – passage from Acts on this theme is the sermon of Paul delivered at the Areopagus in Athens (Acts 17:22–31). Some have taken this passage as a prototype for one kind of inter-faith dialogue. Building upon and to some extent endorsing the religious insights of his hearers ("I see that in every way you are very religious," v. 22; "what you worship as something unknown I am going to proclaim to you," v. 23), Paul goes on to show how these insights are fulfilled in Christ and his gospel. But is this really what Paul is doing at the Areopagus? By the end of the brief summary of his sermon recorded for us in Acts 17, none of the altars are metaphorically left standing, not even the one to an unknown god. Indeed, all men are called upon, not to know more or to supplement their essentially good but inadequate religious instincts, but rather to repent. The exclusive nature of

Jesus' relationship to his father is again brought into play: "by the man whom he has appointed" (v. 31). Paul's words here may indeed be a prototype for interfaith discussions but the discussions he has in mind terminate with the exclusive claims of Jesus and the call to repent from foolish thinking and consequent perverse living.

The entire biblical testimony, not simply a few isolated claims of Jesus but an entire strand of biblical teaching that stretches back through the Old Testament and forward through the preaching and writing of the apostles, compels us to proclaim Jesus as the unique and indispensable focus of God's self-revelation in these last days. God "made his light shine in our hearts to give us the light of the knowledge of the glory of God in the face of Christ" (2 Cor. 4:6). Apart from attention to Jesus, all our talk of God runs the risk of being a comfortable illusion. God determines when and how he is to be known. The Lord of creation and redemption is always Lord of his self-revelation. Jesus is identified by Old Testament prophecy and by apostolic testimony to be the one who alone makes God known in the last days. As the writer to the Hebrews puts it:

> In the past God spoke to our forefathers through the prophets at many times and in various ways, but in these last days he has spoken to us by his Son …
> (Heb. 1:1–2)

2. The Uniqueness of Christ: A Theological Necessity

If understanding Jesus as the unique revealer of God is the inescapable conclusion of an exegesis of the biblical text, are we in a position to understand why this must be so? The answer to this question is most certainly "yes." The reasoning behind these claims for and by Jesus is not a deduction from the text of Scripture but rather is part of the text itself. At least four elements can be isolated for brief comment here.

First and most important of all, Jesus is the unique revealer of God because of his identity as the only Son of the Father who was incarnate at a point in human history. We have seen how this connection is made explicit in John 1 and John 14. It is also an important feature of contemporary theology. As one influential British theologian puts it,

> In the incarnation God has communicated *his divine self* to us in Jesus Christ ... the pivotal issue here ... is the identity (the *tautovth* as Athanasius expressed it) between God and the revelation of himself, between what he reveals of himself and his activity in Jesus Christ and what he really is in himself, in his own ever-living and dynamic Being.[5]

Indeed, it is axiomatic in modern trinitarian theology that true knowledge of God is possible only if God is in himself as he is towards us in Jesus Christ.[6] It is also axiomatic that for any revelation to be genuine and effective much more than a superficial or external connection to our humanity with all its limitations is necessary. Here again Torrance is helpful:

> Only in Christ is God's self-revelation identical with himself, and only in Christ, God for us, does he communicate his self-revelation to us in such a way that it may be communicated to us and understood by us.[7]

The identity of Jesus Christ as the only Son of the Father *and* as genuinely human in every respect whilst never succumbing to sin (Heb. 4:14–16) determines the character and accessibility of his revelation of God. We are not dealing with simply a human interpretation of God – even a faithful and authoritative interpretation of God – when we deal with Jesus Christ. Instead, we are dealing with God himself. Yet at the same time we are not dealing with a revelation so entirely alien to us that we must ultimately resort to the language of darkness and mystery when speaking about God. Jesus genuinely and uniquely makes God known because he alone *is* God as he presents himself to us amidst all the frailty of our human existence. In him God's address of all humanity is direct rather than mediated and, as John Calvin would have put it, this address is tailored to our infirmity.[8]

In other words, the union of the Father and the Son in the Spirit is the ground of the knowledge of God which Jesus brings. In passage after passage, particularly in John's Gospel, appeal is made to this union, this oneness of being, as the guarantee that when we know Jesus we really do know God. He is in a unique position to make known the character and purposes of God. His unity with the Father exists at the most profound level – not just at the level of a common will or a perfect moral coordination but at the level of being. As the Nicene fathers found, we are bound to speak not only of *perichoresis* but also of *homoousios*.[9] This is why the claims of Jesus and the preaching of the apostles are not arbitrary limitations on the points of access to God. Instead, this scandalous particularity arises from just who Jesus is and his unique relationship to the Father. The revelation Jesus brings can be trusted because he is one with the Father. It can be understood by men and women because he is also one with us.

Secondly, it needs to be frankly acknowledged that the exclusive claims of Jesus cannot be excised from the gospel message without doing damage to its basic structure. They are neither incidental nor tangential. The great news of the gospel is that God himself has acted to save us and to make that salvation known. Jesus came to bring light and life to humanity (John 1:4). Apart from him all men and women would remain in darkness and under judgment. The biblical testimony to his humility and truthfulness unravels if he made claims like these and they prove to be nothing but grandiose rhetoric or wishful thinking. Despite the best efforts of two hundred years' worth of critical New Testament studies, no refuge can be taken in the suggestion that these claims were made later by others and not by Jesus himself. Jesus' commission to his apostles and his promise of the Spirit to remind them of "everything I have said to you" (John 14:26) are problematic if these men tampered with the gospel message after Jesus' ascension. Furthermore, we are simply not in a position to differentiate with any degree of certainty between the exact words which Jesus spoke into the Galilean breeze and the words found on his lips in the pages of the Gospels. Yet without this means of escape we are bound to accept the claims of Jesus as his own and must insist therefore that the impeccable character of Jesus and the coherence of the gospel message both begin to evaporate the moment we suggest Jesus is in reality just one of many avenues for knowing God. The one who would make such claims contrary to reality is either deluded or a liar.

However, the eschatological framework of the gospel presents Jesus as the final and climactic revelation of God's character and purpose. His incarnation, his baptism by John, his arrival at the Temple, his transfiguration and the final journey to Jerusalem – not to mention his death, resurrection and ascension – all these gospel events have an apocalyptic character about them (e.g. Mark 13 and Bolt 1995).[10] God himself has intervened in an unprecedented way to bring about a critical turning point in his own plans for the world. The magnitude of these events defies attempts to relativize them in a way that would justify putting Jesus Christ alongside others as merely one means of knowing and relating to the living God. This is all the more striking when they are placed against their proper backdrop: the activity and promises of God throughout the Old Testament.

Thirdly, the alternative if Jesus is simply one access point among many is frankly horrifying. If there are other ways to know God apart from through Jesus Christ – his person, words and work – then strictly speaking these things are not necessary, at least not necessary for all. Why *must* (*dei'*) the Son suffer for some if his suffering is not necessary for others to reach the same destination? What must we say about God if he decrees and endures the humiliation of incarnation and the cross and yet this is just one way among many? What generations of Christians have understood as the ultimate expression of love would become an exercise in some strange form of self-indulgence. In other words, what is not often enough recognized is that it is the character of God which is the ultimate casualty when the uniqueness of Jesus as the savior of humanity and the revealer of God is sidelined or denied.

Finally, the missionary endeavor of the New Testament is inexplicable apart from such a conviction. As we have already noted, the world of the Ancient Near East was very religious.

Sincere and conscientious men and women participated in lively and serious religious practices and faithfully subscribed to the belief structures associated with them. In such an environment why would the apostles and those who followed them persist in calling for repentance and the abandonment of all other religious commitments? Why would they risk punishment and even death for insisting that Jesus alone is God and all must come to him in order to be saved? Why call on sincere and religious people, as Paul did, to forsake their idols and turn to the living God and wait for his Son from heaven (1 Thess. 1:9–10) if the faithful exercise of their own religion would eventually bring them in contact with the same living God? In the ensuing centuries martyrdom was a realistic possibility and yet even when face to face with it men like Polycarp of Smyrna would not turn back from their conviction that the only true God is only truly known in Jesus Christ (witness his "Away with the atheists").[11] Two thousand years of missionary endeavor has been predicated on the uniqueness of Jesus as the revealer of God and the Savior of the world. The world outside of Christ is lost – as we all once were – since, as the apostle Paul put it, "the wrath of God is revealed from heaven against all ungodliness and unrighteousness of men, who by their unrighteousness suppress the truth" (Rom. 1:18).

The identity of Jesus, the coherent gospel message which he gave his disciples to proclaim to the world, the character of God and even the missionary orientation of the New Testament and the Christian movement that grew out of it, are all rendered problematic by the suggestion that Jesus is merely one of many ways to know the living God. There is a deep logic to the biblical presentation of Jesus as the unique revealer of God. The one before whom every knee must bow and of whom every tongue will confess that he is Lord (Phil. 2:9–11) is the one from whom we must all now learn the character and purposes of the one true God. In the light of this, the words of his earliest disciples echo through the centuries: "Lord, to whom [else] shall we go? You have the words of eternal life. We believe and know that you are the Holy One of God" (John 6:68–69).

3. Towards a Recovery of the Concept of Idolatry

Contrary to some recent suggestions, the pluralism of our contemporary situation is not a new phenomenon in world history. An awareness of the "gods of the nations" is evident throughout the Old and New Testaments. Indeed, the apostolic ministry which provided both the pattern and principles for the life of the churches over the past two thousand years was conducted in an environment of intense religiosity and this simple fact, far from being ignored by the apostles, drew from them a call to radical repentance. Since the arrival – and more particularly the resurrection – of Jesus Christ there can be no excuse for searching elsewhere for divine truth, insight or endorsement. The one judge of all men and women has been identified and all are called to come to him (Acts 17:30–31).

The biblical materials – the Old Testament in prospect and the New Testament in face of the realization of God's purposes – simply do not applaud the religious endeavors of those outside of Christ. There is not the slightest suggestion that the religions of the world can be embraced as presenting part of some larger truth. They are never recognized as encouraging expressions of a genuine search for God which stands behind or alongside a true knowledge of God in Christ. Instead, Paul provocatively declares that "the sacrifices of pagans are offered to demons, not to God" (1 Cor. 10:20). Of course, Paul and the other Bible writers understand that genuine love exists amongst those who do not know of Christ or have rejected him (though all human love is tainted by our own selfishness). They also acknowledge genuine philanthropy, justice and truth (of various kinds). But their testimony is resolute: those outside of Christ do not know the God who created them.

The biblical category which embraces any attempt to know God other than in the way he provides is *idolatry*. In the practice of idolatry a god is manufactured which does not correspond with reality because it is not constrained by the way the living God has revealed himself. Of course, the "idol" need not be a physical representation as in the case of Israel and the golden calf. Nor need it take the form of an elevation of "some aspect of the created order to the central place that the Creator alone occupies."[12] Calvin, for one, understood the problem to be far more profound. Idolatry and empty superstition, which so regularly go together, are the inevitable consequence of the impact of sin upon the created human orientation towards God.[13] They are distortions and perversions of how we were made to relate to the true and living God. Futility and frustration has entered into this aspect of human existence as it has in every other aspect. Furthermore, so widespread and diverse is the practice of idolatry that Calvin considered we can rightly understand sinful human nature as "a perpetual factory of idols."[14] In contrast, true religion is properly conformed to God's will.[15]

The search for other pathways to God is inextricably tied to idolatry when it is understood in this most profound sense. However, the appropriate response to such idolatry is not the kind of bigotry that gives way to violence and attempts to coerce conversion from other religions to faith in Christ. We do well to admit with shame that this was indeed the response of some in the past two thousand years. However, this was never the pattern of Christ himself or his apostles. Yet neither is the appropriate response an attempt to rationalize the phenomenon of religious pluralism by suggesting there are many ways to a true knowledge of God, for this flies in the face of the biblical evidence. Rather, the most appropriate response, a response grounded in the gospel and faithful to biblical revelation, is to continue the evangelistic mission of the early church. We need to recover a sense of our world as lost – which is after all the way Christ himself describes it (Luke 19:10) – as a first step to the reformation and revitalization of Christian interface with the world.

4. Conclusion

God has made himself known. He has not left humanity in the dark to grope around with the slim hope of finding some part of the truth about him. However, the deep-seated wickedness of the human heart means that we recoil rather than rejoice that God has at a certain time and in a certain place laid himself bare before the world. Yet the unambiguous testimony of Scripture is that Jesus Christ is God with us. He is the one who makes known the Father. There is no room for alternative pathways or a more generic theism when the truth about Jesus is known. Christian theologians who baulk at the particularity of God's revelation in Christ and seek a more optimistic evaluation of the world's religions are striving against the grain of the gospel itself.

Too much is at stake to pull our punches at this point. At our point in human history, on this side of the cross and resurrection, there is no knowledge of God apart from Christ. The apostle John saw this clearly:

> We know also that the Son of God has come and has given us understanding, so that we may know him who is true. And we are in him who is true – even in his Son Jesus Christ. He is the true God and eternal life.
>
> (1 John 5:20–21)

Notes

1 Hilary of Poitiers, *De Trinitate*, in *A Select Library of the Nicene and Post-Nicene Fathers of the Christian Church, Second Series* (ed. Philip Schaff and Henry Wace; trans. by E. W. Watson, L. Pullan et al. [1898]; reprinted, Grand Rapids, MI: Eerdmans, 1979), I, p. xviii.

2 Karl Barth, *Church Dogmatics* II/1 (ed. G. W. Bromiley and T. F. Torrance; Edinburgh: T&T Clark, 1936–1969), p. 44.

3 Colin E. Gunton, *A Brief Theology of Revelation* (Edinburgh: T&T Clark, 1995), p. 31.

4 There is some debate about whether the words in this paragraph should be included as the words of Jesus which began at verse 10 or whether they are the words of the evangelist.

5 Thomas F. Torrance, *The Christian Doctrine of God: One Being Three Persons* (Edinburgh: T&T Clark, 1996), pp. 142–43.

6 Karl Rahner, "Remarks on the Dogmatic Treatise 'De Trinitate'," in *Theological Investigations* Vol. IV (23 vols.; trans. Kevin Smith; London: Darton, Longman & Todd, 1966), pp. 77–102.

7 Torrance, *Christian Doctrine of God*, p. 1.

8 John Calvin, *Commentaries on the Catholic Epistles* (trans. John Owen [1855]; reprinted, Grand Rapids, MI: Eerdmans, 1948), p. 53. John

Calvin, *The Institutes of the Christian Religion* (ed. John T. McNeill; trans. Ford Lewis Battles; Philadelphia: Westminster, 1960), I.xiii.1.

[9] Torrance, *Christian Doctrine of God*, pp. 91–106.

[10] Peter G. Bolt, "Mark 13: An Apocalyptic Precursor to the Passion Narrative," *Reformed Theological Review* 54.1 (1995), pp. 10–32.

[11] Kirsopp Lake, *The Apostolic Fathers*, Vol. 2 (London: Heinemann, 1913), p. 325.

[12] Vinoth Ramachandra, *Gods that Fail: Modern Idolatry and Christian Mission* (Carlisle: Paternoster, 1996), p. 107.

[13] Calvin, *Institutes*, I.iv.1–4.

[14] Calvin, *Institutes*, I.xi.8.

[15] Calvin, *Institutes*, I.iv.3.

6

The Uniqueness of Christ and the Trinitarian Faith

Veli-Matti Kärkkäinen

1. Introduction

It was no less a theological giant than Karl Barth who made this programmatic statement, the implications of which he himself was never able to pursue:

> The doctrine of the Trinity is what basically distinguishes the Christian doctrine of God as Christian, and therefore what already distinguishes the Christian concept of revelation as Christian, in contrast to all other possible doctrines of God or concepts of revelation.[1]

In the beginning of the third millennium there are two significant developments in Christian theology at the ecumenical and international level that are inspiring a number of new publications, conferences, and debates, namely, the doctrine of the Trinity and the theology of religions.[2] The renaissance of the doctrine of the Trinity, which began in the mid-twentieth century with the groundbreaking work of Barth, has helped revive the relevance of the Christian doctrine of God and its relation to issues such as salvation, community, creation, and eschatology.[3] The challenge of religious pluralism has accounted for the unexpected rise to prominence of issues dealing with how Christianity should relate to other religions.[4]

However, what is most noteworthy and surprising about these two developments is that they have not converged. By and large, the doctrine of the Trinity and the questions of the Christian theology of religions have not been brought into mutual dialogue. This is astonishing in light of the obvious fact that both have to do with God. Indeed, both fields of theological inquiry attempt to identify the God of the Bible and the way God relates to us and the Other.

No wonder, then, that Christian theology in general and evangelical theology in particular have now begun to feel the need to initiate a theological dialogue between the Christian faith in the triune God and the *theo*-logical concepts of other religions. The collection of essays titled *The Trinity in a Pluralistic Age,* edited by Kevin J. Vanhoozer (1997),[5] based on the proceedings of an international conference, explores various topics and theologians on the relationship between the Trinity and pluralism. Writers represent evangelical and moderate classical orthodoxy, yet in open-minded, critical dialogue with differing voices.

The purpose of this chapter is, first, to briefly introduce the main proposals towards a trinitarian understanding of the theology of religions available at the ecumenical and international levels. Second, it will take stock of main contributions to the emerging trinitarian inquiry into the Christian theology of religions. Third, as a preface to the main task, I will briefly summarize the main orientations of trinitarian theologies in contemporary theology, as I see them. Fourth, the bulk of this essay will attempt to offer an outline of key themes and perspectives needed to develop an evangelical theology of religions. Within the confines of a short essay, however, the most that can be achieved is to point to the key issues and suggest some tasks for future work. As such, my proposal is open to discussion and subject to revisions.

2. Trinity and Religions in a Meeting Place

What Barth was to the renaissance of the trinitarian theology in general, Raimundo Panikkar, a cosmopolitan, Asian-born

Catholic theologian and religious scholar, is to the relating of the Trinity to other religions. He was the first to suggest that the Trinity is an appropriate topic with which to tackle religious pluralism, recognising that it is *the* Christian resource; but he went further by claiming that indeed a trinitarian structure can be found in all religions! In his small yet highly significant book, *The Trinity and the Religious Experience of Man*, which was first published in 1973,[6] Panikkar argues for three different kinds of spiritualities, each of which correspond to different "persons" of the Trinity in Christian faith and Hinduism (and perhaps in other religions) too.

It is not insignificant that, following Panikkar, other Roman Catholic theologians have also taken up the challenge.[7] The next major study on the topic did not come until 2000, titled *The Meeting of Religions and the Trinity*,[8] by Gavin D'Costa, another Catholic theologian with an intercultural background. D'Costa takes the postconciliar Catholic trinitarianism as a major resource for highlighting the failure of pluralisms – whether Christian, Jewish, Hindu, or Buddhist – to deliver their promises. He offers an outline but not yet a full program for a trinitarian theology of religions.

Yet another Catholic theologian, the veteran theologian of religions Jacques Dupuis, in his magnum opus *Toward a Christian Theology of Religious Pluralism* (1997),[9] had already made a lasting contribution to the topic of the Trinity and religions; yet, unlike D'Costa, he does not offer a full-scale trinitarian program and his focus is wider. It is significant, nevertheless, that in this book Dupuis expands significantly the theology of religions discourse from his earlier christocentric approach, *Jesus Christ at the Encounter of World Religions* (1991).[10]

The most recent trinitarian theology of religions outside Catholic theology comes from the hand of S. Mark Heim, who originally comes from evangelicalism. His book *The Depths of the Riches: A Trinitarian Theology of Religious Ends* (2001)[11] is perhaps the "most" pluralistic theology of religions yet to appear: on the basis of the diversity in the triune God, Heim advances the thesis that not only are religions different, but they also have different, God-willed "ends" in terms of salvation goals. Heim's book is undoubtedly the most radical challenge to the task of applying trinitarian resources to world religions.

My own recent study *Trinity and Religious Pluralism: The Doctrine of the Trinity in Christian Theology of Religions* (2004) attempts to achieve two goals: first, to offer a critical theological assessment of key trinitarian theologies in contemporary theologies with a view to the Christian theology of religions, and second, to lay out an outline of topics and theological themes needed to begin to develop an evangelical trinitarian theology of religions.

The preceding has not been an exhaustive account, but is representative of the major contributions to the trinitarian approach to religions so far.[12] On the basis of these and related considerations, we can safely conclude that to neglect or downplay the importance of the doctrine of the Trinity for the theology of religions is both shortsighted and detrimental. As mentioned earlier, to develop the theme of Christ's uniqueness among the saviors of the world entails a trinitarian framework. One of the potentials for the future of Christian theology in general and theology of religions in particular is a responsible use of trinitarian resources. Before beginning the pressing task, a brief look at the state of the trinitarian theology in the beginning of a new millennium is in order.

3. Where Are We Now in the Trinitarian Discourse?

What is the state of current trinitarian theology?[13] The following presents my subjective reading of the turns taken at the ecumenical and international level. I believe all of these moves warrant notice by evangelical theology and continued work towards a relevant and faithful understanding of the Trinity in the beginning of a new millennium.[14] Of course, the most that can be done here is to outline the key developments and key players.

First, the doctrine of the Trinity is the structuring principle of Christian theology and thus of the Christian doctrine of God among other gods. In the past, Trinity used to be a more or less necessary appendix to the Christian doctrine of God. In classical theology, the order of the systematic topics demonstrated its place. The tractate on *One God* was discussed first, to be followed by another one titled *The Triune God*. With good grounds, several contemporary theologians from Karl Rahner to Karl Barth to Wolfhart Pannenberg to the Catholic female theologian Catherine Mowry LaCugna have criticized this order since it implies that the doctrine of the Trinity is not an integral part of Christian view of God.[15] In terms of the theology of religions it would mean that one could speak of one God of the Bible without necessarily resorting to Trinity, a topic seen by many other religions, especially by Islam, as a major obstacle.[16]

Placing Trinity in the beginning of Christian theology and the doctrine of God and making it the structuring principle means nothing less than to argue that to speak of God means to speak of Jesus Christ, a topic crucial to the present book. Theologically, it is a brilliant decision from the editor of this book to include a chapter on the Trinity in the discussion of how to frame the uniqueness of Christ vis-à-vis other religions. There is simply no way to proceed otherwise in Christian theology of religions.[17] The Christian God, the one God of the Israelite *Shema* (Deut. 6:4), the Father of Jesus Christ, exists as Father, Son, and Spirit.[18]

Second, the way to know the Christian God – Father, Son, and Spirit – can only be possible through God's self-revelation in the Son. The triune God of Christian faith can only be known on the basis of God's self-revelation, as Barth has insisted, in other words, through his dealings with us. Thus, we "ascend" from salvation history to the inner life of God even though the inner life of God can never be exhausted. This is the essence of what has been called "Rahner's Rule."[19] Technically this means that "economic" Trinity (God for us) is the "immanent" Trinity (God *per se*).

Adopting the Rahner's Rule, third, then means that the doctrine of the Trinity, rather than being an exercise in speculative theology as often was the case in the past – and, again, rightly criticized by many contemporary theologians[20] – is rather an exposition and theological reflection on the biblical salvation history. Although the Bible, not even the New Testament,[21] presents a full-scale doctrine of the Trinity, the structure of salvation history, the coming of the Son, Jesus of Nazareth, to announce and inaugurate the coming of the Kingdom of God in the power of the Spirit, can only be understood in the trinitarian framework; in the words of the eminent Catholic theologian Gerald O'Collins, there is a "trinitarian face" to the history of Jesus.[22]

Fourth, if the Christian God can only be known as Father, Son, and Spirit, it means that history counts. The biblical God cannot be understood as an abstraction apart from the events of history and time. The triune God who became one of us in the incarnation of Jesus of Nazareth and who poured out his Spirit, the Spirit who raised the Son from the dead, can only be known on the basis of his dealings in history and time. In a qualified sense,[23] one can say that what happens here in the world and history, is "included" in the divine life, the "history of God," not only with regard to salvation history (incarnation, cross, resurrection, ascension), but also with regard to creation and perhaps the rest of history. Again, Barth was the first to suggest this idea; Pannenberg and Jürgen Moltmann soon made it a leading theme.[24]

Finally, a unanimous consensus has arisen among contemporary trinitarian theologians that the Christian God is a divine communion. This is the theological conclusion from the biblical idea that God is love. God exists sovereignly and freely as eternal loving communion. Through the same eternal love the Father has shown the Son from eternity, the triune God reaches out to his creation and draws us to participate in the divine life in the Spirit, the bond of communion and the bond of love. Relationality, being-in-relationships, is the proper mode of viewing not only the divine life but also the essence of personhood. Persons exist in communion, in relationships, rather than as mere "individuals." This "rule" of the Eastern Orthodox John Zizioulas has become a received view among most trinitarian writers today.[25]

The rest of this essay will focus on outlining and critically assessing some key themes needed for the development of an evangelical theology of religions with a view to supporting the uniqueness of Jesus Christ among world religions. The following subtopics will be included in the discussion here: (1) the critical role of history as the arena for inquiring into the truthfulness of Christian claims about the triune God; (2) the critical role of Christology for establishing a proper trinitarian theology vis-à-vis other religions; (3) the uniqueness of the God of the Bible who exists as triune; (4) the relationship between the triune God and the church's mission is the pluralistic world; and (5) implications of God as communion for how evangelicals should relate to other religions.

4. History and the Truthfulness of Christian Claims

One of the fallacies of pluralistic theologies is the assumption of "rough parity" between religions.[26] In granting a type of equality to all religions, they commit two theological sins. On the one hand, they eradicate differences among religions (over against the self-understanding of the adherents of the various religions) and on the other hand, they end up denying public truth to any or all of them. In response, we have to argue that while people are not infallible, the self-definition of each religion has to be taken seriously. Furthermore, while it is true that religion plays various roles, such as identity-formation and culture-shaping, it can be argued that the main function of religion is to advance the quest for the ultimate truth. If religion is denied that function, as in atheistic societies, ideology takes that role.

In any society it is given to religion to tackle the ultimate issues of life and death, and it may not be meaningful to talk about religion at all without this component. Even several Asian religions such as Buddhism and Hinduism, often considered to be more tolerant and pluralistic than Christianity and Islam, still each regard themselves as the true religion.[27] Tolerance is not identical to a denial of the truth claims of one's religion, but pluralists such as Hick fail to make a clear distinction between these two.

To argue that the truth claim for Christ only applies to those inside the Christian household is a self-contradictory notion: truth cannot be true only to some people.[28] It either is true or is not. It does a disservice to Christian mission vis-à-vis other religions to try to soften the encounter by reference to a "partial" truth. One way to try to avoid the scandal of conflicting truth claims seeks to refer to "many absolutes": as if there were several unique and universally powerful revelations of truths. As appealing as this sounds to postmodern ears, in fact it is another dead-end. As the pluralist Knitter notes, "many absolutes" may end up meaning "no absolute." To posit more than one "absolute" is to stretch the limits of logic to the point of making it self-contradictory.[29]

Why do I insist on the urgency of pursuing the question of truth for this particular project? For the simple reason that trinitarian faith is anchored in history. Christian trinitarian faith appeals to history and eschatology as the arenas in which the truth question is hoped to be settled finally. The task of theological reflection, rather than assuming truth, is to advance the quest for the truth.[30] Here the idea of the gospel as "public truth," as advanced by the late Lesslie Newbigin, is a most helpful one. According to him, it is not legitimate to reduce faith primarily to the subjective arena any more than it is possible to regard the arena of facts as free from subjectivity. The knowledge he is talking about (following the sociologist of knowledge Michael Polanyi) is committed, yet not subjectivistic, since "it is a commitment which has an objective reference." In other words, it is a commitment "with universal intent." It looks for confirmation by further experience. Significantly enough, Newbigin titled one of his latest articles, a contribution to a symposium dealing with the Trinity and religions, "The Trinity as Public Truth."[31] Thus, the truth of Christian trinitarian faith is an appeal to truth with universal intent. History and eschatology are thus the criteria to which Christian trinitarian faith appeals.[32] In other words, the doctrine of the Trinity in Christian theology and faith cannot be a generic view, but must be a particular view rooted both in history and an expectation of future confirmation. This takes us to the all-important Christological question in relation to the Trinity.

5. The Critical Role of Christology for the Doctrine of the Trinity

In Christian theology in general and trinitarian theology in particular, Christology plays a criteriological function:

> Apart from the divine identity of Jesus as the Son there could not be a Trinity – at least not in the traditional Christian sense. The concept of Trinity expresses the idea that the three Persons that make it up are fully divine: God the Father, God the Son, and God the Holy Spirit.[33]

The implication is that those pluralists who have left behind the contours of any form of orthodox Christology have also given up Trinity. Fortunately, some of them, such as John Hick, are open and honest about that; he admits his view of the divine is modalistic.[34]

There is no doubt that the doctrine of the Trinity cannot be established without a high Christology and a (more or less) classical view of the incarnation. On the other hand, what one believes about God as triune determines one's Christology and pneumatology. Is this a vicious circle where one establishes what one presupposes? Not necessarily. Rather it is a matter of mutual conditioning, based on a methodological choice. In contrast to "Christology from above," the common approach in Christian theology before the Enlightenment, contemporary scholarship (even with vastly radical differences regarding conclusions) takes the route of "Christology from below." This method inquires into the history of Jesus of Nazareth in the biblical testimonies and tries to discern to what extent these interpretations arise integrally from history and from claims by early Christians. Its goal is to inquire into and possibly defend the Christological traditions in which the man Jesus is seen as the Christ. Of course, in the final analysis the method of from above or from below are not exclusive of each other but rather presuppose each other. What is the key issue is the primacy and criteriological role given to the from below method.

My saying this here sounds like an introductory lecture to beginning theology students! Yet, I am insisting on this issue to make my point: our Christology determines to a large extent our view of the Trinity and vice versa. Furthermore, the way to establish the truthfulness (or at least claim to truthfulness) of trinitarian faith is via Christology. There is no other way to argue for the validity of Christian claims to God as Father, Son, and Spirit.

So, history matters, since Christian trinitarian doctrine is necessarily based on the history of Jesus of Nazareth and the Old Testament revelation of Yahweh. The incarnation, cross, and resurrection, as part of salvation history, are historical events. Dismissing their particularity means dismissing the historical basis for a specifically Christian doctrine of God.

Among the pluralists, I find S. Mark Heim's trinitarian theology of religions an interesting exception to the desire to dismiss the question of the truth. He is not willing to give up the historical ground for the emergence of the specifically Christian doctrine of the Trinity since he takes the biblical salvation history culminating in the incarnation of the Word as the crucial revelation and act of God as the key to distinguishing the triune God. According to Heim, Christians' belief in the incarnation affirms that in Jesus the trinitarian relations that constitute God's divinity and the external relations between God and humans participate in each other. This does not, of course, necessarily mean limiting God's presence in the world to the particular history of Jesus of Nazareth, but that the history of the man Jesus makes it constitutive and the criterion for discerning God's presence elsewhere. Heim writes:

> The Trinity teaches us that Jesus Christ cannot be an exhaustive or exclusive source for knowledge of God nor the exhaustive and exclusive act of God to save us. Yet the Trinity is unavoidably Christocentric in a least two senses. It is Christocentric in the empirical sense that the doctrine, the representation of God's triune nature, arose historically from faith in Jesus Christ. And it is so in the systematic sense that the personal character of God requires particularity as its deepest mode of revelation.[35]

In light of Heim's point, I need to criticize those kinds of trinitarian theologies of religions that operate with a truncated

Christology. Implications for trinitarian theology in general and theology of religions in particular are significant and many; in that case, a generic concept of the Trinity emerges rather than one anchored in the history of Jesus of Nazareth. An example of this kind of a generic approach which I find wanting is the view of R. Panikkar. With all its merits, I find his Christology and theological method highly problematic. Panikkar postulates a Christic-principle, which he then connects to the history of Jesus of Nazareth and to other savior figures. Rather than working from below, in keeping with general pluralistic orientations (with the exception of Heim), he follows the from above method, even though very differently from classical Christology. In other words, Panikkar defines the meaning of Christ apart from historical contours and reads the narrative of the Gospels in light of this assumption. Therefore, I wonder if Panikkar has drained the word *Christ* of its historical significance in his radical distinction between the Christ of faith and the Jesus of history.[36]

Following the Sri Lankan evangelical, Vinoth Ramachandra, I would respond that while there is no need for Christians to have a monopoly on Christ, history and universality may not be set in opposition to each other as Panikkar seems to be doing. Wisely enough, Ramachandra also notes, in contrast to many of his evangelical colleagues, that the problem of particularity should not be confused with the problem of the ultimate status of those who are not Christians. "The claim that God has revealed his truth in historical events does not entail, at least without further premises, that those who lack this revelation are excluded from the benefits of that revelation."[37] The question of access to salvation, while not totally unrelated to the issue of Christ's particularity is a separate issue and should not be made a criterion of salvation here.

Furthermore, divesting Christ of salvation history has other disastrous effects not only for trinitarian doctrine but also for the encounter between God and humanity, a topic vital to any Christian theology of religions. Let me quote from my earlier book:

Again, with Ramachandra, I wonder if Panikkar's Christic Theandrism ends up with a non-trinitarian view of the deity. On the one hand, it divests Jesus Christ of full divinity, and on the other hand, it makes the Christian doctrine of the incarnation unintelligible. According to Ramachandra, this leads to the nondualism of Eastern religions in which there is no distinction between the divine and human, and consequently no "encounter" is possible. Panikkar's nondualistic view of the deity seriously compromises the principle of freedom, both with regard to God and human beings. Even when a mutuality between the divine and human is affirmed, "within that mutuality there must be room for that about God which is more than the mutual relation, and also room for that about man capable of denying and seeking to distance himself from that mutuality.[38]

So far I have insisted on the integral relation between Christology and Trinity. This is in keeping with the overall purpose of the present book, namely, to argue for the uniqueness of Jesus Christ among world religions. In order to complete this section one should also talk about the integral relationship between pneumatology (Holy Spirit) and Trinity on the one hand and pneumatology and Christology on the other hand. That space here does now allow me to go into that discourse in no way indicates any lack of importance of that topic. I take it for granted that trinitarian faith entails the full development of both pneumatology and Christology. In this respect, I find the approach of the evangelical theologian Clark Pinnock very helpful, as well as that of the Catholic D'Costa.[39]

Having argued for the necessity of establishing Christological contours for a healthy trinitarian theology of religions, what can now be said about the uniqueness of the triune God of the Bible?

6. The Uniqueness of the Triune God of the Bible

As mentioned, for Barth the doctrine of the Trinity served as a criterion for distinguishing the God of the Bible from other gods. This is the question of the criteria. What concerns me is that in contemporary theology of religions the question of criteriology is not being taken up in the way it deserves.

Christian trinitarian theology that builds on the biblical and classical theological parameters maintains that talk about Father, Son, and Spirit is the only possible way to identify the God of the Bible. This means that the only way to talk about God is to refer to the Father, Son, and Spirit. If so, then vague, "mythological" talk about God becomes problematic, too generic. Hick's "Ultimate Reality" is only a mental concept with little or no relation to history and time.

As already mentioned, the doctrines of Christ and God presuppose and mutually inform each other. Christ's divinity follows from the doctrine of the Trinity and thus makes any kind of pluralistic "theocentrism" a self-contradictory approach. And not only Christ's divinity but also his incarnation must be posited unless we divorce trinitarian faith from "real" history. Therefore, again, any kind of mythologization or "generalization" of the incarnation that divorces the man Jesus of Nazareth from the incarnation works against a healthy trinitarian understanding.[40] Trinitarian doctrine also integrally links the talk about the Spirit to the Father and Son and resists those kind of pneumatological theologies of religions in which the Spirit is made an itinerant, independent deputy.

For classical Christian theology, biblical salvation history and the creedal tradition has served as a fence between what was and was not considered a legitimate contextualization. It is important to note that indeed the main function of the creeds has been that of drawing lines. The creeds do not express the contents of the biblical faith in a timeless, "neutral" way since creeds themselves are already highly contextualized attempts to express the nucleus of the biblical traditions. Yet they do claim to be based on the biblical traditions, and with all their limitations – and perhaps even some distortions – they have helped the church come to a fuller understanding of the essence of the trinitarian faith.

In surveying the key developments of the contemporary trinitarian doctrine, I mentioned that one of the emphases of the revived doctrine of the Trinity is the linkage to history. Apart from the truth question, the role of history comes into the picture again when speaking of the uniqueness of the triune God among other gods. Several implications follow. First, as already mentioned, the basis for discerning the emergence of the doctrine of the Trinity is to look at the biblical salvation history. Methodologically we have to ground the doctrine of the Trinity in revelation, in other words, in the way God reveals himself in salvation history. If the doctrine is based on God's self-revelation, it cannot be made an optional appendix but must remain the crux of the exposition of the Christian God.[41] The clue to the doctrine of the Trinity is to discern how the three trinitarian persons come to appearance and relate to each other in the event of revelation as presented in the life and message of Jesus. It is only on the basis of this triune God that Christian statements about the one God and his distinctive "nature" can be discussed.

Therefore, second, the trinitarian doctrine is not based on abstract speculations nor primarily on alleged similarities among religions. Let us go back to the theology of Panikkar. Having left behind the Christological contours, one is free to base the doctrine of the Trinity on assumed similarities between the *idea* of Trinity among world religions. This is the "cosmotheandric" principle of the threefold structure of reality and of religions that Panikkar postulates so elegantly in *Trinity and the Religious Experience of Man*. There is, of course, no reason to oppose the possibility of similarities among religions when it comes to the idea of Trinity. On the contrary, if we believe – as Christians do – that Trinity is more than just a religious idea, that it is a legitimate theological formulation corresponding to the way the God of the Bible, the Creator of all, actually exists, then it would be astonishing *not* to find parallels. Yet it is quite another thing to base one's theology on the shaky foundation of assumed parallels. I am not, of course, saying that we should shy away from using extra-biblical or extra-Christian vocabulary to express our faith in the trinitarian God of the Bible. What I am insisting is that whatever formulations are used, their adequacy and limits need to be assessed in light of some criteria.

When I am supporting the idea of the uniqueness of the triune God of the Bible vis-à-vis other gods, I am not, however, saying that Christian talk about God/the divine would not be related to general god-talk in religions. To frame the question in the traditional language: Is there commonality between the God of the Bible and the god of the philosophers? For Barth (at least the early Barth), there is no common point between these two discourses. Pannenberg offers a needed corrective. While he insists on the uniqueness of the triune God, based on the biblical revelation as it interprets salvation history, he also insists on the correlation between general god-talk and talk about the distinctively Christian trinitarian God. Taking his clue from the fact that in the Bible the term *god* not only serves as a proper name (*Yahweh*) but also as a general designation (*Elohim*), he argues that specifically Christian god-talk only makes sense in connection with terms for species. Therefore, to make God-talk intelligible, both in Christian theology and in relation to especially the Jewish faith but also other (theistic) faiths, Christian theology would be better not to cut off ties to philosophical and religious discourse. This also guards Christian trinitarian talk from "involuntarily regressing to a situation of a plurality of gods in which Christian talk about God has reference to the specific biblical God as one God among others."[42]

If it can be argued that the triune God of the Bible, the God of Abraham, Isaac, and Jacob, the *abba* of Jesus of Nazareth, is the only true God among the gods, how then is God related to the coming of the kingdom proclaimed and inaugurated by the Son in the power of the Spirit? And even more, how is the coming of the kingdom related to the church? These are questions any trinitarian theology (of religions) needs to address even though a full-scale treatment of these topics is not possible in this essay.

7. The Church, the Kingdom, and the Presence of the Triune God in the World

One of the reasons that I have critiqued in many ways a fruitful trinitarian approach of the Catholic Jacques Dupuis[43] is that he tends to undermine the integral relationship between God and God's kingdom as if the latter would make Christian theology more exclusive. He also tends to resist the integral relationship between God and the church in the world.[44] I see as more fruitful the approach of his younger Catholic colleague Gavin D'Costa. He insists on the integral relationship between the presence of the Spirit and the Father and Son, which then translates into an integral relationship between the triune God and the church. D'Costa contends that the Holy Spirit's presence within other religions is both intrinsically trinitarian and ecclesiological. It is trinitarian in referring the Holy Spirit's activity to the paschal mystery of Christ, and ecclesial in referring the paschal event to the Spirit's constitutive community-creating force under the guidance of the Spirit.[45] In the New Testament, this is expressed in terms of the church being the people of God, body of Christ, temple of the Spirit.

Establishing the close connection between the triune God and the church does not, however, lead to a kind of "ecclesiocentrism" that is blind to either the Spirit's presence everywhere in the world and in creation as the principle of all life or to the Spirit's activity in society and history, peoples, cultures, and religions. Yet to insist on the integral relation between the triune God, the church, and also the kingdom (since as we noticed above, the kingdom is the kingdom of the triune God) makes one's theology of religions authentically trinitarian.

What then is the role of the kingdom of God? Kingdom is, of course, a much larger entity than the church. The church is the sign of the coming of the kingdom of God and is being drawn to the eschatological movement through which God fulfills his purposes in the world. Having created the world, God cannot be God without his kingdom, as Pannenberg has most vocally argued.[46] Trinitarian doctrine, then, rules out the kind of "kingdom-centered approaches" (of, for example, the Catholic Paul F. Knitter[47]) in which the advancement of the kingdom is set in opposition to or divorced from the Father, Son, and Spirit. It is the kingdom of the Father, the coming of which the Son serves as a humble Son in the power of the Spirit. Again, it is negotiable how much "wider" is the sphere of the kingdom than the church. But however that relationship is defined, I see it mistaken to separate the two so much that the church becomes an obstacle to rather than a God-willed agent that participates in the kingdom's coming.

8. Concluding Reflections: Communion and the Encounter with the Other

Many other significant leads should be pursued on the way to a healthy evangelical trinitarian theology of religions; space does not allow me to do so. Let me just mention one key issue. A consensus of contemporary trinitarian theology regards communion as the key to understanding the concept of the triune God. The triune God as a perichoretic communion is a helpful way to negotiate the dynamic and tension between one and many. The Trinity as communion allows room for both genuine diversity (otherwise we could not talk about the Trinity) and unity (otherwise we could not talk about one God). Communion serves as the paradigm for relating to the Other among human beings too. It is not about denying differences nor eliminating distinctives, but about encountering the Other in a mutually learning, yet challenging atmosphere. The Christian, coming from a particular perspective, is both encouraged and entitled to witness to the triune God of the Bible and his saving will, yet at the same time prepared to learn from the Other. This helps the Christian to get to know the Other and may also lead to the deepening of one's own faith. D'Costa's comment is worth quoting here:

> The other is always interesting in their difference and may be the possible face of God, or the face of violence, greed, and death. Furthermore, the other may teach Christians to know and worship their own trinitarian God more truthfully and richly.

D'Costa believes that trinitarian theology provides the "context for a critical, reverent, and open engagement with otherness, without any predictable outcome."[48]

I further agree with D'Costa that other religions are not salvific as such, but other religions are important for the Christian church in that they help the church to penetrate more deeply into the divine mystery. This is the essence of what D'Costa calls the Spirit's call to "relational engagement." The acknowledgment of the gifts of God in other religions by virtue of the presence of the Spirit – as well as the critical discernment of these gifts by the power of the same Spirit – means a real trinitarian basis to Christianity's openness toward other religions. It also ties the church to the dialogue with the Other: wherever the presence of the Spirit – and thus the presence of God – is to be found it bears some relation to the church. Thus, the discernment of the activity of the Holy Spirit within other religions must also bring the church more truthfully into the presence of the triune God. Again, citing D'Costa, "if the Spirit is at work in the religions, then the gifts of the Spirit need to be discovered, fostered, and received into the church. If the church fails to be receptive, it may be unwittingly practicing cultural and religious idolatry."[49] The church better be ready for surprises since there is no knowing a priori what beauty, truth, holiness, and other "gifts" may be waiting for the church.[50]

In the final analysis, trinitarian faith and the "scandal of particularity" of Christian faith are not to be thought of as opposites. According to Ramachandra, this is "a particularity that God takes seriously in his dealings with his creatures." God chose a nation to be the bearer of the cosmic history to the rest, and one mediator to include all. Thus, incarnation is geared toward universality. Particularity is for the purpose of universality, not exclusion. Therefore, Christian faith has always been a missionary faith. Missionary urgency flows from the very logic of the incarnation, death, and resurrection of the messiah of all peoples.[51] As an Asian theologian, Ramachandra further argues that the normativeness of Jesus inherent in trinitarian faith, rather than being something foreign imposed on Asian religions, in fact, "safeguards some of the legitimate concerns of contemporary Asian theologians."[52] Unlike the major Asian religions, Christianity, for example, takes seriously the cause of the poor, fully endorses the equality of all persons created in the image of God, and celebrates humility and self-sacrificial life and service, among other things. The "gospel humanity" results in the creation of a new human community that celebrates plurality under one God.

Let me finish by saying that in this essay of few pages I have not been able to solve the riddle of the relationship between the doctrine of the Trinity and other religions. What I have tried to accomplish is to make more explicit the underlying convictions and understandings that have guided my critical dialogue with leading trinitarian theologians across the ecumenical, theological, and cultural borders, as well as point to the tasks for future work in this area. My all too brief outline has not only been very general in nature but also selective. For example, I have not even touched the question of salvation, not because I do not consider it a worthy question, but because I believe there is only one major divide theologically, and that is the one between pluralists and the rest. My general dissatisfaction with pluralism includes critique of their either too general a view of salvation (the "self-realization" of Hick) or too particularist (the eco-liberation of Knitter).

Many tasks such as the following are left for the future: What exactly is the relationship between the Spirit and Jesus Christ in the outward works of the triune God in the world? Is a distinctively "pneumatological" theology of religions needed as complementing the older, now much rejected "Christological" or should we only aim at a trinitarian one?[53] Are there various forms of trinitarian theologies of religions that are biblical and theologically sound? If so, what are the essential criteria for their soundness (other than discussed above)?

An appropriate conclusion to our study is offered by Vanhoozer in the book he recently edited, *The Trinity in a Pluralistic Age*:

> The Trinity is the Christian answer to the identity of God. The one creator God is Father, Son, and Spirit. This is an identification that is at once exclusivistic and pluralistic.[54] And because this God who is three-in-one has covenanted with what is other than himself – the creature – the identity of God is also inclusivistic. The Trinity, far from being a *skandalon*, is rather the transcendental condition for inter-religious dialogue, the ontological condition that permits us to take the other in all seriousness, without fear, and without violence.[55]

Notes

[1] Karl Barth, *Church Dogmatics* I/1 (ed. G. W. Bromiley and T. F. Torrance; Edinburgh: T&T Clark, 1936–1969), p. 301.

[2] See further, Veli-Matti Kärkkäinen, *Trinity and Religious Pluralism: The Doctrine of the Trinity in Christian Theology of Religions* (Aldershot, England: Ashgate, 2004), p. 1. For Barth's theology of religions in a trinitarian perspective, see ch. 1. This essay is an expanded and reworked version of the final chapter of that book, pp. 164–84.

[3] For an excellent recent survey of contemporary trinitarian theology by a leading Evangelical theologian, see Stanley J. Grenz, *Rediscovering the Triune God: The Trinity in Contemporary Theology* (Minneapolis: Fortress Press, 2004). Also very helpful is the older work of Ted Peters, *God as Trinity: Relationality and Temporality in the Divine Life* (Louisville, KY: Westminster John Knox, 1993).

[4] For an overview, see Veli-Matti Kärkkäinen, *An Introduction to the Theology of Religions: Biblical, Historical, and Contemporary Perspectives* (Downers Grove, IL: InterVarsity Press, 2003).

[5] Kevin Vanhoozer, ed., *The Trinity in a Pluralistic Age: Theological Essays on Culture and Religion* (Grand Rapids, MI: Eerdmans, 1997).

[6] Raimundo Panikkar, *The Trinity and the Religious Experience of Man: Icon-Person-Mystery* (Maryknoll, NY: Orbis/London: Darton, Longman & Todd); the book is also known as *The Trinity and the World Religions*. For an exposition and critical assessment of Panikkar's theology of religions on the basis of his extensive literature, see Kärkkäinen, *Trinity and Religious Pluralism*, ch. 8.

[7] One could guess that the contributions to our topic would come first from the Eastern Orthodox family since that tradition is thoroughly trinitarian in its faith and spirituality. However, the fact that Eastern Orthodoxy for the most part has not been missionary in orientation and has often found itself living under a hostile environment has probably contributed to the stifling of efforts in this field.

[8] Gavin D'Costa, *The Meeting of Religions and the Trinity* (Maryknoll, NY: Orbis, 2000). For an exposition and critical assessment, see Kärkkäinen, *Trinity and Religious Pluralism*, ch. 4.

[9] Jacques Dupuis, *Toward a Christian Theology of Religious Pluralism* (Maryknoll, NY: Orbis, 1977). For an exposition and critical assessment, see Kärkkäinen, *Trinity and Religious Pluralism*, ch. 3.

[10] J. Dupuis, *Jesus Christ at the Encounter of World Religions* (Maryknoll, NY: Orbis, 1991).

[11] Mark S. Heim, *The Depth of the Riches: A Trinitarian Theology of Religious Ends* (Grand Rapids, MI: Eerdmans, 2001). For an exposition and critical assessment, see Kärkkäinen, *Trinity and Religious Pluralism*, ch. 9.

[12] Still another study that deals in a significant way with our topic should be mentioned, idiosyncratic as it is in its approach and bordering on a "universal theology": namely, the book by the senior religious scholar Ninian Smart (in collaboration with his student, the Eastern Orthodox Stephen Konstantine) titled *Christian Systematic Theology in a World Context* (Minneapolis: Fortress, 1991). My reading of that book leaves me wondering if it goes beyond the contours of a specifically *Christian* theology of religions in that Smart and Konstantine build their "trinitarian" doctrine on a mixture of religious traditions which does not easily commend itself to more typical trinitarian approaches.

[13] For some aspects of this discussion, see further Veli-Matti Kärkkäinen, *The Doctrine of God in Global Perspective: Biblical, Historical, and Contemporary Perspectives* (Grand Rapids, MI: Baker Academic, 2004). While that book does not focus on trinitarian theology, it also takes stock of key developments in current biblical, historical, and systematic contributions. A very helpful brief exposition and assessment from an Evangelical perspective can be found in Stanley J. Grenz, *The Social God and the Relational Self: A Trinitarian Theology of the Image of God* (Louisville, KY/London/Leiden: Westminster John Knox, 2001), pp. 33–57 especially.

[14] See also Kärkkäinen, *Trinity and Religious Pluralism*, pp. 4–6 especially.

[15] See, e.g., Karl Rahner, *The Trinity* (New York: Seabury 1997 [orig., 1970]), pp. 15–17.

[16] The radical change of theological climate in contemporary theology is illustrated by Barth and Pannenberg. Barth begins his multivolume *Church Dogmatics* with the discussion of Trinity, even prior to the otherwise crucial doctrine of revelation. Pannenberg, in his first volume of systematic theology, begins the doctrine of God with the discussion of the Trinity, and thereafter takes up the issue of the unity (oneness) of God and God's attributes, routinely discussed first in traditional theology.

[17] This observation also brings the Spirit into the discussion of the Christian God. The Holy Spirit is the Spirit of God and the Spirit of Christ, the principle of communion between trinitarian members. This observation alone, as will become evident in

what follows, makes talk about a one-sided "Christocentrism" or "Pneumatocentrism" a theological bankrupt in relation to other religions.

[18] See further Wolfhart Pannenberg, *Systematic Theology* Vol. 1 (3 vols.; trans. G. W. Bromiley; Grand Rapids, MI: Eerdmans, 1994), p. 259.

[19] "The 'economic' Trinity is the 'immanent' Trinity and the 'immanent' Trinity is the 'economic' Trinity." Rahner, *Trinity*, p. 22 (italics in the text). The designation "Rahner's Rule" goes back to Peters, *God as Trinity*, p. 96. In this context, I am simply referring to this Rule and do not engage in the criticism targeted against it. The critique has to do with how literally you can take Rahner's basic idea without ending up, for example, compromising the freedom of God.

[20] See, for example, Rahner, *Trinity*, pp. 18–19.

[21] See further, Roger E. Olson and Christopher A. Hall, *The Trinity* (Guides to Theology; Grand Rapids, MI: Eerdmans, 2002), p. 6. Barth came close to this idea when he based his doctrine of the Trinity on the biblical idea of Revelation: "God reveals himself. He reveals himself through himself. He reveals himself" (*CD* I/1, p. 296). On a closer look, however, this means constructing the trinitarian doctrine on the *logical* formula derived from the Bible rather than on the structure of the biblical salvation history. Pannenberg is more successful when he takes the coming of the Son, explained above, as the starting point of the trinitarian doctrine. See Kärkkäinen, *Doctrine of God*, pp. 150–51.

[22] Gerald O'Collins, *The Tripersonal God: Understanding and Interpreting the Trinity* (New York/Mahwah, NJ: Paulist Press, 1999), p. 35 (chapter title: "The History of Jesus and its Trinitarian Face").

[23] The need for qualification arises from the obvious problem that if God is too closely tied to history, we may end up not only limiting God's freedom from his creation, but also making God a part of world process (like Process theology).

[24] With regard to Moltmann, many wonder (the present author among them) if he puts too much stress on the role of history in the "coming of God." Yet, as a general principle, what he suggests, namely that Trinity cannot be understood abstractly but rather in relation to the cross and resurrection of Jesus holds as a key theological guideline. See further, Kärkkäinen, *Doctrine of God*, pp. 158–59 especially.

25 One of the defining works in the contemporary trinitarian theology is John Zizioulas, *Being as Communion: Studies in Personhood and Communion* (Crestwood, NY: St Vladimir's Seminary Press, 1985). For a synopsis, see Kärkkäinen, *Doctrine of God*, pp. 135–37.

26 For the role of the trinitarian theology as the critique of pluralisms, see further Kärkkäinen, *Trinity and Religious Pluralism*, pp. 165–66. For a critical engagement with John Hick's pluralistic hypothesis, see ibid., ch. 7 and my "'Universe of Faiths': Theological Challenges of John Hick's pluralism," *Dharma Deepika* [Delhi, India] (January–June, 2003), pp. 5–16.

27 For an exciting account of this phenomenon, see D'Costa, *Meeting of Religions and the Trinity*, part I.

28 See further, Pannenberg, *Systematic Theology*, Vol. 1, pp. 50–51.

29 See further, Kärkkäinen, *Trinity and Religious Pluralism*, p. 167. "A more helpful way to negotiate the tension between acknowledging the perspectival nature of our knowing and thus the particularity of any given position (contra typical pluralism) and refraining from any attempt to issue truth claims (as in relativism) is to follow in the footsteps of L. Newbigin (based on M. Polanyi). Even though there is no detached, 'neutral' point from which to view the world but only a diverse series of perspectives, according to 'critical realism,' reality can be known by locating oneself in the places where reality makes itself known, by viewing it from certain standpoints rather than others. This is no arbitrary subjectivism but (as Polanyi has shown) the approach of even science and philosophy: certain 'plausibility structures' must be posited as the basis for advancing any kind of knowledge. That starting point cannot be posited with any absolute certainty, but it has to be presupposed as a kind of hypothesis. Pannenberg, in fact, treats theological statements as hypotheses to be tested with the help of argumentation and appeal to truth criteria." Ibid., pp. 167–68.

30 See further, Pannenberg, *Systematic Theology*, Vol. 1, pp. 50–52 especially.

31 L. Newbigin, "Trinity as Public Truth," in Vanhoozer, ed., *The Trinity in a Pluralistic Age*, pp. 1–8. For details and bibliographic references, see Kärkkäinen, *An Introduction to the Theology of Religions*, pp. 250–53 especially.

32 In Kärkkäinen, *Trinity and Religious Pluralism*, p. 183, n. 5, I raise the question of whether the view I am presenting here is subject to the postmodernist charge of "foundationalism" believed to be left behind with the advent of postmodernity. Personally, I believe it is not necessarily a bad thing to be foundationalist. The question is,

Which foundationalism? Whose foundationalism? For a person to prefer one narrative/framework/perspective over others with any truth claim that goes beyond my own "ghetto" makes most everybody a foundationalist. Yet one can be, I believe, a "reasoned" foundationalist rather than a naïve one. "Christian trinitarian faith, in my understanding, seeks to find outside the human person the grounds for preferring one narrative over another, that is, in the biblical salvation-history which narrates the history of the triune God in sending the Son in the power of the Spirit to save the world and bring it into an eternal communion. If that is foundationalism, so be it. At the same time, no religious claim, certainly no form of pluralism, is void of 'foundations' in the sense that all kinds of truth claims, even those that claim to be non-truth claims, are perspectival and come from a particular viewpoint." Ibid.

[33] Craig Evans, "Jesus' Self-designation 'the Son of Man' and the Recognition of his Divinity," in *The Trinity* (ed. S. T. Davis and G. O'Collins; Oxford: Oxford University Press, 2001), p. 29.

[34] For details, see Kärkkäinen, *Trinity and Religious Pluralism*, p. 113.

[35] Heim, *Depth of the Riches*, p. 134. This quotation also raises questions with its rather ambiguous statement according to which Jesus Christ cannot be "the exhaustive and exclusive act of God to save us." What is Heim saying here? I am not quite sure what Heim means here, but I fear this statement can be misinterpreted in the way typical pluralistic theologies do, regarding Jesus Christ as one of the savior figures. Rather than seeing Christ as one savior figure, biblical revelation and Christian theology can instead attribute salvation to Jesus Christ even when conscious personal faith may not be required to participate in its effects (post-conciliar Catholic inclusivism being the most typical representative of this view).

[36] For details, see Kärkkäinen, *Trinity and Religious Pluralism*, ch. 8.

[37] Vinoth Ramachandra, *The Recovery of Mission* (Downers Grove, IL: InterVarsity Press, 1996), p. 89.

[38] Kärkkäinen, *Trinity and Religious Pluralism*, p. 174.

[39] See further, Kärkkäinen, *Trinity and Religious Pluralism*, chs. 6 and 4, respectively, as well as my "Toward a Pneumatological Theology of Religion: Pentecostal-Charismatic Contributions," *International Review of Mission* 41.361 (April 2002), pp. 187–98.

[40] It is another issue to negotiate the possibility of God's presence "outside" the incarnation. Why should we limit the mode(s) of the presence of the Almighty?

41 In the confines of this essay, a detailed study of the emergence of the doctrine of the Trinity in the New Testament cannot, of course, be attempted. Suffice it to say that its basis lies in the self-distinction of the Son from the Father. Jesus' differentiation from and service to the Father and the coming of the Father's kingdom forms the basis for a distinctively Christian doctrine of the Trinity. The Spirit is introduced by virtue of his involvement in God's presence in the work of Jesus and in the fellowship of the Son with the Father, as a constitutive element of the biblical concept of God.

42 Pannenberg, *Systematic Theology*, Vol. 1, p. 69; see also Kärkkäinen, *Trinity and Religious Pluralism*, pp. 85–87.

43 There are a number of merits to Dupuis' proposal such as a healthy pneumatological and Christological integration as part of the trinitarian theology.

44 Kärkkäinen, *Trinity and Religious Pluralism*, pp. 59–66.

45 For details and bibliographical references, see Kärkkäinen, *Trinity and Religious Pluralism*, pp. 69–72. D'Costa finds the biblical support for this mainly in the Johannine Paraclete passages (John 14–16). In my view, those Johannine passages are only one instance of a larger and more convincing New Testament approach; see ibid., pp. 77–78.

46 Pannenberg, *Systematic Theology*, Vol. 1, pp. 311–13 especially. This is no limiting God's freedom since it is in his sovereign freedom that God has created the world.

47 See further, Kärkkäinen, *An Introduction to the Theology of Religions*, pp. 313–14.

48 D'Costa, *Meeting of Religions and the Trinity*, p. 9.

49 D'Costa, *Meeting of Religions and the Trinity*, p. 115.

50 D'Costa, *Meeting of Religions and the Trinity*, p. 133.

51 Ramachandra, *Recovery of Mission*, p. 233.

52 Ramachandra, *Recovery of Mission*, p. 216.

53 See further, Amos Yong, *Beyond the Impasse: Toward a Pneumatological Theology of Religions* (Grand Rapids, MI: Baker Academic, 2003), for a distinctively pneumatological theology of religions.

54 Here I do not find the term *pluralistic* helpful for the simple reason that the term is already used in such a variety of ways that adding one more, in this case Vanhoozer's quite idiosyncratic definition, only adds to the confusion. A term like *inclusivistic*, even though that term is also widely used, may better serve the purposes of this quotation; in fact, that is the way Vanhoozer defines his term "pluralistic" in what follows in the same quotation.

55 Vanhoozer, ed., *Trinity in a Pluralistic Age*, pp. 70–71.

7

The Uniqueness of Christ in Relation to Jewish People: The External Crusade

Ellen T. Charry

The question of the uniqueness of Christ in relation to Judaism is quite different from the uniqueness of Christ in relation to any other religion or worldview. This is because in its very formation, the church dug a grave, or perhaps more accurately, built a mausoleum for Judaism. This complicates things considerably, because the Jewish people never realized and certainly never accepted that they are the church's great mausoleum of enshrined dead ancestors. Jews believe themselves to be quite alive, because the Jewish people are the people of God. Consequently, they are not at all sure what the church is, although they are certain that it is not the people of God. The church, however, is quite sure that the Jewish people are no longer the people of God and so they are theologically dead. Jews are both self-deluded and arrogant to think that they remain the people of God after the advent of Christ.

The theological relationship between these two great traditions, each of which claims to be the people of God, cannot be grasped by slogans like "Christianity grew in Jewish soil," or that "Judaism is the background or even foundation of Christianity," and so relevant to Christian origins. It is not that "Christianity is Judaism's daughter" and so inherited Jewish Scripture, leaving Judaism behind and moving on. Nor will it do to point to the fact that Jesus was Jewish, and bow politely to his family. None of these historical observations conveys the theological consequence of the church's claims about Jesus for the Synagogue.

The church erupted as a hot theological and literary polemic against the synagogue and quickly turned into an *ad hominem*, and eventually physical crusade against Jews. Only the Christian side of the crusade was covered by "journalists," however. From the Jewish side, all we have left are some oblique allusions to the struggle, and in Middle Ages Christians burned much of that (not only the parchments but on occasion Jews along with them).

The crusade never ended and no treaty was ever drawn up, let alone signed by the combatants. Even though they won every battle fought, the crusaders could not admit victory, either because some of the enemy always escaped, because enemy look-alikes kept appearing who had to be defeated, or perhaps because doubts about how successful their crusade really was lingered in the Christian psyche. Because of this enduring insecurity, the crusade dragged on for 2000 years, and now literary landmines litter the landscape. We might name it the Eternal Crusade of the Church against the Synagogue. No one tallied the fatalities, although statistics are now slowly being recovered, and "photos" disclosed. Recently, an armistice of sorts has been suggested. There were a few attempts to grapple with these issues in the late twentieth century. Of these from the Christian side, perhaps the only thoroughly theological attempt was Paul M. van Buren's trilogy, *A Theology of the Jewish-Christian Reality*. With such history, though, it is difficult to envision what the terms of a peace treaty might be.

To understand the Eternal Crusade we must first identify what was at stake. One way of putting the issue is that it is about who are the people of God – the Jewish people or the body of Christ, for each side claims the title for itself. Yet the ecclesiological issue is also a strictly theological debate about who understands God correctly. Is he utterly one, or is he triune, that is, Christologically qualified and humanized?

Recall that Jewish and Christian traditions as we know them now took shape at the same time. Judaism is not Israelite religion as found in the "Old Testament," but the literary and liturgical deposit of the hermeneutics of the Pharisees and their theological descendants that began in the first century and continued through the fifth. Judaism's orienting texts emerged from these centuries – the various midrashim and the Talmud in two forms, one from Babylonia, the other from Palestine, both comprised of the Mishnah from the earlier period of the Tannaim (ca. 20–200), and the Gemara from days of the Amoraim (ca. 200–500). The Tannaim and the Amoraim are collectively referred to as Israel's sages. Although Christianity began explosively in the first century, it took normative shape from the second through the fifth. All revolutions must be institutionalized to be successful. Even though we now have many forms and styles of Christianity, almost all of them pivot around two central doctrines, the Trinity and the incarnation. These teachings were not formally defined until the fourth and fifth centuries, respectively, by conciliar decision. Key to understanding Jewish-Christian history is the fact that Judaism evolved slowly and gently by majority vote, with minority voices carefully recorded, while the church's conciliar decisions emerged from fierce theological debates, political intrigue, formal condemnation, state-sponsored coercion, and even physical violence. Victors often destroyed their opponents' writings on the ecclesiastical principle that error has no rights. Christian combativeness helps account for the Eternal Crusade that, while it began as a crusade against Judaism often slipped over into being a crusade against Jews because they withstood the attacks on Judaism. Judaism, by contrast, has no formal structure comparable to the conciliar practice of anathematizing heterodox views, not even for Christianity itself. For Christians, Jews were simply another segment of the phalanx of errors to be vanquished in order to proclaim the gospel.

Both traditions took shape over against Graeco-Roman paganism and one another. Christians define themselves as not pagans and not Jews. Jews define themselves as not pagans and not Christians. Yet even this way of putting it is not quite nuanced enough. Perhaps more precisely, the early Christians redefined the people of God as the body of Christ based on what they believed and heard about Jesus of Nazareth. Membership requirements were extremely strict and demanding as Matthew and the Johannine corpus report. Anyone who did not agree with this and adhere to it scrupulously could not be a member of the people of God. Christian ferocity about right doctrine begins at the beginning.

The Synagogue defined itself as the people of God that keeps itself free from the taint of pagan idolatry by obeying God's Law. To the extent that it was interpreted as similar to the religion of the Canaanites, the Greeks, and the Romans, Jews read Christianity as another in a long line of offenses against God. So defining itself as not Christian was simply an extension of "not pagan," whereas Christians, when they said, "not pagan, not Jewish" referred to two distinct and venerable traditions. Christians stated this explicitly. Gregory of Nyssa, for example, in his great catechetical oration defines Christianity as a median between paganism and Judaism. One of the "reporters" from the Christian "front" called those who did not join the new body hypocrites. This is extremely unfortunate, since it turned a proper ecclesiological argument into an *ad hominem* attack that enabled the Eternal Crusade to expand from a polemic against the Synagogue into an attack on Jews. Over the long haul, the fact that this was a theological debate was quite obliterated from view, and the Eternal Crusade took a dark turn.

In short, the Eternal Crusade was set up as great battle for truth against error, with the Christian side bent on eradicating error and the Jewish side bent on protecting itself from same.

1. Christianity Jewishly Speaking

1.1 Jewish disinterest in Jesus

Jews do not doubt that Christians claim that Jesus Christ is the only savior of the world, and unique in this sense. What Judaism does not accept is that he is the savior of the world, the Son of God, or the second Person of the Trinity incarnate. With Islam, it returns a definite NO to any and all of these claims. Christ is unique in that he is the only Jew whom Gentiles worship as God. There are several reasons for this flat denial. Since the nineteenth century, there has been a movement among European Christians to evangelize Jews. The fact that various forms of Hebrew Christians are currently encouraged by some Protestant denominations in the form of some blend of Christian doctrine with Jewish culture as a missionary strategy does not change the fact that, theologically speaking, Judaism has no place for a savior as Christians do, either within the fold or without.

One reason is that Scripture (that Christians call the Old Testament) does not talk about a savior in the sense that the church claims Jesus is. The idea arose only after Jesus was soteriologically identified. Israel may need a deliverer (perhaps like Elijah) anointed or appointed by God to liberate her from her earthly troubles, but that concrete rescue of the group has no relation to the claim about saving people from their sins that Christians came to make about Jesus. Instead of liberating his people from Roman oppression, had he lived, Jesus would have brought a bloodbath upon Israel. Thus, one popular conception of the disagreement between Christianity and Judaism – that the former believes that Jesus is the messiah while the latter sees no evidence for this claim, and so is still waiting – is quite misinformed. The two communities are like ships passing in the night on this point. Their conceptions of messiahship and redemption share no common ground. Jews think in the concrete historical terms of Scripture, while Christians think in the spiritual terms of Greek philosophy. In this, Jews follow Scripture. Both Judaism and Christianity see Elijah as a messianic forerunner (Mal. 4:5). Perhaps it will be helpful to designate the Jewish view "rescue" and the Christian view "salvation" to help keep this difference clear. Three Hebrew verbs designate rescue in the Hebrew Scriptures: *pdh*, *g'al*, and *ysh'h*. The first two generally connote ransom or redemption of a person, the nation, or land from an assigned social or ritual status to be delivered into the hands of competent protectors. It can be effected by persons or by God. The third term is more diffuse. It is the root of the names Joshua, Isaiah, Hosea and Jesus. It connotes rescue from dire circumstances, not by established procedure, but by divine intervention. Still, the three terms are not definitively differentiable, and undue weight should not be placed on any one of them.

A second reason that Jews are not troubled by Christian soteriology is that the Synagogue does not think soteriologically – Jews do not theologize in the Greek style that Christians use. The Synagogue has no doctrine of the Fall or of original sin that unites humanity as a despairing mass before God and from which one cannot extricate oneself without divine aid. The question is not whether Jesus is our savior or someone or something else is. Of course, Jews also read Genesis 3, but they never interpreted it as theologically significant as Paul may have and Augustine certainly did. The term "Fall" itself appears only once in the Apocrypha (4 Esdras 7:118), but Protestants do not accept that as canonical. Further, the Synagogue holds tightly to our ability to obey God, following the tone of Deuteronomy, explicitly chapter 30:15–20. Jews never discussed the bondage or the freedom of the will because they never doubted that we can obey God, for why would he give us commandments that we could not keep? He would be confused. The idea that we can decide only for ill and not also for good was introduced by Augustine at the beginning of the fifth century. It is not a scriptural notion. By that time, the Synagogue had proceeded on other grounds, and was little influenced by Augustinianism.

The synagogue says NO to Christ because saying YES would betray the command of God to remain a people set apart religiously, physically, culturally, and socially from paganism by observing the commandments. There is a deep ambivalence within Jews about this theologically commanded apartness. While the preceding is true theologically, Jews have also wanted political, economic and social acceptance from the host cultures in which they live. To outsiders this seems contradictory so that Jewish loyalty seems split. This is the reason that Jews do not distinguish moral from ritual commandments and even today may scrupulously heel to rabbinic practices that are plainly not rational. Rationality is not the point, however, when it comes to the commandments of God. Nor is Judaism a set of ethical principles, despite some nineteenth-century Jewish apologetic efforts to this effect. Perhaps it is worth noting here that Judaism and Christianity operate with quite different notions of grace. For Christians grace is God's acceptance of us though we sin, while for Jews grace is God's Law that provides his people his way of remaining his own.

While it agrees that God covers sin, the Synagogue sees no need for a mediator although the Temple priesthood is gone. Confession of sin, repentance, prayer, and almsgiving, and finally death replaced sacerdotal mediation and provide sufficient access to God. Jews do not need an advocate with "the Father" because they do not experience the gnawing guilt and constant fear of damnation so central to Western popular piety and theology, as we see it in Christian art and preaching, and that is presupposed in Luther's insistence on *sola gratia*, for example. The fact that Augustine claimed a universal need of salvation based on a universally sinful human state never entered Jewish thought or practice. This is the primary reason why Jews do not evangelize. We know that both pagans and Christians were attracted to Judaism, but this was not due to evangelism. Indeed, under Christian rule it eventually became illegal to become a Jew in the Roman Empire, while Christians forced conversion on Jews and their children. They do not believe that they possess a great truth or solution to "the human condition" that others need, because they do not worry about "the human condition." Therefore they do not find anything lacking in their tradition in this regard. They are not anxious about their salvation because the need for it never took hold.

Synagogue Jews simply want to obey God as their sages have taught them to – not for any reward but out of gratitude, because they are privileged to be God's own. They do not, however, gain salvation thereby. In this connection, we should add that Paul's polemic against circumcision and food taboos has been read in light of Romans 7 that depicts Jewish practice and teaching as psychologically burdensome and unworkable. This has no echo anywhere in Jewish literature. The Law, of course, did keep Jews and Gentiles apart, and it was an impediment to pagan conversion. Jews, by contrast do not find "the Law" oppressive (boring, perhaps) because it is God's means of protecting his people, not a test for Jews to prove themselves to him or earn his favor. Jewish religious practice does not win God's favor but is its proof! Even though purity practices became rather intricate, the goal of purity was to keep

Israel from harm in a hostile pagan environment, not to earn "salvation." Paul's polemic against the Law as works-righteousness quite misunderstands the purpose of the Law, or intentionally distorts it in order to attract pagans. Jews can obey the commandments that are sweet in the Jewish mouth (see Psalm 119, for example) because they ensure the survival of the people of God. Not keeping the commandments would lead to the perdition of the Jewish people, and that would surely be to spurn God's loving kindness, but it would not affect the fate of Jewish souls.

One further note should be added. From the way Scripture has been interpreted, it may appear to Christians that Christ is so clearly the meaning of the Law, the prophets, and the psalms that Christianity is the logical or obvious intention of Judaism. While readily acceptable to Christians, this exegesis/eisegesis is not at all obvious to Jews, however. We will consider this more carefully when we turn to Judaism Christianly speaking.

One reason that Christologization of Scripture seems natural to Christians is because Christian canonizers, like their Jewish counterparts, arranged the biblical books to support their theological claims. The texts were ordered to promote theological continuity between Scripture and the literature about Jesus. They put the book of the prophet Malachi at the very end of their arrangement of the prophets because it ends with "Lo, I will send you the prophet Elijah before the great and terrible day of the Lord comes. He will turn the hearts of parents to their children and the hearts of children to their parents, so that I will not come and strike the land with a curse" (Mal. 4:5). They then connected Malachi to Matthew's genealogy, making Matthew the first canonical Gospel because it links Jesus back to Abraham, creating theological unity between Scripture and the apostles' writings. These moves authenticated Jesus by embedding the accounts of his life in Jewish history. We will return to this theme below.

This linkage did not work for Jews, however, because their Bible follows the Masoretic ordering that concludes with 2 Chronicles that ends with King Cyrus announcing the repatriation of the exiles and the rebuilding of the Temple in Jerusalem. Both communities ordered the texts to support their own theology. Their different orientations could not be made clearer than by looking at these significant decisions.

Since Jews carry no plaguing guilt before God, they have no need of justification through Christ's death. More pressing than the wrath of God was the wrath of Rome. Jesus Christ could not be God's anointed rescuer of Israel when his controversial activities threatened to bring the military might of Rome down on Israel (John 11:47–50). Surely Jesus' provocative personal style also rendered him controversial. The Gospels present him as angry and confrontational with authorized and respected Jewish leaders, and on occasion even simple Jews. His militancy and divisiveness demanded utter loyalty that intentionally disrupted family, social, and economic life across the land. He did not argue points of law politely with the elders in order to arrive at consensus or majority rule, as was their means of maintaining order. Rather, he disregarded the entire orderly process of the development of the tradition, unsettling the populace with his "field preaching," agitating large crowds and setting them against their leaders. Jesus was not a team player. He did not play by the rules. On the contrary, he was a rude loose canon when relations with Rome required authorized leadership to maintain order, and mediate prudently between a restive populace and its edgy occupiers. Palestine was a tinderbox. Finally, Jesus had to be sacrificed, not to appease God on our behalf as later theology would argue, but to appease Rome on Israel's behalf. Once the historical reality faded other considerations could appear.

Another set of issues emerged from Jesus' teachings. These overturned the structure of authority that enabled Israel to maintain her identity and trust in God amidst foreign domination and a dramatic transition from being a nomadic to a settled people with an agricultural economy. Impugning authorized interpretations of Scripture and the work of Jewish law would leave Jews adrift with no way to organize their communal life.

The preceding perhaps suffices to explain both why Jews have no trouble accepting the Christian claim to the uniqueness of Christ as well as why they have no theological interest in him. Virtually the only serious theologically constructive interest in Christianity by a Jew came from Franz Rosenzweig in his impenetrable *Star of Redemption* in 1921. From a first-century perspective, the body of Christ remains a Jewish heresy, though never officially declared so, since Judaism has no formal procedure for excommunication. As it took shape theologically, however, it is more nearly apostasy, as we shall see below. For the Christian part, the Jewish people looks like stubborn resistance to the revealed Word of God humanized.

1.2 Summary

To speak of Christ in relation to Judaism is painful, for it is impossible to do so without evoking centuries of vituperation, violence and counter-violence, and reciprocal hostility, fear, and contempt. Jews have said NO to Christ for two millennia, enduring humiliation, persecution, oppressions, degradation, and death in order to act upon their integrity as the people of God. While a few said yes out of true faith in him, others were baptized under threat of banishment, death, torture, or other forms of coercion of adults and children. This was especially the case during the Counter-Reformation in Spain. In the nineteenth and early twentieth centuries Jews apostatized for the sake of social advancement, and were looked on by other Jews as traitors. It has been commonplace for Christian polemic to attribute the Jewish NO to Christ to Jewish disobedience to God, stubbornness, misreading Scripture, corruption, arrogance, perhaps even stupidity (the *ad hominem* argument referred to above). Perhaps the two most blatant examples of this literary genre are John Chrysostom's eight discourses against the Judaizing Christians delivered in Antioch during Holy Week, sometime between 387 and 389, and Luther's 150-page treatise "On the Jews and their Lies" of 1543. It should, however, not go unnoted that patristic theologians wrote at least twenty-six separate treatises "against the Jews." What a vexing lot they were.

Once the Eternal Crusade expanded from being properly theological to being *ad hominem*, and Jews began to suffer legally and physically simply because they were Jews, they came to despise the body of Christ based on their experience.

Apart from theological objections, Christian treatment of Jews exposed Christian claims of love, reconciliation, and forgiveness as empty. Jews had little outlet for their hurt, fear, and anger, so sporadic outbursts of spontaneous rage and contempt had to suffice, as in Alexandria in the mid-fourth century. Since the Christians had legislative authority, outbursts of resentment and revenge often eventuated in further physical suffering for Jews, both spontaneous and legal, until all they wanted was to be left alone. They suffered civil disabilities in Christian lands until Napoleon. Pockets of tolerance arose from time to time, and Jews rose to high levels in government and the arts. The two most important examples of this are medieval Muslim Spain and modern Germany. The first was wiped out by the deportation and forced conversion of Jews (and Muslims) from Spain at the end of the fifteenth century in order to unify Spain as a Catholic domain. The second ended in disaster with Nazism. Jewish survival itself is a triumph for and of God, and sometimes it had to be achieved at a high price. Interestingly, the divine command to remain a people apart – even to the point of divorcing foreign wives (Ezra 10) – set the pattern for Jewish recoil from interaction with Christians in marriage, trade, and fellowship. Sadly, even this was taken amiss by Christians, and even today, Jews are criticized for being clannish. This is ironic, given the fact that Jews were prohibited from most professions and education, and enclosed in ghettos for centuries, partly for their own protection. Their consignment to banking in the Middle Ages was because this was prohibited to Christians.

1.3 Jewish rejection of Christ

We have seen that Jewish disinterest in Christ stems from a lack of perceived need for him, plus aversion to his style and that of his followers. Rejection of him, on the other hand, was on theological grounds. Although the Eternal Crusade makes it difficult to distinguish the theological rejection of Christ from the historical reasons that Jews are simply not attracted to him and so cannot take him seriously because emotional antipathy stands in the way, important theological issues loom. The

Jewish NO to Christ is deeper and more serious than a perceived lack of need for the salvation he offers or the understandable suspicion and contempt for people who speak of the love of God, yet defame, abuse, and kill Jews. It is even deeper than the scripturally informed judgment that Jesus was not the messiah that God had promised. Strictly theological issues pivot around ecclesiology, mission, and trinitarian doctrine.

1.4 Ecclesiology

Paul and the Gospels initiated offensive theological doctrines that would become formalized only in later centuries. Paul claimed that in his death, Christ brought about a new people of God comprised of Jews and Gentiles. Paul, Matthew, and Luke argue that through Christ, God embraced Israel's enemies and had to explode the Jewish people as the people of God to do so.

According to Paul, Christ's death means that the Jewish people are no longer the people of God, but the body of Christ is. Jews who fail to join this body are lost to God. This eventually led Jews to conclude that Christianity is a different religion, although the Eternal Crusade must deny this, claiming that the church, not the Jewish people, is Israel. Christ's death separated Israel from the Jewish people. Matthew redefined the people of God along the ethical lines suggested by Jesus' teaching, rather than as the Jewish people. In both of these interpretations Jews are welcomed into the new people of God.

With Luke, however the conviction that God reaches out to Gentiles through Christ becomes even sharper. In preaching in the synagogue in Nazareth, Jesus seems to be telling the faithful that God did not send him to rescue and heal them, but their enemies! This implied, or at least could be read as suggesting not that the people of God is now Jews and Gentiles, as Paul and Matthew suggested, but Gentiles instead of Jews! No wonder the worshippers tried to kill him!

Despite the important differences among the three, the followers of Jesus exploded the Jewish people as the people God, flatly denying Israel's calling as God's people set apart for God in the midst of Roman paganism and cruelty that would defile her. To appreciate the ecclesiological offense here we might pause over the Synagogue's doctrine of election. According to Scripture, God called Abraham, and after him, Moses as the founding ancestors of a particular family set apart by God. This is not a reward because they had any value or virtue of their own that qualified for this election (Deut. 7:7–9). On the contrary, their value lay precisely in their ordinariness. God rescues and punishes Israel by turns precisely to show the world that Israel is not one among the nations, but set apart for a different way of life. By maintaining this distinctiveness Israel testifies to God, pointing the nations toward him through herself. That is why Jesus' interpretation of 2 Kings 5 and 1 Kings 17, according to Luke 4, is indigestible.

1.5 Missiology

From another perspective, the ecclesiological debate is a missiological debate. Israel's mission, to be a light to the nations, is not to hand on a higher moral code received from God in order to civilize the nations, but to be a living witness to God's claim on all people, as Elijah and Elisha do in their context, Jonah and Ruth do in theirs, and even Pharaoh does in Exodus 12:32. Paul is by no means unaware of the scriptural weight of this biblical Israelology of faithful witness that lets non-Israelites see God through Israel. In order to counter it with support for his own radical teaching, Paul had to pervert scriptural texts and read the Gentiles into texts that clearly refer to Israel. He was a masterful if infuriating exegete, interpreting texts in the service of his call to the Gentiles that divided Israel from God. He taught that Israel no longer needs to point the nations toward God that they should turn to him, because they are already members of God's household through the cross of Christ. In him, God created a new multinational people of God – and here is the rub – without even telling anyone about it until afterwards! This is quite out of order for Jews whose ancestors accepted the covenant at Sinai (Exod. 19, 24). At least they had some inkling of what they were getting into.

1.6 Trinitology

The ecclesiological explosion would have been quite enough to set first-century Palestine ablaze. Yet there is more. Johannine theology laid the foundation for the later claim that Jesus was not only with God and could lead others to abide in him, but that he was God, consubstantial, *homoousios* with the Father. This claim went beyond blasphemy to apostasy. It may have been poor judgment to suggest, as the Gospels did, that Jesus was God's anointed savior. And it strained credulity to claim that the Jewish people is no longer the people of God. But to say that Jesus is God!? This, Jews concluded, was beyond the pale. Christians, they concluded, do not worship God but had invented a new religion and worshipped a new god.

In sum, we see that many issues are involved in the Christian claims about Jesus in relation to Judaism. Christians traded in the sacred commandments of God for faith in an unknown itinerant preacher who claims to be God's anointed savior, but who in fact succors Israel's enemies and incited the wrath of Rome against his own kin. Beyond that, claims about Jesus were expanded to suggest that he was the Son of God in a way that other Jews are not. Fourth-century theologians, using the Greek philosophy at their disposal, would expand this scriptural claim to suggest that to be the Son of God meant *being* God, or, as Athanasius put it, consubstantial with the Father. Trinitarianism was apostasy.

Jews do not believe that their calling is fulfilled in Christ, but rather that Christ negates God's will for them. They are bewildered by Christian failure to grasp that demurral of Christ is faithfulness to God. For their part, Christians are perplexed at Jewish suspicion of Christ, for they believe that he fulfills Israel's mission to bless all people, even ol' Pharaoh, as God's people. In short, Jews do not understand why Christians do not understand their NO to Christ, while Christians would compromise themselves if they accepted that NO. Theologically, Jews and Christians can only speak past one another, if at all. Here we have looked primarily at the Jewish side of the story, and every story has two of those.

2. Judaism Christianly Speaking

2.1 Christian interest in Judaism

Christians, of course, see the whole story through very different lenses because they have very different needs. While Jews have little interest in Christ or his followers except to protect themselves from them, Christians are interested in Jews not only for missionary purposes, but for theological reasons because the church defines itself over against the Synagogue. This is the basic reason for the Eternal Crusade. The church is always a bit theologically insecure because it must always contend with the Jewish claim that the Jewish people, and not the body of Christ, is the people of God. This is one reason why the claim to the uniqueness of Christ is so central. It must always justify its claim because it is universal.

While Jews live and think in the here and now, and focus on the safety and identity of the people of God (i.e. Israel), Christians took the Greek philosophical path and are oriented toward ideas and their conceptual analysis. Philo and Paul are Hellenic Jews who left us a body of writing in which Christians are interested, but Jews were not persuaded by either approach. This is one reason why even though they share some texts, Jews and Christians do not really share Scripture. Once Christians read God's life with Israel trinitarianly, Jews and Christians no longer shared a common Scripture. It is the same reason that theological interaction between Christians and Jews is almost impossible.

Christians claim that they worship the God of the Jews and so naturally expect to be able to talk about him together meaningfully, even though they may disagree in the end. Yet, even this turns out to be a false hope. This is not only because of Jewish fear of Christian evangelism, but also because the Christian doctrine of God, that exegetes the paradox of the divine simplicity and the divine complexity, never piqued Jewish sensibilities. Thus, there are not even parallel theological problems that Jews and Christians could worry about together or try to persuade one another of. They share no common framework within which meaningful theological disagreement could happen.

Christians may wish Jews were delighted and honored by the fact that God chose to save the world through one of their own, indeed, an untutored artisan. Christ spells, not the end but the full flowering of God's promises to all people as his people. Sadly, what one sees as flowering the other sees as destruction. Both examine the same history, and both claim divine authority, but draw quite different conclusions. Christianly speaking, the fulfillment God's promise that his people will be as numberless as the stars in the sky and the sand of the sea has plainly happened, while Jews are forever seeing God's people as on the verge of extinction at the hands of his enemies. What is stubbornness in the face of the plain facts to one is faithfulness to God to the other. While Jews can never view their destruction as the triumph of God's promises, Christians (most of them Gentile by now) can never accept that God's grace and love could be real yet exclude them!

2.2 Ecclesiology (1)

Christianly speaking, however, the issue is deeper than examining empirical evidence. Ultimately the question of who are the people of God leads to a question about God, as noted above. The German word *Aufhebung* sustains the paradox of sublation in which extinction and preservation co-exist in the precipitate. Accomplishing the purpose of the thing entails its obliteration, as the acorn must die to achieve its destiny – to become a tree. Similarly, Christ makes real not only God's promise to the nations through Abraham, but also the vision of Isaiah 2 that all nations shall stream to the house of the God of Jacob, on an easy access highway made straight and planed.

That Jews fail to welcome Gentiles into the covenant looks stunningly rude to Christians, even though their making it illegal to become a Jew did not encourage Jews to welcome Gentiles. To Gentiles, Judaism should gladly commit suicide so that God's love for themselves may spread to the ends of the earth through Christ. But more than table-fellowship is at stake here.

Paul did away with conversion to Judaism (and hence with Judaism as Jews could recognize it) in order to proclaim that

God is God of all without going through Judaism. For him, the Jewish people has a new mission – or rather never understood her mission in the first place. Israel's mission to the Gentiles has changed from witnessing to God by being Jews who point Gentiles toward God to witnessing to God's love for Gentiles by embracing Christ. To continue being the people of God now that Christ has come requires destroying the wall of hostility between Jews and pagans that Israel believes is necessary to sustain the people of God, *halahkic* conversion remaining the narrow passageway between the two. Again, what is resistance to the will of God to one is faithfulness to the other. Paul's ecclesiological move corrected a self-centered tribal doctrine of God that ignored God's promises to the Gentiles scattered throughout Scripture.

While sociologically speaking, today Jews have to defend their theological right not to be Christians, and Christians welcome those Jews who do accept Christ into the household of God (as if they have not been in his household all their lives), theologically the situation is quite the reverse. Theologically speaking as we see it in Acts, it can only be that Jews welcome Gentiles into the household of God. So, the burden of proof lies with the church to explain how *she* is the household of God. Given what we have observed so far, the issue for Christianity in relation to Judaism is not whether Christ is unique, for he surely is. The issue is rather, the authority Christians have to claim that the cross of Christ defines the people of God and its message as the only way for anyone to be related to God: in the strength of weakness and humiliation, not the power of military might, the right of birth, or the expertise of education.

Christian theology had a lot of work to do. First it had to demonstrate that while it looks like God moved house (from the Jewish people to the body of Christ) he really has not. Neither has he torn down his old house and built a glittering new one on the same spot, nor has he built on a new addition exactly either. It is more like he has remodeled his house, knocking down walls between small rooms to create large open spaces, and redecorated. Indeed, nobody claims that God moved house. To the Jews it looks like nasty riffraff built a flashy house next door, and they have, not surprisingly, turned out to be bad neighbors. Christians deny this. They claim that God hired them as a team of craftsmen, laborers, and decorators who simply followed his design plans for redoing his original house. As this little parable suggests, the issue of who is the people of God is contended, and claims and counterclaims are easily misread. God's compassion for all people sustains the Eternal Crusade from generation to generation.

2.3 Ecclesiology (2)

The crusade against the synagogue is necessary in order for Christianity to legitimate itself theologically. Christians are not claiming to be squatters, nor do they think that they pushed the original residents out. Most invited them to stay but, offended, they rushed out in a huff. Neither have the Christians built a new building, claiming that theirs is the true house of God while the other one was false. If none of these, they do have to make clear what they *are* claiming, for they are theological upstarts, mavericks. They must make careful arguments and this because it is not just that they appear rude in claiming to be following orders in remodeling the house and then inviting strangers in. It is that they appeared out of nowhere and do not even seem to know where they are going. Indeed, the disciples themselves acknowledge how confused they are and often look foolish and befuddled in the Gospels. Their religious descendants have to legitimate themselves in order to authenticate their claim that the only way to God is through Jesus Christ. Indeed, we have noted that in himself, Jesus had no authority, let alone his later followers. His authority comes from the claim that he is the Logos – the meaningful order of God of which the world partakes as his creation – become a real person so that we could see and touch and love him concretely as we love one another. We will return to this shortly.

Of course, Christians are no more able to let go of their side of this struggle than are Jews. Those who truly understand the threat that Marcion posed to the church realize that unless Christ truly enables Gentiles to be God's own, they remain theological pretenders. There is only one God, one correct way of understanding him, and one correct way of worshipping him, one correct way of knowing him, and one correct way of being loved by him.

Further, Christians know that they are making claims that strain credibility. They have to authenticate these claims theologically for two reasons. One reason is that they must be able to convince others, not to speak of themselves, that they worship the God of Israel and not some other, lest they be pagans in an Israelite house. The other is that they must show that their claims do not confute the common (Hellenic) view of God, lest they be idolaters. They must be theologically as well as intellectually respectable, for Judaism stood on one side and philosophy on the other, each scrutinizing this upstart church from its own perspective.

At first, Christian claims made sense to no one who had credibility in that day, but paganism collapsed with the fall of Mediterranean civilization. By then, Christian vocabulary, practice, and literature were sophisticated and well established, and bore all the marks of every tactical battle in the Eternal Crusade. Subsequently, there could be no altering that. All the battlements and fortifications were in place, and the weapons and uniforms at the ready. Yet, in spite of the Eternal Crusade against them, the Jewish people endured.

To extend our little parable, the basic Christian strategy is to claim that although the Jewish people truly and with good reason thinks that it is the exclusive legitimate resident of God's house, they are but its builders and first tenants. To legitimate the Christians, Paul argued that God had always intended to invite everyone, and that the long-time residents had simply not read all the fine print on the original contract (i.e. Gen. 12:3b).

There was, of course, plenty of wrangling about appropriate comportment, dress, and language and whose was right, but the real issue had to go back to the names on the contract. Since the Jewish side had no journalists, and each side claimed that God judged in their favor, Paul's position hit the papers, and to all intents and purposes he won this basic battle. The ecclesiological battle was settled de facto, because Paul created "facts" on the ground – churches everywhere. Since their entrance requirements seemed less challenging, at least surgery was not required, Christianity spread quickly and broadly. Gentiles could call God "Father" without becoming Jews.

2.4 Hermeneutics and doctrine

The next and more protracted plank of the strategy of the Eternal Crusade required highly trained soldiers, because the work was not only labor intensive, but required great skill. The theological equivalents of land, naval, and airborne units had to be trained, outfitted, and operationalized so that the claim to the uniqueness of Christ would be a tour de force. Homilies, polemical treatises, commentaries, letters, mystagogy, mysticism, painting, sculpture, illustrated manuscripts, and architecture were all enlisted in the crusade for Christian orthodoxy against all opposition. Although other opponents were also targeted as needed, shrapnel from the Eternal Crusade against the Jews is evident always, everywhere, and forever.

In order to legitimate the claim that they worship the God of Israel, Christians naturally turned to Scripture (again, that is Hebrew Scripture). There was no real doubt that Scripture was Scripture, although one noisy objection (from Marcion) had to be put down. Perhaps one reason that the Crusade was unceasing is because Marcion's desire to sever the body of Christ from the God of Israel remains a constant temptation. The nomenclature "Old Testament" and "New Testament" itself attest to Marcion's enduring allure. For without Scripture how could the body of Christ claim to be the people of God? Ironically, in order to interpret Scripture for their own purpose, Christians had to know Hebrew, and there was only one way to learn it: from Jews. Origen and Jerome both "plundered the Egyptians" in this case, Jews, to translate and analyze the original texts that would so forcibly be turned against the Jews. This began a long history of Jewish self-betrayal.

As the Gospels and Paul's letters began to gain a hearing, the Christians had to show that Jesus did not come from nowhere. He had to be authenticated scripturally, that is, by God. If they do indeed worship God, Christians had to explain who Jesus is;

they could not simply assert that he is God (or the Word of God, or the Son of God, or the Christ, or the Son of Man) loudly and think they had addressed the issue. This would turn into a two hundred year doctrinal struggle. But the problem is front and center in the Gospels and the evangelists do not shy away from it. Jesus' short and provocative itinerancy and his bold self-proclaimed identity had to be justified in terms that people could understand: Scripture and tradition on one hand and philosophy on the other. Worries about keeping his identify quiet, about who knows what and when they know it indicate how explosive these claims are.

Matthew's opening genealogy, the stories of Jesus' baptism and the account of the transfiguration, for example, reflect the pressing need to explain Jesus theologically; healing miracles were not enough, although they generated a lot of excitement. Otherwise, Jesus could easily be dismissed as a kook, and indeed was by some. The Gospel of John, for example, is unabashed about Jesus' confrontational, rude style (even to his mother: John 2:4), his intentionally speaking in riddles so that no one could understand him, and his alienating people who tried to support him with suspicion and his infernal and outrageous demands (e.g. to hate your parents). Scripture and tradition were the tools to counter instinctive reactions to Jesus, both pro and con. These were all they had to forward a theologically persuasive view of this difficult man. Thus, for the sake of the Gentiles, Paul and the Gospels turned God against the Synagogue by forwarding God's presence in Christ. One way of viewing the explosion that is the apostles' writings is as a massive hermeneutical confrontation. Christians said that Jesus is the definitive hermeneutical key to understanding Scripture and the people of God, while skeptical Jews insisted that their sages were Scripture's only legitimate interpreters and that was on behalf of the Jewish people's faithfulness to its calling as God's people as God's witness to the nations. So, the crusade was equally about who is the people of God, and about how we shall understand Scripture.

After the first century, people started praying to Jesus, it again became a burning necessity to make it clear to everyone that they worship the God of Israel, not Jesus of Nazareth. Now it became not the identity of Jesus of Nazareth that took center stage but the identity of Jesus Christ, the Son of God. This was a philosophical challenge that led to formal trinitarian doctrine. Once the trinitarian doctrine of God was in place, the practice of praying to Jesus was properly recognized to be inappropriate, and proper trinitarian prayer was offered to the Father through the Son, in the Holy Spirit. This proper trinitarian liturgical sensibility has long since been lost. Collects are now offered to God through Jesus Christ or again directly to Jesus: "Jesus we just want to ..." revealing a Unitarian or perhaps Arian theology. Now, under the pressure of inclusive language, trinitarian liturgical language is being lost altogether, so that the Arian implications of early locution are mooted. There are not even grounds to argue that prayer should be trinitarian. The way from prayer to Jesus to trinitarian doctrine and then trinitarian prayer was arduous, but it had to be taken, lest Christians find themselves to be worshipping either a man or some God other than the God of Israel, the creator of heaven and earth.

The need to explain Jesus was so pressing that even though his first followers had interpreted him scripturally, by the time they were known as Christians, his next generation of followers felt that more was needed. Paul had already begun to interpret Scripture Christologically, and this was later picked up by others. Reading Scripture Christologically used a very different hermeneutic. It moved beyond the historical claims that God was again at work in Judaism of the first century in Jesus, to argue that although the incarnate Christ had only appeared of late, he was in fact the true (and only) intent and meaning of Scripture all along. Christ became the hermeneutical key by which to understand the Law, the Prophets, and the Psalms, over against Jewish, Marcionite, Arian, Gnostic, or Judaizing readings. Following the vituperative language of the Gospels, Jews came to symbolize all scriptural and doctrinal falsehood. Christological reading became a central strategy for arguing both trinitarian doctrine and soteriology. Thus, even when arguing against other foes, theologians were sealing the doors of the mausoleum. More on this below.

Doctrinal controversies and crises called for explaining the catholic faith against theological error, and Jews were, as noted above, swept up into the lot. Greek and Latin theologians knew that they had to account for their worship and creed, and the crusade against error advanced a notch. The early emergence of a baptismal creed (the Apostles' Creed) that begins, "I believe in God the Father, the Almighty, creator of heaven and earth" implies the Marcionite alternative against which the catholic faith had to be articulated. It is unfortunate that the repudiation of Marcion did not force elaboration of the first article of the Creed. The entire fourth century was given to the contestation of the second and third articles that resulted in their elaboration and elongation into the definitive Nicene-Constantinopolitan Creed. In its codified form, the energy is all in the second article, even though the third received some further clarification from its earlier form. Had there been further discussion of the first article, perhaps it would have as it should have been explained by adding "who redeemed Israel from Egypt." This would have utterly repudiated Marcion (who still lurks in many corners of the church) and perhaps laid a stronger foundation for later Christian history. As it stands, the entire history of God with Israel is bypassed by the Creeds. The omission lent a blind eye toward the more violent aspects of the Eternal Crusade. Beyond this, it deprived the body of Christ of a clear vision of the fullness of its life in God. Indeed, christocentrism or even christomonism is perhaps the source of the deepest Christian self-misunderstanding because it tries to jump over the struggle for Christian self-definition as the people of God, and leaves the impression of something like the people of Christ that simply will not do. A second-person unitarianism, even if inadvertent, would lend support to the Jewish claim of Christian idolatry reinvigorating the Eternal Crusade all over again.

We have arrived at the place where we can see that much Christian doctrine developed in order to support previously existing belief and practice. Jesus had to be the incarnation of the divine Logos or both human and divine, lest salvation not be of God. In light of salvation through the cross, Jesus had to be both human and divine. The body of Christ of both Jews and Gentiles had to redefine the Israel of God. These issues recurred in various forms because Christians had to show that in adoring Jesus and hanging their salvation on him they were relying upon God, and not apotheosizing a man as the Romans did their emperors. If the body of Christ really is the "new" or even worse, "true" Israel (as if the Jewish people had been false to its scriptural self-understanding in rejecting Jesus) it had to be clear that it was the God of Israel that they worshiped and not Zeus or Jupiter in Jewish dress.

It has become common to say that the catholic faith was worked out in response to heretical challenges. But when we push the question we see that popular belief and practice sent theologians to create the doctrines that supported popular piety against the perennial possibility that Christians were being creative, and this could not be tolerated.

In addition to ecclesiology and trinitology, Christology and soteriology were also intimated. Although the Christological debates arose from the need to defend themselves against the Jewish charge that they worshipped a man, Christological doctrine was influenced primarily by non-Jewish sources, since there was virtually nothing to draw on in Judaism. As we have noted, turning to philosophy only had the effect of further alienating Jews, of course.

Soteriology was not quite as simple. Here Christians did and still do scour Scripture for adumbrations or precedents by means of which their soteriological (and sacramental) claims could be justified. The church built Judaism's mausoleum when it went beyond legitimating Jesus by explaining him in scriptural terms (as do the stories of the transfiguration and Jesus' temptation in the desert), and employed typology. Typology argued that the true meaning of scriptural events lay in their Christian application. For example, the goat sent out into the desert bearing Israel's sins (Lev. 16:10, 21–2) combines with the sacrificial lamb of the Passover to become Christ, the Lamb of God who carries away the sins of the world (Israel having been redefined as Jews and Gentiles). Or, Israel's crossing the Red Sea and being fed manna in the desert become baptism and Eucharist. These two hermeneutical strategies are quite different and have different implications for the claims about Christ in relation to Judaism. The former recognizes that Jesus must fit into Scripture's story of God's dealings with

Israel. Typology, by contrast, has already left scriptural authority behind because later the legitimacy of Christ is taken to be self-evident. Now Scripture merely points toward the truth revealed in Christ. For the former, Israel (that is, the Jewish people) is the Israel of God, while the latter speaks of the mausoleum toward which one must tip one's hat. Here Scripture has no meaning without Christ, so, before the incarnation it was not possible to grasp it correctly at all. Christ is the true meaning of Scripture. Calvin, although he uses the sacramental typification noted here, has a rather nuanced view of these matters. His treatment of Christ in relation to Scripture is what we might call "relative." His instincts are decidedly anti-Marcionite and so he must interpret Scripture and the apostles' writings about Christ continuous and consistent. He teaches that the grace of God revealed in the incarnate one in the first-century Palestine is simply a clearer presentation of the grace of God revealed through God's history with Israel. In this he disagreed with Luther who pitted the Law against the gospel in a way that retains Marcionite overtones. Christian soteriology comes in two forms, one associated with the East and one with the West. The former is divinization and the latter atonement. Divinization derives from Greek sources and receives no support from Jewish sources. Atonement soteriology, while it has no parallels or analogues in Judaism could be elaborated from scriptural passages on forgiveness of sin.

3. Conclusion

The Christian attitude toward Jews has been dubbed trium–phalist. A closer look, however, reveals that triumphalist bravado covers a theological insecurity that continuously needs to address two major concerns. First, Christians must continuously demonstrate that the body of Christ is the people of God and the Jewish people is not. Second, it must argue that in worshipping Jesus they are worshipping the God of Israel and that by not worshipping him Jews are not worshipping God.

Interestingly enough, the notion of heresy has now quite faded from view. Yet the language of the Eternal Crusade, grounded as it is in the apostle's writings, is now hard-wired into Christian preaching, teaching, and interpretation. Christian claims about the uniqueness of Christ in relation to Judaism need to be articulated again in every generation as long as Jews endure, for they refuse to give up their identity as the people of God. Finally, theologically speaking, Jews and Christians each hold the other to be apostates. As painful as all this may be, it cannot be avoided, especially by evangelicals seeking to bring the light of Christ to those sisters and brothers who, as John's prologue put it even then, could not grasp it.

References

Cohen, Hermann, *Religion of Reason out of the Sources of Judaism* (Atlanta, GA: Scholars Press, 1995)

John, Chrysostom, *Discourses against Judaizing Christians, Fathers of the Church ; V. 68* (Washington: Catholic University of America Press, 1979)

Luther, Martin, *Luther's Works*, Vol. 47 (ed. by Jaroslav Pelikan for Vols. 1–30 and Helmut T. Lehmann for Vols. 31–55. 55 vols. Philadelphia: Fortress Press, 1961)

Nyssa, Gregory of, "The Great Catechism," in *Gregory, Bishop of Nyssa* (eds. W. Moore and H.A. Wilson; Grand Rapids: Eerdmans, 1988), pp. 471–509

Rosenzweig, Franz, *The Star of Redemption* (Notre Dame, IN.: Notre Dame Press, 1985)

Strack, Hermann Leberecht and Günter Stemberger, *Introduction to the Talmud and Midrash* (trans. Markus Bockmuehl; Edinburgh: T. & T. Clark, 1991)

Van Buren, Paul M., *Discerning the Way: A Theology of the Jewish Christian Reality* (New York: Seabury Press, 1980)

——, *A Theology of the Jewish-Christian Reality: Part II, a Christian Theology of the People Israel* (New York: Seabury Press, 1983)

——, *A Theology of the Jewish-Christian Reality: Part III, Christ in Context* (1st edn.; San Francisco: Harper & Row, 1988)

8

The Uniqueness of Christianity in Relation to Buddhism

Paul S. Chung

1. Christian Theology and the Others in Global Context

It becomes an inevitable reality in global context that a way of dealing with the gospel/culture question turns into a gospel/religions question without further ado. For Christians, the question of the gospel/culture nexus is often a difficult agenda to handle, because they are afraid of mingling the sacred with the profane. They are afraid of syncretism, in other words, tainting or polluting Christ with bad elements in profane cultures. In addition, it is believed that non-Western cultures are too inferior to be compatible with or approachable to Christianity.

However, theology is profoundly challenged to face the religious others and to recognize difference in postmodern, global context. In the Western tradition of Christianity the other was labeled in a different way: it was pagan until the sixteenth century, and then unenlightened in the age of Reason. It was called primitive in the nineteenth century, and just different in the twentieth century. A century ago the privileged citizen of any developed Western nation – white male Protestant – did not have to confront the other; women, slaves, native peoples, and homosexuals were of course not invisible, but were successfully deproblematized, and unrecognized. The unproblematic nature of otherness in earlier times was a result of the prevalence of what Jean F. Lytord calls "metanarratives." Metanarratives shape a view of the world. In the power of metanarratives the voice of the other is unheard, the presence of the other as other is unnoticed. In postmodernity, the abandonment of metanarrative means the encounter with the other. The category of the other in postmodernity represents the postmodern spirit of deconstruction and resistance to the status quo.[1]

To avoid the mistakes in the past there have been a number of theological attempts at paying attention to differences and distinctive qualities of other cultures and religions. Karl Rahner carried out a ground breaking paradigm shift in recognizing other religious people as anonymous Christians. Rahner's theory of anonymous Christians is based on the supernatural existential which is built into us by God's free initiative of grace. In other words, God's self-communication in Jesus Christ is the source of our longing search for God. Thus the members of other religious traditions can live as anonymous Christians in the sincere practice of their religious beliefs. However, Rahner's idea of the anonymous Christians would be offensive to non-Christians by forcing them into a category that they do not acknowledge. Would a Christian be happy when he/she is called an anonymous Shamanist?

The recent shift of interest in ecumenical and global theology points to the fact that Christianity is required to reflect on pluralist demands of other religions. A term like the theology of religions makes a universal demand to include all religions and ideologies into the mystery of God as the Great Integrator. Such a pluralistic strategy, rejecting claims for a specific, particular, context-bound way, does not recognize the privilege of Christianity in any absolute sense, and even stresses total rejection of the postmodern incommensurability of religions and ideologies. However, it would be naive to assume that a theology of religions is so autonomous as to become a project of reducing all differences of religious languages into one Integrator.

Paul Knitter, beyond the conservative exclusivist approach
and liberal inclusivist approach as well, calls for a new
paradigm of the pluralist position, which means "a move away
from the insistence on the superiority or finality of Christ and
Christianity towards recognition of the independent validity of
other ways. Such a move comes to be described by the partici-
pants in our project as the crossing of a theological Rubicon."[2]
Likewise, Panikkar symbolizes the history of Christianity in
relation to other religions by using the metaphor of three sacred
rivers. Panikkar's metaphor of a river is exemplified up to the
point of calling for a pluralistic plunge into the river Ganges.
His poignant question is like this: "Does one need to be
spiritually a Semite or intellectually a Westerner in order to be a
Christian?"[3]

In an attempt to bring Christianity over the Rubicon into the
pluralistic theology, Knitter makes note of three principal
strategies, that is to say, three bridges across the Rubicon. The
first is a "historico-cultural bridge" in the name of historical
relativity, in light of which exclusivist and inclusivist as well
appear presumptuous with their excessive attachment to the
truth claim of Christian absoluteness. The second is the
"theologico-mystical" bridge in the name of the mystery, in
which the divine mystery exceeds human linguistic and
conceptual formulation. The third is the "ethico-practical"
bridge in the name of justice and peace.

The situation of inter-religious reality is well expressed by
Hans Küng: "No world peace without peace among the
religions, no peace among the religions without dialogue
between the religions, and no dialogue between the religions
without accurate knowledge of one another."[4]

However, the metaphor of crossing over a theological Rubicon
(reminiscent of Caesar's crossing of the same river in 49 B.C.)
would be subject to skepticism due to its formidable project of
assimilating the other, difference, and uniqueness within its own
integrating framework. Or a calling for a pluralistic plunge into
the river Ganges – due to its radical relativistic pluralism – would
blur a postmodern hermeneutic concept of fusion of horizon and
its history of effect in that a specific, particular, context-bound
uniqueness would be established.

The pluralist group is blamed for falling prey to the loss of one's own religious identity and uniqueness. According to Pannenberg, the strategy of pluralism is accused of reviving the old German liberal theology of Harnack and others in the nineteenth century. What is more important for Pannenberg is to take in earnest the final future of God at the center in favor of genuine pluralism in which the Christian has the promise of God in Christ. Christian uniqueness in a pluralistic context issues from the eschatological finality of Jesus Christ.

In critically speaking of a pluralistic theology of religion, Moltmann sheds light on not losing identity, but on attaining a deeper understanding of identity in engaging in dialogue with other religions. What is promising for Moltmann is to bear witness to the truth of one's own religions without falling victim to the relativism of multi-religious reality. Dialogue is formed in the following way: "From anathema to dialogue – from dialogue to co-existence – from co-existence to convivence – from convivence to cooperation."[5]

Listening to the challenges of other religions would be an integral part of Christian theology in our global context. Without engaging in serious conversation with the religious others, a Christian systematic theology would fall into the gray zone of imperialist exclusivism. However, the debate in inter-religious context is complicated and provocative, but still has no satisfactory solution. Only further dialogue will tell where it goes with the hermeneutics of suspicion and retrieval.

2. Situation in Buddhist-Christian Relation

There has been more dialogue between Christianity and Buddhism in particular, since the Second Vatican Council, which has affirmed a "more dynamic, evolutionary concept of the reality" of the church by putting an end to the long-burdened European, Greek, rationalistic theology. In considering the relationship between Christianity and other religions, conversations are encouraged for learning from and sharing with religions outside Christianity.[6]

On the Protestant side Tillich made a contribution by articulating his encounter with Buddhism in a systematic manner. Because of Tillich's approach to a dialogue between Buddhism and Christianity in terms of his method of correlation, Buddhism appears more and more as a living religion in polar tension to Christianity. Tillich thinks that all religions find a sacramental basis for themselves. If this basis is properly balanced and united with mystical and prophetic elements, the religion of the concrete spirit comes to birth, and theonomy appears with an eschatological reservation. This theonomous element is part of the structure of the religion of the concrete spirit. His approach based on a dynamic typology of Buddhist-Christian relation becomes an example for "making inroads into Buddhist spirituality" in the dialogical-personal way.[7]

Masao Abe, in accepting Tillich's dialogical approach, however, makes it possible to facilitate a Buddhist-Christian encounter at a deeper level in which he makes some corrections to Tillich's insufficient understanding of Buddhist ideas. In addition, I have a special apprehension for Barth's approach to Buddhism. In light of the name Jesus Christ Barth sees the affinity between the Reformation principle of grace and Pure Land Buddhism. The name Jesus Christ is not confined to Christianity, but it is God's eternal Immanuel for the world and the entire race. Barth's approach is to find symptoms of the kingdom of God in Buddhism, in which God's strange voice outside the walls of Christianity plays a decisive role in leading Christianity to self-criticism and radical openness towards religious others.[8] Barth's understanding of Buddhism was responded to and corrected by his Japanese disciple Katzumi Takizawa at a deeper level for making clear similarity and difference on both sides.[9]

A mutual renewal and transformation in dialogue with a school of Amida Buddhism and the bodhisattva teaching in Japanese Mahayana Buddhism is proposed by John Cobb. According to John Cobb, inter-religious conversation can benefit both religions. Each renews and deepens the other, and both maintain their difference. Cobb brings a teaching of justification in Shinran (1173–1262), the founder of the true teachings of Pure Land Buddhism to Luther's theology of justification. According to Shinran, a human being is to be saved by the Amida-Buddha, and reborn in the Pure Land. Therefore, it suffices for receiving grace and salvation to recite and pray with the name, "Nembutsu" (Namu-Amidabutsu=Amen, Amida-Buddha).

Cobb's interest in carrying out the mutual transformation through the praxis of dialogue may become clear in his insistence that Amida Buddhism can deepen and renew its self-understanding in encounter with Christianity, as conversely Christianity does the same with respect to Buddhism. His phrase of buddhized Christianity would occur in being renewed by Christ as the principle of the Transformation. Christ is the Way, not the exclusive Way, but allowing different ways in itself, and can serve as the inspiration for correcting, renewing and transforming every religious way. Cobb's attempt is a crossing over to Mahayana Buddhism and a coming back to Christianity in favor of mutual transformation. This may be a hermeneutic strategy for transforming Christianity, including Buddhist insights and achievements, though not displacing or dislocating the centrality of Christ.[10]

David Tracy pays more attention to the affinity between the Mahayana Buddhism of Nagarzuna (represented by the contemporary modern Kyoto school such as Nishida, Tanabe, Nishitani, Takeyushi, Abe and others) and French deconstructive postmodern philosophy like that of Gilles Deleuze and Jacques Derrida. Be that as it may, Tracy does not ignore the difference between the Buddhist idea of nonduality, namely a metaphysical, yet anti-metaphysical character of Mahayana Buddhism, and French postmodern celebration, without reservation, of Nietzschean difference and dissension.[11] To develop an analogical imagination in Buddhist-Christian dialogue and to engage in such dialogue as a committed Christian theologian, Tracy proposes to take three elements into account. Firstly, self-respect for one's own tradition, secondly a self-exposure to the other religion as the terror of otherness, thirdly an attitude of willingness on the side of the dialogue partner allowing for the process and challenge of mutual questioning and inquiry, even a willingness to risk one's own understanding in the presence of the other which might constitute the dialogue in an authentic sense.[12]

A Buddhist-Christian dialogue teaches us that the two religions do not work in the same way, nor in totally different ways. As the dialogue continues and develops, dialectics between suspicion and retrieval of the hermeneutics would come into focus. To become a Christian in the reality of religious pluralism seems to choose between two options. That is, a militantly exclusivist fundamental way of rejecting the wisdom of other religions as chimera or a tolerant liberal way of relativizing the uniqueness of Christianity not only for the sake of affirming other revelations and ways of salvation, but also even running the risk of plunging Christian identity and uniqueness in the river of pluralism. However, there is a need of carrying out inter-religious dialogue at a deeper personal level so as to seek a unique way beyond exclusivism or pluralistic relativism, while remaining a committed Christian with openness to the mystery of God in the world.

3. Justification in Buddhist-Christian Context: Luther and Shinran

When Luther's teaching of justification is seen in Buddhist-Christian relation we see a striking parallel with a teaching of other power in Pure Land Buddhism. According to Buddhist tradition (in *Larger Sutra of Immeasurable Life*) Amida Buddha was Dharmakara who lived in India a million years ago. After long practice, as the bodhisattva Dharmakara, he achieved Buddhahood and became Amida. After enlightenment, he refused to reside in nirvana, instead, he made forty-eight vows to save people by bringing them to the West Pure Land.

Shinran (1173–1262) is regarded and revered as the founder of the school of the true teaching of the Pure Land, which is often referred to merely as Shin Buddhism. It is the dominant lineage, although the Chinese Pure Land's representative Shan-tao (613–681) describes his teaching in the same terms. Shinran's uniqueness in Buddhist tradition is his paradigm shift from self-awakening to nirvana to the universal grace of the absolute Other Power in Amida Buddha.

Before we deal with Shinran's doctrine, it is necessary to turn attention to his teacher, Honen (1133–1212). Honen's understanding of Buddhism is articulated only in the three disciplines of "percepts, concentration, and wisdom," although there are many doctrinal systems in Buddhism. The decisive turning point, which would put an end to Honen's struggle, occurred finally in his reading of a commentary on the *Meditation Sutra*: "Whether walking or standing, sitting or lying, only repeat the name of Amida with all your heart. Never cease the practice of it even for a moment. This is the very work which unfailingly issues in salvation, for it is in accordance with the Original Vow of that Buddha."[13] This passage led Honen to abandon other practices and instead focus on reciting the name of Amida. The exclusive practice of nembutsu (Amen, Amida-Buddha) itself became thus central and fundamental to Honen's teaching.

In association with Honen, Shinran, however, in his own experiential perspective, interprets the Pure Land teaching to be justified historically in the meaning of Amida Buddha's primal vows. He was strongly convinced that the final enlightenment could be attained not through the self-striving discipline, but through the principle of absolute Other Power. Shinran maintained that human effort is incapable of purifying itself sufficiently to achieve enlightenment. As we have already mentioned, Honen stressed that nembutsu means exclusive invocation, i.e. the mere repetition of the Namu Amida Butsu. However, Shinran did not feel nearer to enlightenment, although having practiced nembutsu for many years. So he abandoned the nembutsu itself as a practice or means to attain enlightenment. When all human efforts fail, people could be open to and trust fully in Amida's vows. The self-discipline-oriented path to enlightenment are regarded as subordinate or a preparatory stage for trust in and surrender to Amida's promise of salvation. This is ensured in the eleventh vow: "May I not gain of perfect awakening if, once I have attained buddhahood, the humans and gods in my land are assured of awakening, and without fail attain liberation."[14]

Because everybody receives their faith from Amida Buddha, the spiritual equality of all the faithful is affirmed. If the religious life is understood as an expression of gratitude for the Buddha's compassion and the assurance of our final enlightenment through our faith/trust in the Buddha's vows, the concrete manifestation of this gratitude is the recitation of the name of Amida Buddha. However, gratitude beyond recitation is expressed by a compassionate concern to share the teaching with others. Of course, ethical duty is not necessary for salvation, not to mention causative of it. Rather it is a means by which the compassion of the Buddha becomes real in the world.

Shinran made a distinction between dharmakaya-as-suchness and dharmakaya-as-compassionate means out of the formless, nameless dharmakaya-as-suchness. Amida Buddha, appearing in the form of bodhisattva Dharmakara, stated the forty-eight vows of great compassion, and after having fulfilled the vows, finally became the Buddha of Immeasurable Light and Life. Therefore, Amida Buddha can be called a mediator – if we use a Christian metaphor – between the formless Buddhahood (Sunyata) and all sentient living creatures in the world of samsara. The primal vow is thus the expression of the embodiment of Amida's karuna (compassion) and parajna (wisdom). However, Amida Buddha for Shinran is not merely the manifestation of the dharmakaya-as-suchness, but Sakyamuni Buddha is also the most important of such manifestations including the possibility for human beings to become mediators.

What is distinctive in the concept of faith in Shinran is that faith as the realization of Buddha-nature is placed and seen in Amida's compassion and promise to deliver all beings, as is well expressed in his vows. For Shinran like Luther, a forensic meaning of faith is connected with the belief in the name of Amida, which is *extra nos* (outside us) imputed to us as meritorious and efficacious for us. At the same time, this objective dimension refers to an inner transformation of one's mind for the ethical responsibility.

A paradigm shift from the egocentric character of religious effort to its altruistic nature marks Shinran's interpretation of soteriology on the basis of universality of the Buddha's vow. Let me conclude the teaching of salvation in Shinran by comparison with a remark of Honen: "Even sinners enter into the life of nirvanas, how much more the righteous? (Honen) while if the righteous enter into the life of nirvana, then how much more in the case of sinners? (Shinran)"

The difference between Honen and Shinran lies in the point of fact. For Shinran an evil person possesses the capacity to receive Amida's grace of salvation, that is, Buddha-nature. The statement that an evil person attains birth so naturally would run counter to the primal vow of Amida Buddha. If a good person attains birth through the self-power, it would be in contrast to Amida's primal vow. Therefore, abandoning attachment to self-power and entrusting oneself whole-heartedly to Other Power, one will enter the life of nirvana in the Pure Land. For this reason, Shinran said, "even the virtuous man is born in the Pure Land, so without question is the man who is evil."[15]

Let me compare Shinran's understanding of universal salvation through faith alone to Luther's teaching of justification. As a matter of fact, justification for Luther means the doctrine on which the church stands or falls (*articulus stantis et cadentis ecclesiae*). The teaching of justification, when properly understood, is faith in Christ. Faith in Christ for Luther implies a double meaning of being declared righteous by God on the one hand, and of being acquitted, renewed in terms of the divine promise and grace on the other hand. In the first place, Luther put emphasis on *sola fidei* in God who justifies the unrighteous and reckons him/her as righteousness. And next, faith is described as the reception of divine promise. At this point, faith is not understood as human work or repentance to receive divine grace. Rather "justification is received by faith, that is, in the shape of faith."[16]

The double dimension of justification, that is imputation of Christ's righteousness in the forensic sense as well as in a process of transformation, is solely grounded in Jesus Christ who is present in faith, because the justifying faith "takes hold of and possesses this treasure, the present Christ" (LW 26:130). Christ who is really present in faith is the subject and object of justification and at the same time, the ground for effective transformation of human life. "The righteous man himself does not live; but Christ lives in Him, because through faith Christ dwells in Him and pours His grace into Him, through which it comes about that a man is governed, not by his own spirit, but by Christ's" (WA 2. 502,12–14).

Luther grounds himself on the basis of Paul alone by opposing the caritas idealism. No *fides caritas formata* (faith formed by charity), but *fides Christo formata* (faith formed by Christ) meant a paradigm shift in breaking through his Reformation. From the beginning Luther's teaching of justification which is based on a life in union with Christ ("happy exchange") expresses a dynamic relation of faith to love. In other words, life of the justified is a life in which faith is active in love. The Christological hymn (Phil. 2:4–11) is the basis for Luther to think that God's own humility in the most radical sense refers to the embodiment of God's freedom in love. God's self-giving love shapes effectively and finally the freedom in humility that the justified are called to follow in his/her faith. This refers to the evangelical episteme in characterization of Luther's justification forensically and effectively, as well.

In a similar structure of thought-form Shinran found himself in his understanding of faith, totally saved and yet totally lost. This paradox of religious experience would be compared to Luther's concept of *simul peccator et simul justus*. This refers to the similarity in difference.

Be that as it may, Shinran's understanding of faith as a gift of Amida seems to presuppose Buddha nature in all human beings and be connected inseparably with it. If an evil person comes to nirvana, his/her Buddha nature should be in accord with Amida's compassion in the sense of identification between nirvana and samsara. Paradoxically speaking, Amida's grace can be only realized through the Buddha-nature in human beings. However, in matters of justification and salvation, Luther would oppose *imago Dei* (or to use the metaphor *imago Buddha* in a Christian way) as the point of contact capable of receiving, realizing and fulfilling the grace of God.

In addition, Luther's forensic concept of justification cannot be properly understood without its effective and transformative dimension of justification. The real presence of Christ, i.e. the *inhabitatio Christi* in the believer constitutes a central motif in Luther's idea of justification. Unlike Shinran whose interest is not in real presence of Amida Buddha, the union with Christ in Pauline perspective is taken by Luther to include both a relation to Christ and unity with him. If Christ as the *favor dei* articulates the forensically declared righteousness, Christ as the *donum dei* elaborates the aspect of effective righteousness. Because there is still residual sin in human being in a post-baptismal sense, justification, like the process of salvation in trembling and fear is based on Christ's forensic and effective work and is in need of renewal effected by the Holy Spirit in the ministry of word and sacrament.

Moreover, in matters of soteriology Luther's experience of *Anfechtungen* (inner struggle) is quite different from Shinran, albeit there would be an existential resemblance. Luther's experience with God's wrath and love on the cross of Jesus Christ is historical, concrete and experiential, while Shinran's faith in the Other Power of Amida is based on the myth of the bodhisattva named Dharmakara. The latter is not much concerned about the history. Unlike the story of Jesus Christ, the Amida story is more metaphysical, more spiritual rather than objective and historical reality and fact. Furthermore, the Buddhist perspective on salvation is not in accord with a sacrificial image of the nailing and blood on the cross. This is difference in similarity.

Luther's understanding of divine suffering on the cross, which is the foundation of *theologia crucis* tends to elaborate divine immanence in deep solidarity and compassion with people who suffer, rather than a manifestation of Other power as sunyata. Unlike Shinran's iconoclastic and anti-liturgical direction, Luther is deeply convinced that human being shares through faith in participation in God's compassion which is highlighted in celebration of the word and sacrament.

However, when it comes to encounter with wisdom of Pure Land Buddhism, a Buddhist spirituality of universal compassion helps us to deepen and actualize an inclusive tendency in Luther's own thought which has been by and large neglected in the historical development of Lutheran tradition. The most moving compassion and the ethical aspect of a Bodhisattva are found by the following passage of the *Bodhicaryāvatāra* :

May I become the protector of those without protection, the guide for those on the path, the boat, the bridge and the causeway for those wishing to go the other shore.

May I become a lamp for those desiring a lamp, a bed for those desiring a bed, a slave for all beings desiring a slave.

May I become the wish-fulfilling gem, the miracle urn, a successful mantra, a universal remedy, the wish-fulfilling tree and the wish-fulfilling cow for all beings.[17]

A Bodhisattva suffers for suffering, as God in Jesus Christ suffers for suffering. The spirituality of embracing the others can be brought up and taken up into God's wounded heart on the cross for all. Luther's extraordinary sense of the gospel can be reread and rediscovered in listening to the God's strange voice outside the walls of Christianity. At this point I find Luther's reflection on Ishmael very meaningful and indispensable for Christian openness to the world: "For the expulsion does not mean that Ishmael should be utterly excluded from the kingdom of God … The descendents of Ishmael also joined the church of Abraham and became heirs of the promise, not by reason of a right but because of irregular grace" (LW 4:42–44).

Basically, Luther's teaching of justification characterizes and shapes our Christian identity in terms of humble attitude before God and openness to the mystery of God in the world. What is extraordinary for Luther's theology of creation lies in the fact that God is in cooperation with human being for the preservation of creation, while rejecting this cooperation in regard to justification. "All creatures are God's larvae and mummery that he will let work with him and help in all sorts of creating, but that he otherwise can and does do without their help, so that we cling only to his word" (WA 17 II, 192, 28–31). They are invited to God's future in the new creation of all things. The end of the world is not the darkness of death or hell, but the new creation of all things. God's Spirit moves human beings and the cosmos open to the future of God. Luther's theology of "God with us" in its particular sense moves in the direction of inclusive and cosmic dimension of God's grace in Jesus Christ.

As a matter of course, we do not ignore a double outcome of judgment or confessional exclusivism. Universal salvation and a double outcome of judgment are biblically attested in mutual tension. Nevertheless, according to Luther, we sinners are saved only by God's gracious act in Jesus Christ. Besides, this grace comes to us while we are still sinners. I hear this inclusive tendency from Luther's commentary on 1 Timothy 2:4. "This is an exclusive proposition that is expressed in universal terms ... He causes all men to be saved" (LW 28:260). Given this fact, Luther would tend to affirm inclusive dimension of *sola fidei* in embracement of the others. Christ crucified and risen sharpens the universality of Christ's saving justification for all and empowers an ecumenic pluralism that beyond relativistic pluralism is meant to supply a perspective of assuming responsibility for its corresponding unity.[18] In so doing, Luther's conviction of justification on the basis of *fides Christo formata* gains more in prominence when it comes to encounter with people of other faiths.

4. Toward Christian Uniqueness as Embrace of the Others

"But what about you? ... Who do you say that I am?" (Mark 8:29). Publicly Jesus calls himself into question among his disciples. Reading from the Bible in the synagogue of Capernaum, Jesus proclaimed his mission: "The Spirit of the Lord is on me, because he has anointed me to preach good news to the poor. He has sent me to proclaim freedom for the prisoners and recovery of sight for the blind, to release the oppressed, to proclaim the year of the Lord's favor" (Luke 4:18–19). The exclusive claim of the gospel for the crucified God was foolishness to the Greeks and it remains as a stumbling block to many contemporary Hellenized Christians who felt ashamed of the cross. To the Athenians in front of the Areopagus Paul bears witness to *Solus Christus* in a conviction that everybody lives, moves and has his/her being in the universal reign of God (Acts 17:22, 27b, 28). Therefore, the exclusivity of Christ cannot be fully understood apart from its dimension of embracing the others.

In Buddhist-Christian context Christian uniqueness lies in witnessing the particular and inclusive dimension of the gospel without doing harm to the wisdom of religious others, and by recognizing the different as different. Justification by faith alone refers not to the selfish private encapsulation of God's salvation in Jesus Christ in the interest of excluding and condemning others, but refers to a universal dimension of the Spirit in favor of them. "The wind blows wherever it pleases" (John 3:8).

As Pannenberg states,

Jesus of Nazareth is the final revelation of God because the end of history appeared in him. It did so both in his eschatological message and in his resurrection from the dead. However, he can be understood to be God's final revelation only in connection with the whole of history as mediated by the history of Israel. He is God's revelation in the fact that all history received its light from him.[19]

The uniqueness of Jesus of Nazareth which is the highest expression of God's cosmic plan of salvation becomes manifest especially in his passionate solidarity and compassion with others, that is, the deviant, the irrelevant, the marginalized, the oppressed, all in all the lowest of the low (Matt. 25). Christian uniqueness is not supposed to be sought in thrall to a Western rationality culture or a tradition of onto-theology.

The eschatological kingdom proleptically present in Jesus appears and is active in various ways of other religions. In the history of world religions Jesus Christ holds a unique place as the key to the future of the world and its salvation on the basis of his death and resurrection, but without the exclusivism of the others, nor falling into the sheer relativism of neo-liberal pluralists.

A strange, even uncomfortable, ominous voice stemming from outside the walls of Christianity (Karl Barth)[20] serves as an inspiration for setting Christians free from being captive to the excessive project of the Enlightenment in the West, and leading them to a humble attitude and radical openness towards God's future. When it loses God's other voice, a

Christian uniqueness would fall into the gray zone of a deaf faith. In this regard, the theological language of God's saving grace in Jesus Christ is not based on a scientific objective claim seeking one unequivocal meaning of the gospel, because the reader cannot discover and recover the meaning of the gospel as it actually was. However, the effective history (H.-G. Gadamer) does not necessarily lead to sheer relativism or a pluralist theology of religion. A Christian theology of religions in favor of Christian uniqueness does not in fact stand in opposition to the reality of pluralism itself, because God is the One who accepts the world's pluralism and integrates all its variety and pluriformity through his universal grace in Jesus Christ into the coming kingdom of God.

Buddhist-Christian conversation is meaningful in so far as it gives rise to a common language and improves a mutual enrichment and transformation without losing each unique-ness or doing harm to other areas in which dialogue partici-pants have never been. The conversation with others is likened to a game in which we do not even take the initiative of getting into the game.[21] The game of conversing with others produces an intensification process that can lead to a reflective distancing from the relativity and inadequacy of all religious beliefs. Through this hermeneutical circle, participants return to their own religions experiencing them in a more profound way. A deeper understanding of Christian uniqueness would occur in the process of a fusion of horizons. This hermeneutical process enables participants to witness their uniqueness, to get into dialogue with mutual humility and openness, and finally helps to enrich and renew each tradition before the future of God.

Let me conclude my reflection on Christian uniqueness in inter-religious context with a prophetic voice of Karl Barth regarding the so-called true words of God *extra muros ecclesiae*:[22]

We may think of the mystery of God, which we Christians so easily talk away in a proper concern for God's own cause … We may think of the disquiet, not to be stilled by any compromise, at the various disorders both of personal life and of that of the state and of society, at those who are inevitably driven to the wall. We may think of the resolute determination, perhaps, to attack these evils. We may think of the lack of fear in face of death which Christians to their shame often display far less readily than non-Christians far and near ... Especially we may think of a humanity which does not ask or weigh too long with whom we are dealing in others, but in which we find a simple solidarity with them and unreservedly take up their case. (*CD* IV/3.1, p. 125)

Notes

[1] Cf. J.-F. Lyotard, *The Postmodern Condition: A Report on Knowledge* (Minneapolis: University of Minnesota Press, 1984).

[2] *The Myth of Christian Uniqueness: Toward a Pluralistic Theology of Religions*, eds. John Hick and Paul Knitter (Maryknoll, NY: Orbis, 1987), p. viii.

[3] R. Panikkar, "The Jordan, The Tiber, and the Ganges: Three kairological Movements of Christic Self-Consciousness," in *The Myth of Christian Uniqueness: Toward a Pluralistic Theology of Religions* (eds. John Hick and Paul Knitter; Maryknoll, NY/London: Orbis/SCM, 1987), p. 92.

[4] Hans Küng, "Christianity and World Religions: Dialogue with Islam," in *Toward a Universal Theology of Religion* (ed. Leonard Swindler; Maryknoll, NY: Orbis, 1987), p. 194.

[5] J. Moltmann, *Experiences in Theology: Ways and Forms of Christian Theology* (Minneapolis: Fortress Press, 2000), p. 20.

[6] Second Vatican Council, "Pastoral Constitution on the Church in the Modern World," No. 5. Cf. "Declaration on the Relationship of the Church to Non Christian Religions," No. 16.

[7] P. Tillich, *Christianity and the Encounter of World Religions* (Minneapolis: Fortress Press, 1994), p. 38.

[8] For the strange voice outside the walls of Christianity in Karl Barth's theology, *Kirchliche Dogmatik* (Zürich, 1932–67), I/1, p. 83; IV/3, p. 122.

[9] K. Takizawa, *Reflexionen über die Grundlage von Buddhismus und Christentum* (Bern: Peter Lang Verlag, 1980).

[10] John B. Cobb, Jr. *Beyond Dialogue* (Philadelphia: Fortress, 1982), pp. 142–43.

[11] David Tracy, *Dialogue with The Other: The Inter-Religious Dialogue* (Grand Rapids, MI: Eerdmans, 1990), pp. 70–71.

[12] Tracy, *Dialogue with The Other*, p. 73. Cf. David Tracy, *The Analogical Imagination: Christian Theology and the Culture of Pluralism* (New York: Crossroad, 2000), pp. 446–57.

[13] Harper Havelock Coates and Ryugaku Ishizuka, *Honen: The Buddhist Saint* (Kyoto, 1925; repr. New York/London: Garland Publishing, 1981), p. 187.

[14] Luis O. Gomez, *Land of Bliss: The Paradise of the Buddha of Measureless Light* (Honolulu: University of Hawaii Press, 1996), p. 167.

[15] Cf. Hee-Sung Keel, *Understanding Shinran: A Dialogical Approach* (California, Fremont: The Nanzan Institute for Religion and Culture, 1995), p. 31.

[16] Cf. Paul Althaus, *The Theology of Martin Luther* (trans. R. S. Schultz; Philadelphia: Fortress Press, 1979), pp. 230–31.

[17] Cf. Francis Brassard, *The Concept of Bodhicitta in Śantideva's Bodhicaryāvatāra* (Albany: State University of New York Press, 2000), p. 47.

[18] Cf. Ted Peters, *God – the World's Future: Systematic Theology for a New Era* (2nd edn.; Minneapolis: Fortress Press, 2000), pp. 348–63.

[19] Wolfhart Pannenberg, "The Revelation of God in Jesus of Nazareth," in *Theology as History*, (ed. J. M. Robinson; New York: Macmillan,1967), p. 104.

[20] For the strange voices of God outside the walls of Christianity, cf. *KD* I/1, p. 83, *KD* IV/3.1, p. 122.

[21] Cf. David Tracy, *The Analogical Imagination: Christian Theology and the Culture of Pluralism* (New York: Crossroad, 2000), p. 115.

[22] For a relation between Barth and religious pluralism, see Paul S. Chung, *Martin Luther and Buddhism: aesthetics of suffering* (Eugene: Wipf & Stock, 2002), pp. 315–32.

9

Jesus Christ – Eschatological Prophet and Incarnate Savior
A Christian Proposal to Muslims

Ng Kam Weng

1. Jesus, the Eschatological Prophet

One of the reasons given by the Islamic authorities in Malaysia to explain why the unrestricted public viewing of the film *The Passion of the Christ* would not be allowed was because the film depicts images of one of the prophets of Islam. More than that, it was also because "Christianity teaches Christ as crucified and resurrected and that is an offence to Islam."[1] Evidently, theological concerns are paramount behind the authorities' censorship policy. This recent event in Malaysia epitomizes the ongoing debate between Christians and Muslims regarding the status of Jesus.

Some Muslim officials attempt to back up their theological veto by providing an array of historical objections to Christianity. For example, it is common for Muslims to reject the Gospels on grounds of historical inaccuracies and textual corruption. Muslims appeal to the Gospel of Barnabas – even though its inauthenticity has been demonstrated long ago in the original publication by Londsale and Laura Ragg[2] – simply because this Gospel included a prediction of the coming of Muhammad. Other Muslim apologists, not content with rejecting the crucifixion of Jesus, claim that the historical Jesus escaped to Kashmir after evading execution by the

Romans. It appears that theological pre-understanding here pre-empts independent historical investigations. For Muslims, since Muhammad is the final seal of the prophets, Jesus could not have achieved a finished work of salvation.

Muslims assert the utter transcendence of God. Divine revelation therefore takes the form of revealed commandments rather than a revealed person. The issue that separates Christians and Muslims is whether or not the claim that Jesus Christ as the decisive revelation of God compromises the utter transcendence of God. Resolving this issue requires an inquiry into the prophetic calling of Jesus. We need to ask whether Jesus' ministry went beyond mere proclamation and constituted an adequate, if not decisive, act of divine salvation for humankind.

Both Muslims and Christians apply the title "prophet" to Jesus. However, the distinctive Islamic emphasis on prophethood should not be missed. In general the Muslim teaching of prophets includes the following: (1) A messenger/apostle (*rasul*) is sent with divine Scripture to guide and reform mankind; (2) All God's prophets were trustworthy, knowledgeable, and most obedient to God. Allah protected them from serious sins and bad diseases; (3) Denying any of the prophets constitutes unbelief (Surah 4: 150–151); (4) Many prophets were mocked and rejected (Surah 15:11; 17:94). Some prophets were delivered by God, e.g. Noah (Surah 21:76; 26:118; 29:15; 37:76), Lot (21:71, 74; 26:170), and Moses (Surah 28:20–22; 26:65). Some of the prophets, however, were killed "wrongfully" (e.g. Abel, Zechariah, and Yahya or John the Baptist), c.f. Surah 2:61, 87, 91; 3:21, 112; 4:155; 5:70. Finally, and most importantly, for Muslims Muhammad is "the seal of the prophets" (Surah 33:40).[3]

Islamic traditions have described Jesus as an ascetic prophet. A famous hadith has Jesus saying,

> My seasoning is hunger, my undergarment is fear of Allah, my outer-garment is wool, my fire in winter is the ray of the sun, my lamp is the moon, my riding beast is my feet, and my food and fruit are what the earth brings forth (that is, without cultivation). At night I have nothing and in the morning I have nothing. Yet there is no one on earth richer than I.[4]

In another hadith, Ka'b al-Akbar reported that Jesus "was an ascetic in the world, longing for the next world and eager for the worship of Allah. He was a pilgrim in the earth till the Jews sought him and desired to kill him. Then Allah raised him up to heaven; and Allah knows best."[5]

More significantly, Jesus holds an honored position among the prophets, being none other than the eschatological prophet who brings his work to completion at the end of time. As one hadith testifies, "And there are none of the People of the Book who will not believe in him before his death. On the day of Resurrection he [Jesus] will be a witness against them" (Al-Bukhari Vol. 4. Book 55.657).[6]

However, Christians will be startled by Muslim teaching that Christ's return will include judging Christians for their folly. According to Al-Bukhari (Vol. 4. Book 43.656), Jesus will descend as a Just Ruler. He will break the cross and kill the pig and bring war to an end. Such Muslim eschatological expectation can only bring a sense of foreboding for the Christians.

Despite their high estimate of Jesus, Muslims assert Muhammad's superiority: Jesus wandered as an ascetic, but Muhammad brought glory and triumph to God as a ruler-saint and bequeathed us a comprehensive legal system as well as a blueprint for building a perfect political order. Several implications arise from this evaluation: Since Islam is the final and perfect revelation (Surah 5:3, 5), the Gospels cannot be final. The Gospels retain truth to the extent that they are prophecies concerning the coming Muhammad.

For Muslims, Jesus is only a prophet, albeit a most honored prophet; he is not the son of God, much less an incarnate God. It is natural for Christians to react to this diminution of Jesus' status by avoiding any discussion about Jesus' prophetic vocation. However, dialog must begin with common ground. Discussion about the prophetic vocation of Jesus can be an opportunity to nudge Muslims to reconsider whether their understanding of Jesus is prematurely truncated. The question raised is, to what extent God is personally involved in the sending of his prophets, especially the prophet [Jesus] who manifests the full embodiment of God's spirit and who not only proclaims salvation but attests to his message with signs and wonders. Christians should urge Muslims at least to be willing to listen to the self-testimony of Jesus and assess the Bible on its own terms.

One may begin with the Old Testament which understands a prophet to be a person who, "because he is conscious of having been specially chosen and called, feels forced to perform actions and proclaim ideas which, in a mental state of intense inspiration of real ecstasy, have been indicated to him in the form of divine revelation."[7]

Reginald Fuller argues that the category of the eschatological prophet remains the best category for understanding Jesus' historical mission and

> gives a unity to all of Jesus' historical activity, his proclamation, his teaching with *exousia* ("authority"), his healings and exorcisms, his conduct in eating with the outcast, and finally his death in the fulfillment of his prophetic mission. Take the implied self-understanding of his role in terms of the eschatological prophet away, and the whole ministry falls into a series of unrelated, if not meaningless fragments.[8]

The Old Testament also looks forward to the coming of an eschatological prophet. This teaching has its origin from the Deuteronomic tradition of Moses found in Deuteronomy 18:15, "The LORD your God will raise up for you a prophet like me from among your own brothers. You must listen to him." Moses was a prophet, a proclaimer of the word, a mediator between God and the people (Deut. 5:5) and sometimes a suffering mediator (Deut. 1:37; 4:21, cf. Num. 12:6–8 and Exod. 33:11).

According to the New Testament, Jesus fulfilled these prophecies. The Gospels tell us that Jesus had visions and ecstatic experiences – baptism and transfiguration. His insight and supernatural knowledge is evidenced by his prophecy of his death in Jerusalem and the destruction of Jerusalem by the Roman legions in A.D. 70. He taught with divine authority, but he also enacted symbolic actions that were characteristic of the Old Testament prophets. After the miraculous feeding of 5000 (John 6:1–15; cf. Mark 6:30–44; cf. Matt. 14:13–21; Luke 9:10–17), the crowd declared that "Surely this is the Prophet who is to come into the world" (John 6:14). They were recalling the miraculous provision of manna in the Exodus event (Exod. 16:4–8). At the Feast of Tabernacles, during the ritual pouring of water at the altar, Jesus declared "If anyone is thirsty, let him come to me and drink. Whoever believes in me, as the Scripture has said, streams of living water will flow from within him" (John 7:37–39). The significance of Jesus' claim was not lost to the crowd, given the traditional belief that the eschatological prophet would repeat the miracle of dispensing water at Horeb (Exod. 17:1–6; Num. 20:2–11). Their verdict was, "Surely this man is the Prophet [after Moses]" (John 7:40, c.f. Mark 6:4; Deut. 18:15–19). Edward Schillebeeck elaborates,

> Like Moses, he [Jesus] communicates the law and justice (Isa. 42:1f) , but now to the whole world; the suffering servant-like Moses is "the light of the world" (Isa. 49:5–9; 42:1–6); and like Moses he is the mediator of the covenant (Isa. 42:6; 49:8), leader of the new exodus, this time from the Babylonian captivity. The twelve tribes are gathered together again as a result of this exodus (Isa. 49:5; 43:5f). In this new exodus the eschatological prophet greater than Moses will again strike water from the rock and offer "the water of life" to his people (Isa. 41:18; 42:20; 48:21; 49:10; see the Gospel of John). The suffering servant is the Moses of the new exodus (Isa. 43:16–21); expiating sins, suffering for his people, the Mosaic servant has all the marks of the figure who in early Judaism is in fact called the messianic eschatological prophet like Moses ... the royal messianic prophet Moses, the *divus*.[9]

Jesus' symbolic actions came to a climax when he rode into Jerusalem riding on a donkey. The crowd proclaimed Jesus to be no ordinary prophet but *the* prophet with a messianic mission, who comes in the name of the Lord (Matt. 21:9). Jesus was the fulfillment of all Old Testament prophecies concerning the eschatological prophet – particularly those in the book of Isaiah – not only in the proclamation of the Jubilee (Luke 4:18–19; cf. Isa. 61:1–2) but in his prediction of vicarious death for sinners (Isa. 52–53). Later, the early church pointed to the resurrection of Jesus as evidence that God vindicated him as the eschatological prophet foretold by Moses (Acts 3:12–26; 7:2–53; cf. Deut. 18:15–19).

In fulfilling the Old Testament prophecies, Jesus endowed his prophetic office with eschatological significance. The Old Testament prophets proclaimed the word. Jesus himself is the Word. The OT prophetic message was given to Israel. Jesus is the light of God given to the world. In other words, the category of eschatological prophet elevates rather than restricts Jesus' universal significance, since the qualifier "eschatological" points to his universal paradigmatic significance. To quote Schillebeeckx again,

> Certainly in the New Testament, the term eschatological prophet implies that this prophet is significant for the whole history of the world, and significant for the whole of subsequent history … Thus eschatological prophet means a prophet who claims to bring a definitive message which applies to the whole of history.[10]

For first-century Jews, the arrival of the kingdom of God should be evidenced by Israel's return from exile, the defeat of evil (especially Israel's enemies) and the return of Yahweh to Zion. The Messiah would fulfill these covenant promises of God to ancient Israel. The messianic significance of Jesus becomes clear.

> Jesus applied to himself the three central aspects of his own prophetic kingdom-announcement: the return from exile, the defeat of evil, and the return of YHWH to Zion … He regarded himself as the one who summed up Israel's vocation and destiny in himself. He was the one in and through whom the real "return from exile" would come about, indeed, was already coming about. He was the Messiah.[11]

More astoundingly, Jesus further claimed that "as true king, he not only had authority over the Temple, but would share the very throne of Israel's god [sic]."[12] Jesus' sense of vocation required him to "enact in himself what, in Israel's Scriptures, God had promised to accomplish all by himself … He would embody in himself the returning and redeeming action of the covenant God."[13]

To be sure, these messianic claims were accompanied by prophecies that Jesus would be killed by the elders of Israel

(Mark 8:31). Jesus saw his prophetic vocation as one that required him to die in Jerusalem, "for surely no prophet can die outside Jerusalem" (Luke 13:33). These prophecies were fulfilled when the Jewish elders colluded with the Roman authorities to put Jesus to death. The Jewish leadership was concerned to kill one they saw guilty of blasphemy in claiming to have the authority to sit at God's right hand. For the Roman authorities, the occasion provided a convenient reason for taking pre-emptive action against a potential political rebel. In contrast, the early church saw Christ as the power of God and the wisdom of God. Christ "has become for us wisdom from God – that is, our righteousness, holiness and redemption" (1 Cor. 1:24, 30). Indeed, "None of the rulers of this age understood it, for if they had, they would not have crucified the Lord of glory" (1 Cor. 2:8).

1.1 Islamic rejection of the crucified Prophet-Messiah

Christians buttress evidence for the historical factuality of the cross by appealing to eyewitness accounts and reports found in non-Christian historical sources (Josephus, Tacitus). The Christian witness to the crucifixion is plausible since it is inconceivable why Christians should invent the crucifixion which declares that their founder died an accursed death (under divine judgment) on the cross. As such, an outright denial of the crucifixion would be tantamount to a willful blindness to historical reality. Muslim critics therefore grudgingly acknowledge that historically a crucifixion did occur. However, they suggest that someone other than Jesus was crucified. They argue that Christians have misunderstood the significance of the cross because they are victims of an illusion. God, they claim, replaced Jesus with someone that bore his likeness.

Muslim scholars bypass the historical record with an appeal to the Qur'anic revelation: Surah 19:33 – "So peace is on me the day I was born, the day that I die, and the day that I shall be raised up to life (again)!" Surah 3:55 – "Behold! God said: 'O Jesus! I will take thee and raise thee to Myself and clear thee (of the falsehoods) of those who blaspheme; I will make those who follow thee superior to those who reject faith, to the Day of Resurrection: then shall ye return unto me, and I will judge between you of the matters wherein ye dispute'" and Surah 4:157–159:

> That they said (in boast), "We killed Christ Jesus the son of Mary, the Messenger of God"; – but they killed him not, nor crucified him, but it was made to appear to them, and those who differ therein are full of doubts, with no (certain) knowledge, but only conjecture to follow, for of a surety they killed him not: – Nay, God raised him up unto Himself; and God is Exalted in Power, Wise – And there is none of the People of the Book but must believe in him before his death; and on the Day of Judgment he will be a witness against them.

Synthesizing these verses, Muslims conclude that God took Jesus to himself (in heaven) and replaced Jesus with someone else to be crucified on the cross. But the problem with this substitution theory was not missed out even by Muslims themselves. For example, the great Muslim commentator Razi wondered if such a denial would not put them on a slippery slide, for if we deny incontrovertible eyewitness reports then surely, all human testimony regarding divine laws and prophecy would be equally questionable. If we reject what the normal human senses perceive, then we are denied all possibility of attaining the truth. Equally problematic would be a question of divine integrity. A God who makes the onlookers misperceive the person on the cross to be someone else must be a God of deception.[14]

The substitution theory suggests that Islam was influenced by early Gnostics who denied the crucifixion. It is therefore ironic that Christians have stepped forward to defend the integrity of the Qur'anic witness by suggesting that the substitution theory represents a misreading of the Qur'an by later interpreters. David Brown offers a suggestion that would make the Qur'anic witness more rational:

> These verses are intended to be a rebuke to the Jews, and particularly to Muhammad's contemporaries in Medina, for

various acts of unbelief ... the reference to the crucifixion does no more than dispute the claim made by the Jews that they had disposed of the Christian Messiah and repudiated his claim to be an apostle of God by crucifying him. In particular, the phrases "they did not kill him, nor did they crucify him", do not necessarily mean that there was no crucifixion, but that, even if there was, it was God who was responsible for all that happened during the last hours of the Messiah's life and that the Jews had done whatever they did only by permission of God's will. A similar figure of speech occurs in 8:17 in which the Muslims' action at the Battle of Badr are attributed to God and not to their own volition; they did in fact fight and kill, but only by God's permission and direction. These verses, therefore, do not explicitly deny the Christian story of crucifixion, for they refer primarily to Jewish claims against the Christians.[15]

Such an exegesis of the Qur'an takes history more seriously and opens new grounds for dialog. But it is doubtful this approach will be well received by Muslims. Indeed, the persistence of the substitution theory in Islamic tradition only confirms its theological consistency with central Islamic doctrines. In particular, the denial of the crucifixion arises from the Muslim belief that God does not need "intercessors" or atonement or crucifixion. There can be no intercessor or mediator since, a priori, such a mediator would share common qualities ("association") with God. In any case, there is no need for drastic intervention on God's part since the human predicament is not so serious in Islam. According to Islam, all human beings are born *fitrah* (sinless). To be sure, one cannot deny human failings before God. But in contrast to Christianity which teaches sin as a rebellion against God, Islam teaches sin to be ignorance of God. Adam sinned because he misunderstood God's commands. Ismail Faruqi stresses that,

> Adam therefore did commit a misdeed, namely, that of thinking evil to be good, of ethical misjudgment. He was the author of the first human mistake in ethical perception, committed with good intention, under enthusiasm for the good. It was not a "fall" but a discovery that it is possible to confuse the good with the evil, that its pursuit is neither unilateral nor straightforward.[16]

A second reason why Muslims reject Jesus' crucifixion arises from Islamic faith in divine justice. In particular, God cannot abandon his prophet to tragic and unjust fate. Indeed, as the Qur'an testifies, God gives victory to those who seek to further his cause (Surah 22:40; 40:51):

> O you who believe!
> If you will aid (the cause of) God,
> He will aid you, and plant your feet firmly (Surah 47:7);
>
> Nay, God raised him up unto Himself; and God is Exalted in Power, Wise (Surah 4:158).

Herein lies an ironic twist in the denial of the cross or the messiahship of Jesus. For the Jews Jesus could not be a prophet sent by God since he was crucified. The Muslims reverse this logic – if Jesus was a prophet sent by God then he could not have been crucified. Muslims appeal to other examples of God's protection of his prophets such as Abraham and Lot (Surah 21:71), Noah (Surah 21:76–77), Moses (Surah 28:18–28) and lastly Muhammad (Surah 28:18–28).

God by definition will protect his prophets. God will not abandon his prophets or allow them to be mistreated by his people. Prophetic mission cannot be prematurely aborted by violent opposition. Hence, there is no place for the crucifixion in the arena of history.

Finally, Muslims cannot accept that Jesus accomplished a definitive work of salvation by dying on the cross. Jesus' mission was merely preparatory in comparison to the work of the final prophet, Muhammad. The Qur'an asserts in Surah 61:6 – And remember, Jesus, the son of Mary, said: "Children of Israel! I am the messenger of God (sent) to you, confirming the Law (which came) before me, and giving Glad Tidings of a Messenger to come after me, whose name shall be Ahmad." Likewise we read, "We sent Jesus the son of Mary, confirming the Torah what had come before him: We sent him the Gospel: in it was guidance and light and confirmation of the Torah that had come before him: a guidance and admonition to those who fear God" (Surah 5:46 cf. Surah 3:3).

It is evident that such a theological framework does not allow for the cross to be the locus for the finished work of salvation. In other words, if Jesus himself anticipated a later, "seal" of the prophet, he could not have accomplished salvation and divine reconciliation on the cross.

2. More Than an Ordinary Prophet

How do we adjudicate the difference between Christians and Muslims regarding the prophetic mission and status of Jesus? Obviously, the issue cannot be answered in abstraction. For this reason, it is unfortunate that the controversy revolving around the incarnation of Christ has overshadowed his actual life lived out in history. It is of vital importance that Christians present their doctrine not as an imposition of a philosophical grid on the historical facts. Their proclamation of Jesus as God's incarnation should be seen as a compelling conclusion based on a respectful handling and faithful interpretation of the historical data. In other words, reading about the life and works of Christ must lead us to ask what manner of man was Jesus: Is he a remarkable man; is he a prophet; is he more than a prophet and what then?

Jesus' hearers were impressed by his unconventional wisdom. It is reported that he confounded the learned teachers of Israel in debates. Indeed, they were astounded by his authority and profound wisdom. Unlike normal teachers who merely quoted from earlier authorities Jesus pronounced acute and astute judgments on spiritual controversies and acted with uncharacteristic ethical freedom. Such are the hallmarks of a prophet.

Like the Old Testament prophets, Jesus confirmed his words with miraculous deeds. He urged the stubborn Jews who had difficulty accepting his words to believe, at least, on the basis of his miraculous works. On the other hand, Jesus' miracles must be viewed in proper perspective. Miracles would have satisfied both the Jewish and Islamic desire for signs and worldly success. However, the suggestion that Jesus should have resorted to miracles to win over the Jews underestimates the stubbornness of an unbelieving heart. After all, the Pharisees, like Pharaoh of old, rationalized away the miracles, either as works of the prince of devils or the illusions of court magicians.

The miracles of Jesus provided some evidences to support his prophetic claims but they alone could not bring about the moral-spiritual transformation demanded by Jesus. Spiritual transformation or being born again is the result of being brought into a spiritual and living relationship with Jesus. It is precisely such a relationship that the powerful elite rejected; they felt too self-sufficient to require divine empowerment. Instead, Jesus' teaching secured sympathies mainly from the hard boiled underclass of an oppressed society who knew only too well its moral inadequacies.

Admittedly, immediate success through miraculous signs would constitute a tempting strategy to achieve worldly success. Indeed, history shows that some of Jesus' followers veered from the wisdom of their master when they sought to attain success in terms of power rallied around the "flag and sword" in their missionary enterprise. By doing so, they had ascribed to politics and military might an undue importance in the light of what is truly important in spiritual terms.

The Christian may challenge the Muslims to re-examine why the success of prophets should be gauged in terms of immediate worldly success such as securing social power. Is not the sword of Caesar efficacious only for temporal rule? Indeed, such temporal concerns can detract one from a more important encounter with God that leads to spiritual transformation. The sensitive reader should already detect a fundamental shift in our expectation of prophetic vocation, that is, a vocation that goes beyond bearing a message. It must be one which initiates a new, transforming relationship with God.

2.1 Revelation to inform and to transform

Jesus exercised a prophetic vocation in continuity with the Old Testament prophets but his ministry evidently burst the bounds of traditional prophetic vocation. The Old Testament prophets were merely messengers but Jesus was the incarnate Word and Mediator. Herein lies the fundamental difference between the Christian and Muslim estimation of Jesus, and, consequently, their different understanding of divine revelation.

Karl Barth highlights the distinctiveness of Jesus' prophetic vocation. For Barth, revelation is testimony to the Lordship of God. That is to say, only through God is God known. "God reveals himself as the Lord" means that he reveals what only he himself can reveal *himself*.[17] Christ steps into human history while always remaining Lord and God. He meets us as Immanuel, God with us. The event of revelation is identical with Jesus Christ in all that he was and said and did (CD 1.1.127). Barth concluded that Jesus Christ is thus not one who came simply to tell us about God but is himself the divine word and action of God for us. Revelation is God's self-disclosure and God's saving action at the same time.

In other words, the revelation of Jesus Christ goes beyond conveying information. H. R. Mackintosh echoes the multi-faceted dimensions of Jesus' prophetic office:

> Revelation explicitly includes the bestowing on man of the gift to recognize and believe it. The imparting of the Spirit, creating faith within, is an essential element of revelation itself. The event called revelation, in the New Testament is both things – a happening *to us* and *in us* ... in other words, the revelation is revelation only when by the Spirit it "gets through" to man.[18]

Christianity envisages a richer sense of revelation than Islam does. For Muslims have only the revelation of Divine will; God the Revealer remains himself unrevealed. He sends his message but is himself withdrawn in transcendence. In Kenneth Cragg's words:

> Revelation is not a personal self-disclosure of the Divine ... There remains beyond the revelation the impenetrable mystery of the Divine. What the revelation does is to give men to know how God wills that men should live. It has a practical intent ... the substance of what God reveals is His will rather than His nature, and the end of revelation is obedience rather than perfect knowledge. God sends rather than comes.[19]

Understandably then, Islam becomes a religion that focuses on the law rather than metaphysics. On his part, Cragg argues that the Christian understanding of the revelation of the personality of God is more plausible:

> For the revelation is not simply a law to be followed, or a set of facts to be believed or even a history to be accepted. It is the offer of a relationship. It *brings*, it is true, a law to obey and involves facts and history, but it *is* essentially a relationship to be received and experienced. Its doctrine of God means fellowship with God: its doctrine of man means repentance, forgiveness, and regeneration. All that it proclaims and asserts, it offers and imparts. It is a proclamation unto experience.[20]

The Gospels make clear that Jesus was not only bringing a special message. He personified what God reveals. He was not only an "emissary" but the personality in and through whom God is known. Whereas in Islam the Qur'an is the very "text" of divine truth, the New Testament is the access to the Christ-expression of God. The Scripture has its being by derivation from the prior and primarily reality of "the Word made flesh" (John 1:14).

The Christian understanding of revelation is morally realistic and spiritually fitting. Many sincere seekers confess that spiritual insight remains inadequate at the level of abstraction. They long for an embodiment of spiritual precepts in the context of human relationships and the ordering of community. It is therefore reasonable to expect that God will not only reveal the requirements of his law, but personally exemplify them through an obedient life lived out in the ambiguities of human interactions. That is to say, both divine revelation and the personal intervention of God are necessary since nothing less would be adequate to overcome the predicament of the human condition. Indeed, unless one realizes the magnitude of the obstacles to religious fulfillment, one will not be open to the deeper dimensions of revelation emphasized by Christians who insist on the necessity of God's personal revelation in Jesus. In Barth's words, "He comes therefore as helper, as a redeemer, as one who brings another and proper order ... he comes as the kingdom of God in person."[21]

How did Jesus translate God's revelation into saving action of God? He did so by manifesting the truth and glory of God that entails judgment to overcome wrong and establish righteousness, and so bring man his salvation. The category of Royal Man aptly captures how Jesus' vocation brings about saving action. First, Jesus' existence transforms accepted values in his favoring the lowly and in his fellowship with sinners. In fellowship and conformity with this God who is poor in the world the royal man Jesus is also poor, and fulfills this transvaluation of all values, acknowledging those who (without necessarily being better) are in different ways poor as this world counts poverty.

Second, Jesus did not consciously seek to replace the existing social orders with new orders that presume to be more just. He preached in the synagogues and accepted the cultus of the Temple, the order of the family, the socio-economic orders of his day and even subjection to Roman imperialism. Neither did Jesus align himself with any of the contending parties for power. His actions and attitudes are genuinely revolutionary given the fact that he transcends all party lines and political programs, either conservative or progressive. Indeed, he places all programs and principles under scrutiny. Jesus relativised each of them by the higher demands of the kingdom of God. Jesus' "royal" freedom brought a sense of crisis to all entrenched social relationships, principles and powers that had hitherto presumed to have unquestioned authority.

The manifestation of Jesus' royal character is always attenuated by his self-humiliation. Still, the clues to his royal character could be seen in the distinctiveness and dignity with which he encountered his fellowmen. For example, Jesus always demanded a decision in response to him, given his unforgettable uniqueness and authority. Indeed, so powerful and lasting was his presence that the early church's witnesses were compelled to assert that the same presence was effectively working among them after his death and resurrection. As one who demands to be followed, Jesus simultaneously gives others the freedom to do so.

The Muslim asks why the world remains very much the same. Is this not evidence of the incompleteness of Jesus' mission that will be completed by Muhammad the later and final prophet? For these Muslims, the "incompleteness" of Jesus' achievement was evident given the continuation of Roman power and the tenacity of Jewish religion. Ali Shariati suggested that in the face of these insurmountable obstacles, only the ascetic option was available to Jesus. Unfortunately, Jesus' ministry was counted as deficient and that was judged evident when the ascetic ideals of Jesus became so influential that it stunted social development in the Middle Ages. On his part, Shariati was looking for the "Ideal Man" who holds the sword of Caesar in his hand and the heart of Jesus in his breast. For him, it was precisely because Jesus lacked the first quality that his mission was judged to be partial in its success and inferior to Muhammad's.[22]

But if Jesus was assigned an inferior role, why do Muslims still hold onto an eschatological expectation of the return of Jesus? Investigation into this peculiar attitude provides an unexpected opportunity to penetrate deeper into the Muslim perception of Jesus in the light of Muhammad. Cragg finds a helpful entry in the words of Khalid Muhammad Khalid:

> He [Jesus] was the love which knows no hatred, the peace which knows no restlessness, the salvation which knows no perishing. And when we realize all these things on earth, we shall then comprehend the return of Christ ... He is peace and love and truth and good and beauty. With Muhammad the faithful we declare: "Christ, not Barabbas, the true not the false, love not hatred, peace not war, life not extinction."[23]

This characterization represents one high point in the Muslim perception of Jesus. But Cragg observes that although Islam provides Jesus with an eschatological dimension, the final worth remains assigned to Muhammad. After all, Muhammad acted with the historical realism which is perceived to be wanting in Jesus. The tension involved in juxtaposing the two founders of faith is evident, "If Islamic traditions need to anticipate a Christ-style future, Jesus needed to anticipate a Muhammad-style future, the one in eternal the other in temporal terms. The Gospel may have it right in the ultimate;

the Qur'an has it right in the concrete."[24] Nevertheless, notwithstanding the high estimation accorded to Jesus, he remains subordinate to Muhammad.

Indeed, the "non-success" of Jesus only underscores the fact that the ultimate "kingdom of God" was yet to come. We are told that Jesus' partial attempt serves as a foretaste of the success of Muhammad in bringing in the kingdom. For this reason it is important to realize that though Islamic theology assigns Jesus the role of defeating the *Al-Dajjal* (Anti-Christ), nevertheless, the fact that the eschatological Jesus will eventually have to resort to force only proves that the Islamic dimension was lacking in Jesus' first coming. As Cragg put it in such ironic terms, "We have a Jesus in emphatic, final espousal of Islam: we have a Muhammad in ultimate accomplishment only through the agency of Jesus."[25]

It is therefore premature for Christians to rest cozy on the high honors granted to Jesus by Muslims. Such honors are partial and still amount to a diminution of Christ. After all, the universal and final moral exemplar is not Jesus but Muhammad. This is the natural outcome arising from the assumption that Jesus failed in his historic mission. In contrast,

> Muhammad became the universal exemplar. The assumption, theologically unexamined, was that in *this* particular – Muhammad in Arabia A.D. 570–632 – the universal made itself manifest. The good, worthy to be the timeless example, was available for recognition and imitation, *in this life at that time*. This meeting of the universal and the particular, the plural and the singular, the eternal and the temporal, is the ultimate mystery of all existence.[26]

The Christian response would be to insist that to judge the mission of Jesus to be a failure is to ignore the eschatological consummation waiting to be fulfilled in Jesus' second coming. Indeed, to use a language that echoes Muslim Jihad, Jesus is prosecuting the war of the Lamb to bring about final victory or consummation for the kingdom of God. Thus we read Barth's paraphrase of Revelation 11:15, "the kingdoms of this *world* are to become the kingdoms of our Lord and of his Christ" immediately, undialectically, incontrovertibly, irresistibly … Then he will be not only the Reconciler, then he will be the Redeemer, the Savior of the world" (Titus 2:13).[27] Christian eschatology looks forward, not merely to a better future but also to a future which in its perfection includes and surpasses absolutely all the matters of history. The appropriate posture from the Christian perspective is to hope while waiting for God's sovereign timing. We recall that when the disciples asked the resurrected Jesus when he would restore the kingdom of Israel, Jesus replied, "It is not for you to know the times or dates the Father has set by his own authority" (Acts 1:7).

3. Beyond *Shirk* to Salvation

But Muslims reject the Christian eschatological hope with their insistence that such a projection is premised on the questionable claim that God was in Christ. This rejection is further reinforced by the theological objection to the crucifixion on grounds that there is no need for atonement. If human beings are born good and innocent (*fitra*), if sin is only forgetfulness and not rebellion, then what is needed is not atonement but education. Obviously, conflicting theological anthropologies have to be resolved here. But at this juncture our question is, how does the revelation of Jesus Christ answer the human predicament? If indeed sin is rebellion, then how can God provide reconciliation without compromising his holiness? If revelation is proof of divine compassion how then is Christ the focal point of divine compassion?

The Christian view is that precisely because God is the loving and holy Creator, he is not free to be indifferent to rebellion within creation. What kind of a God is he who chooses to remain indifferent while evil men continue to flout his law and oppress the weak and righteous? God could have opted to command and coerce obedience at a distance or through angelic intermediaries. However, he chooses to remedy the fault from within creation himself. Such concerns form the basis of Cragg's searching question, "Can God remain sovereign apart from redemption?"[28] The incarnation of Christ and his atoning work on the cross indicate that because God is sovereign he is prepared to condescend himself and bear the price of reconciling rebellious human beings to himself.

It is precisely at this point that the most fundamental difference between Islam and Christianity becomes evident. One cannot evade the uncompromising insistence of Islam that there can be no association with God. God does not forgive the association of a partner with himself: a lesser sin than that he forgives to whom he wills (Surah 4:48, 116).

To be sure, the Qur'anic insistence was a forceful rejection of polytheism common among Arabs at that time, which included teaching that God had wives (Surah 72:3), sons (Surah 2:116; 6:100–101; 10:68; 17:111; 18:4; 19:91–92; 21:26; 25:2) and daughters (Surah 6:100; 16:57; 17:40; 37:149–153; 43:19; 53:27). It was all too easy within the context for Muhammad to misunderstand the designation "son of God." For example, Surah 4:171 and Surah 5 rejects the Trinity on grounds that it amounts to tri-theism.

The rejection of association with God and of the idea that God begets is emphatically found in Surah 112:1–4:

> Say: He is God, the One and Only;
> God, the Eternal, Absolute;
> He begets not, nor is He begotten;
> And there is none like unto Him.

Undoubtedly, Muslims protest that acceptance of the incarnation would be tantamount to an *apotheosis* of a man. To acknowledge the deity of Christ is seen as committing the sin of *shirk* (sin of association). To this, Cragg deftly points out that similar but unacknowledged logical moves are involved even for the Muslims' understanding of the revelation of divine will.

It is undeniable that linking eternal attributes to anything other than God poses an immediate logical problem. In other words, if Christian revelation is challenged to answer the charge of an *apotheosis* of man, by the same token, the charge of an *apotheosis* of language confronts the alternative Islamic understanding of revelation. God may transcend the boundaries of human language and religious experience. But surely, asked Cragg, his transcendence cannot negate our human God-talk and human religious activities like prayer and worship. Indeed, such admission is a pre-requisite to any possible appreciation of Jesus as the focal point where divine expectation and human response meet. Craig also counters that:

> We do not do justice to that unutterable transcendence, however, if we plead it to negate what *is* given in revelation. Surpassing mystery is one thing, total enigma would be another ... There could be no obeying a wholly elusive Lordship ... Revelation becomes a sorry joke if its claims are no more than a tantalizing stance, an "as-if" which derides us when it most enjoins. "We have not created the heaven and the earth and all they hold together as if We jested" (Sura 21:16, 44:37). We must not equate the frailty of language with the futility of faith.[29]

Reservation about the possibility of God's revelation in Christ is understandable for Muslims endued with great zeal to preserve the transcendence and sovereignty of God. The Christian response must be to stress that the question whether the incarnation did or did not occur has to be settled eventually by an investigation of the historical records, and that our conceptual formulation of God should be shaped in a response to how the one God has actually revealed himself to be. The Christian must patiently and firmly assert that:

> If God is personal, knowledge of Him must be a personal revelation. He can never be only prepositional ... And the "Who" cannot be known except in Self-communication. Words, teaching, ideas, propositions, must become "the Word" – experience, fellowship – before revelation is complete ... Revelation is not simply recorded in a book; it is embodied in a Person.[30]

To be sure, the Christian must remain sensitive to the Muslim's misgivings that in the teaching of the incarnation of God in Christ, the unity and sovereignty of God were compromised nevertheless. Cragg, on his part, expresses reservation at the propriety of translating the word *shirk* into the English word "association." This, he considers as misleading. With his considerable competence in Arabic, he argues that the actual restriction is a "plural" worship, alienating what alone is divine to what is not, as idolatry in all its forms.[31]

Divine revelation therefore includes creating relationships that need not be rejected on grounds of *shirk*. On the contrary, the divine-human relationship is a logical conclusion of divine rule over his creatures. Semitic religions point to a God who is vitally concerned with man. This concern flows from the Creator/creature relationship, which is further characterized by the giving of the law and revelation, guidance and reminder, command and submission. Does this Christian view of "God in Christ" somehow unwarrantably and improperly "compromise" God? Cragg answers that "God in Christ" is consistent with the nature of God to rule, to respond and to care. We see parallels in Islamic language of "sending" and "mission" in the prophetic sense of *risalah*. That is to say, the Creator has a stake in the creature. Divine intervention in human affairs cannot compromise God since he is only exercising his authority over what he inherently owns. One may even push the argument further and affirm that "It was an act of divine benevolence God was obliged to perform. The concept of divine justice requires requital of evil, compensation for innocence, and what is salutary for man."[32]

Muslims rightly reject any attempt to ascribe ultimacy to anything outside of God. The Christian shares this insistence but goes further by insisting that such negation should be redemptive. In this regard, God's sovereignty should include his ability to enact the drama of redemption within the flux of history. Otherwise God would remain in splendid isolation and irrelevant to humankind.

By the same token, there is no reason why we have to accept the Islamic restriction of prophethood that negates the possibility of the Incarnation. Indeed, the life of Christ confirms a prophethood that is deepened, if not climaxed, in a one-for-all incarnate revelation of God. As the writer of the book of Hebrews testified:

> In the past God spoke to our forefathers through the prophets at many times and in various ways, but in these last days he has spoken to us by his Son, whom he appointed heir of all things, and

through whom he made the universe. The Son is the radiance of God's glory and the exact representation of his being, sustaining all things by his powerful word. (Heb. 1:1–3)

Notes

[1] *http://www.asianews.it/view.php?l=en&art=584.*
[2] *The Gospel of Barnabas* (tr. L. and L. Ragg, Oxford: Clarendon Press, 1907).
[3] David Shenk and Badru Kateregga, *Islam and Christianity: A Muslim and a Christian in Dialogue* (Grand Rapids, MI: Eerdmans 1981), pp. 34–38.
[4] Muhammad 'Ata ur-Rahim, *Jesus, Prophet of Islam* (Omar Brothers, 1978), p. 223.
[5] Muhammad 'Ata ur-Rahim, *Jesus, Prophet of Islam*, p. 222.
[6] *Hadith Al-Bukhari*, MSA-USC Hadith Database. Internet edition found in *http://www.usc.edu/dept/MSA/reference/searchhadith.html*. A handy one volume collection of the hadiths can be found in the *Summarized Sahih Al-Bukhari* (trans. Muhammad Muhsin Khan; Darussalam Pub, 1996).
[7] J. Lindblom, *Prophecy in Ancient Israel* (Philadelphia: Fortress, 1962), p. 46.
[8] Reginald Fuller, *Foundations of New Testament Christology* (Charles Scribner's Sons, 1965), p. 109.
[9] Edward Schillebeeckx, *Interim Report on the Book Jesus and Christ* (London: SCM, 1980), pp. 65–66.
[10] Schillebeeckx, *Interim Report*, p. 67.
[11] N. T. Wright, *Jesus and the Victory of God* (Christian origins and the question of God, vol. 2; London/Minneapolis: SPCK/Augsburg-Fortress, 1996), pp. 477, 517.
[12] Wright, *Victory of God*, pp. 643–44.
[13] Wright, *Victory of God*, p. 653.
[14] For discussion on this view see Chawkat Moucarry, *Faith to Faith* (Leicester: Inter-Varsity Press, 2001), pp. 134–37.
[15] David Brown, *The Cross of the Messiah* (London: SPCK, 1969), p. 31, quoted in Colin Chapman, *Cross and Crescent* (Leicester: Inter-Varsity Press, 1995), p. 198.
[16] Ismail Faruqi, *Islam and Other Faiths* (Islamic Foundation, 1998), p. 120.
[17] Karl Barth, *Church Dogmatics* I/1 (ed. G. W. Bromiley and T. F. Torrance; Edinburgh: T&T Clark, 1936–1969), p. 353.

18 H. R. Mackintosh, *Types of Modern Theology* (Nisbet, 1937), p. 281.
19 Kenneth Cragg, *Call of the Minaret* (Oxford: Oxford University Press, 1964), pp. 47–48. See also his discussion in *Jesus and the Muslim* (George Allen & Unwin, 1985) and *The Christ and the Faiths* (London: SPCK, 1986).
20 Cragg, *Call of the Minaret*, pp. 277–78.
21 Barth, *CD* IV/1, p. 216.
22 See Kenneth Cragg, *Jesus and the Muslim*, pp. 51, 52.
23 Cragg, *Jesus and the Muslim*, p. 52.
24 Cragg, *Jesus and the Muslim*, p. 53.
25 Cragg, *Jesus and the Muslim*, p. 59.
26 Cragg, *Call of the Minaret*, p. 100.
27 Karl Barth, *Credo* (London: Hodder & Stoughton, 1936), p. 122.
28 Cragg, *Call of the Minaret*, p. 312.
29 Cragg, *Jesus and the Muslim*, p. 200.
30 Cragg, *Call of the Minaret*, p. 290.
31 Cragg, *Jesus and the Muslim* p. 204.
32 Cragg, *Jesus and the Muslim*, p. 202.

10

The Law of Love According to Confucius and Paul

Cruciform Love and *Ren Ren* (Benevolent Persons) of Becoming Fully Human

KK Yeo

I was raised in an atheist family with deep devotion to the teaching of Confucius. I became a Christian in high school and thought then that to be a Christian Confucianist was not to destroy my cultural tradition but to fulfill it. I acknowledge Christ to be the only Lord and savior, but believe that, whereas Christ can save Chinese culture, Confucian thought can contextualize the gospel of Christ for the Chinese. Over the years, the cross has become the most meaningful of symbols and the event that has enabled me to construct my Chinese Christian identity.[1] In this chapter I want to highlight the radical commandment of Jesus Christ in loving one's enemy, in contrast to the sacrificial love in Confucian thought. Before that I will compare and contrast the interpretation of the love commandment of Paul with the understanding of *ren ren* (benevolent persons) of Confucius. The purpose is to show that to be a full Confucianist is to be a Christian, and to be a Confucianist Christian is to practice love as taught by Confucius and Christ. I will use the Analects as my resource on the teaching of Confucius, and the New Testament, especially Pauline writings, on the teaching of Christ.[2]

1. Law of *Ren* (Love) in Life of Holiness

1.1 Ren (benevolence, fully human) and co-humanity

1.1.1 The semantic of ren

The word *ren* – benevolence or love – is a key concept in the teaching of Confucius. In the relatively short book of the Analects, the word is used no less than eighty times. *Ren* can be used either in the narrow sense of one's desirable virtues (e.g. in Analects 9:29, 14:28) or more often in the broad sense of the encompassing ethical ideal (e.g. 14:4).[3] In Analects 12:22, *ren* is equated with love (for fellow human beings).[4] In Analects 22:12, when asked the meaning of *ren*, Confucius replied that *ren* is to love people (*ai ren*). According to Analects 22:12, the translation of *ren* as "benevolence" or "love" is apt. But *ren* is not just loving one's fellow beings (12:22); it is to be empathetic/conscientious (*zhong*) and merciful/reciprocal (*shu*, Analects 4:15). *Ren* also carries within it all the moral qualities that govern the relationships between two or more human beings.[5]

1.1.2 Ren as co-humanity

Confucius regards *ren* as the fountain head of all virtues. The Chinese character for *ren* is composed of two ideograms: "person" connotes self or a human being, and "two" connotes relation.[6] Etymologically, *ren* is to be translated simply as human-relatedness, and human-relatedness is defined specifically as love, which is the cardinal principle of human relationships.[7] As vividly expressed by Fang Ying-hsien, "in terms of two semiotic foci: *ren* is (1) the tender aspect of human feelings, namely, love, and (2) an altruistic concern for others ..."[8] Fang's first point on feelings is a modern psychological projection on Confucius' thought world, but his second point is well taken. For Confucius says, "In order to establish oneself, one must establish others" (Analects 6:30). To be truly human is to be responsible to and for others, and "the others" are not specified in Analects 6:30; they could be family members, friends, superiors, or enemies. But the emphasis on edifying and caring for others is clear.

1.2 Ren ren: To be a benevolent person is to become fully human

Benevolence is universally cherished whether it is expressed culturally as *ren* or *agape* (sacrificial love, divine love). Confucian *ren* and Pauline *agape* are not the same; one concerns with love that extends from family to others in a structured society, the other concerns with self-sacrificing love for others in extending the family of God. The different ways of extending love between Confucian and Pauline ethics can be traced to their different understanding of heaven (*tian*) and God (*Theos*). Confucius lacks Paul's understanding of personhood or personality of God, but he does share Paul's awe and reverence before death. Because of this lack of God awareness, the move forward or aspiration for Confucius is not to God but to full humanity, i.e. to creatively fulfill the mandate of heaven by being *ren ren* (a benevolent person). Thus, to become a benevolent or humane person, one has to follow the established norms, the rites (*li*), the way (*dao*), to be moral (*de*) and to love (*ai*) others. If "one observes the rites and rituals and overcomes oneself, one will be benevolent" (Analects 12:1).[9] Conforming to the rites and being guided by virtues, one will not only have a sense of shame when one fails to do so, but one will also be able to reform oneself when that occurs (Analects 2:3). Confucius believes that once on the road of desiring and pursuing benevolence (*ren*), one will have the resources to continue (Analects 4:6). In contrast to Confucius' forward move to full humanity, Paul's cry of helplessness in his moral and spiritual frustration confesses his captivity in law of sin and his own wretchedness. Paul also cries for help from "God – through Jesus Christ our Lord" (Rom. 7:24–25). The moral resources for Confucius are rites (*li*) and virtues (*de*), the spiritual resource for Paul is "law of the Spirit of life" in Christ Jesus (Rom. 8:2). Despite these differences, Confucius' understanding of *ren ren* may be comparable with Paul's understanding of Jesus Christ as the "best humanity" who loves sacrificially.

Confucius advocates that one must desire and pursue benevolence – "Is benevolence really far away? No sooner do I desire it than it is here" (Analects 7:30).[10] According to Confucius, a benevolent person (*ren ren*) desires (*yu*) benevolence and finds it close by. In contrast, Paul confesses that evil lies at hand (Rom. 7:21), and that an "unspiritual [person], sold as a slave to sin" (Rom. 7:14) cannot do the good he or she wants to do, instead only do the evil he or she does not want (Rom. 7:18–20). Confucius would say that "there is benevolence in me," but Paul says that "there is nothing good in me" (Rom. 7:18). In Galatians 5:16–17 Paul speaks of "desires of the sinful nature." The different moral tones and views of anthropology between Confucius and Paul – one sees the resourcefulness in human beings, the other sees the depravity – can be traced to their different assumptions of heaven (*tian*) and God (*Theos*), as we have mentioned earlier. These different views of God (theologies) result in different ethics. Consequently, Confucius uses the word "desire" (*yu*) to mean a resolved preference for the highest principle of life – love, whereas Paul uses the words "covet" (*epithymia*) and "will" (*thelô*) to mean desire captivated by sin.

Despite the differences between the ethics of Confucius and that of Paul, they share a common view on a person of love as one who seeks to edify others. This is what Confucius means by *ren ren* and what Paul means by Christ's sacrificial love on the cross. When Confucius was asked by his disciple, Zi Gong, if there were people who gave liberally to the common people and brought relief to many and, if so, were they to be considered *ren ren* (benevolent persons)? Confucius replied that they were more than benevolent, they were perhaps sages (a sage is superior to *ren*). He mentioned that the sage-rulers, Yao and Shun, would find it difficult to accomplish so much as that – giving sacrificially to all people and bringing help to the multitude. Both Yao and Shun had practiced benevolent government by appointing people who were gifted and trustworthy (Yao used Shun as regent and Shun used Yu) rather than their unworthy sons (Yao's son Dan-zhu and Shun's son Shang-jun) (Analects 6:30).[11] Confucius explained what *ren ren* means: A *ren ren* (benevolent person) is one who establishes others in order to establish oneself (in ritual), and who helps others to succeed. Roger T. Ames and Henry Rosemont, Jr explain that "correlating one's conduct with those near at hand can be said to be the method of becoming"[12] a *ren ren*.

By this measure one could say Jesus Christ qualifies to be a *ren ren* and a sage, for his passion shows his preoccupation not with death, but with his faithfulness to give himself completely for the sake of humanity. Christ died on the cross as a fully human because of his *ren* (sacrificial love). Jesus exhibits the spiritual and moral quality to be fully human by his complete trust and his love for all despite the reality of human sin.

1.3 Spirit and law, li and ren

There is a subtle difference between the ethics of Confucius and Paul with regard to love (*ren* or *agapê*) and the law (*li* or torah): Paul sees that *agapê* (divine love) supersedes the *torah* (love fulfills the requirement of the law), whereas Confucius sees the mutually supplementary roles of *ren* (love) and *li* (ritual propriety).

In Galatians 5:18 Paul writes that those led by the Spirit are not under the law. They are not against the law, in fact they fulfill the law. The fruit of the Spirit fulfills the law – "Against such [fruit of the Spirit] there is no law" (Gal. 5:23). However, the works of the flesh oppose not only the Spirit, but also violate the law (Gal. 5:17). There is no law that runs against the fruit of the Spirit. Similarly, in Confucius' thought ritual propriety (*li*) is grounded in and fulfills *ren*, *li* should not go against *ren*. In order to be *ren* (benevolent), one must be persistent in the daily practice of following *li*, the rites/rituals (Analects 12:1). This is true especially for political rulers and those who seek to cultivate virtues in themselves in order to be leaders.

Despite the emphasis on rituals and rules in his ethics, Confucius is aware of the dual dangers of ritualism and legalism. Paul wrestles with his opponents in Galatia on how to make the Jewish law meaningful to the identity of the Gentile Christians. Though the problems are not the same, the responses of Confucius and Paul to *li* (ritual propriety) and *torah* (Jewish rules of life and faith) are similar in that, both use love (whether *ren* or *agapê*) to subvert law (whether *li* or *torah*), and consequently fulfilling the spirit of the law. We shall see in the next section how "loving one's neighbors" for Paul means fulfilling the law. Here we look at how similar it is for Confucius to speak of fulfilling *li* (rites) by means of *ren* (love).

Confucius grounds *li* in *ren*. It is possible for a person to love another merely for the sake of duty (although that would be a religious achievement and a noble task). But Confucius teaches that loving for the sake of filial piety can be superficial. The example is given in the Analects (2:7) – which I have used a number of times already: "Merely to feed one's parents for the sake of piety without reverence ... even dogs and horses are fed" (Analects 2:7). Merely doing what is expected of *li* (rites) is right and dutiful, what is essential however is the higher principle of *ren* (benevolence). Therefore, *li* must be grounded in *ren*.[13] *Li* (ritual) without *ren* can degenerate into formalism or insensitivity that make one less and less human. Analects 3:3 also says, "If a person is without *ren* (love), what has he/she to do with *li* (ritual or ceremonies)?"

Scholars are divided on the question of interpreting the relationship between *ren* and *li*. Analects 12:1 seems to put *li* over *ren*. In the essay "*Ren* and *Li* in the Analects," Shun summarizes the debate as follows:

> According to Xu Fuguan, one of the most important innovations of Confucius is the discovery of the ideal inner life, which he characterizes in terms of the *ren* ideal. Confucius gives the traditional *li* rules a justification in terms of the *ren* ideal, thereby giving *ren* evaluative priority over *li*. And, according to Lin Yu-sheng, *ren* is an ideal inner life that has ultimate value, whereas *li* derives its value from *ren* through the instrumental role it plays in the cultivation and development of *ren*. Accordingly, *ren* has evaluative priority over *li*, and provides a perspective from which one can justify the revision of a *li* rule.

This way of interpreting Confucius contrasts sharply with that proposed by Zhao Jibin and Cai Shangsi ... According to Zhao Jibin, Confucius regards the content of *ren* as determined by *li*, and the observance of the *li* practices of his time as providing the sole criterion for distinguishing between the possession and lack of *ren*. In doing so, Confucius has given *li* a priority over *ren*. Furthermore, because the ideal is just to observe the existing *li* practices, this conception of the relation between *ren* and *li* is opposed to any revision of or departure from the existing *li* practices. Cai Shangsi proposes a similar interpretation. According to him, *li* is the most important concept in Confucius' moral thinking, and it is *li* that distinguishes human beings from other animals. Observance of *li* is the criterion for the possession of *ren*, and Confucius' conception of the *ren* person is just the conception of someone who follows the existing *li* rules in all areas of life.[14]

This is a significant debate for at least two reasons. The first being that if Xu and Lin's reading is correct, then Confucius' teaching can constantly be *reinterpreted* in new contexts and be made relevant based on the conviction that *ren* (love), being the highest principle of life, can change the cultural norms of every land. Wherever Zhao's and Cai's reading is preferred, however, with priority given to *li* over *ren*, Confucianist ethics have tended to be conservative.

Second, the two readings have implications for the cross-cultural hermeneutic advanced here. The former reading (*ren* over *li*) allows the ideals of Confucius' teaching to be more easily applied to other cultures than would the latter reading (*li* over *ren*). While the latter reading defines more precisely than the former the essence of Confucianist anthropology, it seems rigid and therefore difficult to translate across cultural divides. There is no intention here to resolve the tension between these two readings, since each reading has its textual support (with perhaps greater textual support for the first reading),[15] thus making the two interpretations plausible. But I do want to continue this cross-cultural reading of the texts and state up front that my bias prefers the first reading because of my cross-cultural commitment. This commitment is to find meaningful connections across cultures through the comparative readings of texts. I borrow from Galatians to read the Analects, and in the same manner I constantly borrow the lenses of virtue from the Analects to read Paul's letter to the Galatians.[16] To speak of "Paul's way of *ren ren*" is an example of viewing Paul's reinterpretation of the law via the lens of Confucius' new understanding of *li* (rites) by means of *ren* (love).

2. Paul's Way of *Ren Ren*: Love for One's Neighbors

Can love become legalistic and rigid? Can *ren* become *li* and a law? Can the ritual of love overcome ritualism? These questions Confucius was concerned with can be phrased in the language of Paul: Can the "law of Christ" – to bear one another's burden and to love one's neighbor (Gal. 6:2) – ever become a rule of life that binds the Gentile and Jewish Christians? Paul thinks that the law of Christ or the law of love can guarantee greatest good and maximum freedom for the Christians in Galatia.

In Galatians 5:13–15 Paul suggests that for Gentile believers a life pleasing to God and a life of freedom ought to include the yoke of the law as stated in Leviticus 19:18. Paul's emphasis here on the necessity to fulfill the whole law recalls his earlier argument in Galatians 3:10, 12, and 5:3. The entirety of the law must be upheld if one wishes to receive the blessings the law provides. For those who can do so the law is a blessing; for those who cannot the law becomes a curse.

Here, Paul's hermeneutic of loving one's neighbor as a way of loving God is actually commonly used by New Testament writers to maintain the continuity between the Jewish law and Christ. New Testament writers reinterpret the fulfillment of the whole Mosaic law in terms of the one commandment in Leviticus 19:18 (see Matt. 5:43; 19:19; 22:39; Mark 12:31; 12:33; Luke 10:27; Rom. 13:9; Jas. 2:8).[17] Among the New Testament writers, Paul, and possibly James also, best understand the radical gospel of Jesus since both Paul and James highlight "loving your neighbor" as the *summation* of Jewish law.[18]

2.1 *Fulfillment of the whole law via Leviticus 19:18*

In Galatians 5:14 the whole law is said to be fulfilled in one word (*en eni logo*), i.e. the one commandment, of Leviticus 19:18. The whole law (*ho pas nomos*) refers to the *unity* of all requirement of the laws. It is different from *holon ton nomon* ("the entire law") in Galatians 5:3 which refers to all the precepts of the law. Scholars disagree on how the law is fulfilled. Peter Stuhlmacher postulates that the "Zion Torah" is inaugurated by the messiah in the eschatological age through his obedient death so that the Mosaic law, promised to all nations (Mic. 4:1–4; Isa. 2:2–4; 25:7–9; Jer. 31:31–34; Ezek. 20; 36:22–28; 40–48), might be made relevant to the Gentiles.[19] Paul may have been influenced by this interpretation of the messiah, but more evidence of such a messianic movement is needed. Galatians makes no mention of the death of the messiah as fulfilling the Jewish law: It contends that the messiah died as a curse to lift the curse of the law (Gal. 3:13–14), but the language of fulfillment is absent. Stuhlmacher's interpretation would make sense if one were to link the obedient death of the messiah to the love commandment of Leviticus 19:18, but again (Gal. 5:14) no link is stated. It makes better sense to say simply that the ceremonial requirements of the laws are not applicable to Gentiles, that only the moral-spiritual commandments are apt – which can be summarized by the one commandment of Leviticus 19:18.

2.2 Paul's reinterpretation of the whole Law into "Law of Christ"

"Carry each other's burdens, and in this way you will fulfill the law of Christ" (Gal. 6:2). Bearing one another's burden is to encourage solidarity in the community. The "burden" (*baros*) is not spelled out – Paul's intent is to be general – but it covers all the human frailties and troubles found in a community.[20]

Though the phrase "fulfill the law of Christ" (Gal. 6:2) may recall Galatians 5:14 ("the entire law is summed up in a single commandment" [Lev. 19:18]), the phrase occurs only here in the New Testament. The closest to it in the New Testament is 1 Corinthians 9:21, which has *ennomos Christou* (under Christ's law). Here Paul explains that for the sake of those outside the law (i.e. the Gentiles), he identifies with those outside the law (i.e. Gentile believers) even though he believes himself to be "under Christ's law."[21] A similar occurrence is in James 2:8. Though James 2:8 does not use the phrase "the law of Christ," his interpretation of the love commandment in Leviticus 19:19 as the "royal law" (*nomon basilikon*) seems to link the two thoughts found in Galatians 6:2 with Galatians 5:14. Galatians

5:14 does not contain the words "the law of Christ"; Paul's point in 5:14 is on fulfillment of the entire law. The common understanding is that the new law of Christ, or the "royal law" of God is not an abolition but fulfillment of the Jewish law.

That Jewish law as a whole needs to be fulfilled even in the Messiah age is part of Paul's theological conviction. By subsuming the whole of the law under the law of Christ, Paul constructs a new reality and a new identity for Gentile Christians. The Gentile Christian movement owes its roots and identity to its Jewish neighbors. It is true that Gentile believers are not required to observe the "works of the law," but that does not mean they are lawless people. They have the "law of Christ" to fulfill.

2.3 The significance of Paul's reinterpretation of the law

Paul's reinterpretation of whole law by means of one law (Lev. 19:18) and into "the law of Christ" is significant in the following aspects.

First, the law, in spite of all its multiple precepts, does have *a unity*; in other words, the whole is greater than the parts. How can the fulfillment of one commandment keep the spirit of the law alive? Paul sees the summary of the law in the love commandment, thus understands the purpose and essence of the law as captured by "loving one's neighbors."

Secondly, the use of Leviticus 19:18 as fulfillment of the whole law is to be understood as *love for humanity*. Intrinsic to the teaching of Leviticus 19:18 is God's will for humanity, viz., to be the people of God is to be a people characterized by love. Love as the ethical dimension of God's will for humanity occupies the main argument of Paul in the last two chapters of Galatians.

The giving of the law is a sacred event in which God wills his people to be his own among the nations and to be people characterized by love. The purpose of the law is to differentiate and to form the identity of the people of God – not to alienate them from other nations but so that their moral and theological identity might convey to other nations the will of God – for all to love one another.

Even though Paul has already shown that the law's function to mark the identity of the people of God ended when the messiah came, he does not seek to eliminate the law altogether. Paul knows the strength and the danger of using the law for moral formation. In this respect, Paul's theology is similar to Confucian ethic. Paul redefines the relationship between God and human beings in terms of grace and love in what God has done in Christ. The people of God are shown to love others as God has loved them. Thus, Paul interprets the law with the emphasis on *loving others*; this is similar to Confucius' ethic of *ren ren* – people who *love others*.

Thirdly, the commandment of love can be said to be *Jewish in origin but fulfilled by the faithfulness of Christ for the sake of Jews and Gentiles*, and thus to become "the law of Christ." As such, it is appropriate to speak of Christ being the end and the fulfillment of the law. And, it is appropriate to speak of bearing "each other's burdens, and in this way you will fulfill the law of Christ" (Gal. 6:2).

The law of Christ is the reinterpretation of the Mosaic law through Christ's "faithfulness unto death." One can even say the whole Christ event is hermeneutically summed up by Leviticus 19:18 – if one were to abstract the principle of love for humanity from the love of God in Christ. The law of Christ does not speak of a new law totally different from Mosaic law. In fact, the law of Christ is Mosaic law but read anew in light of the Christ event.

According to Paul, it is this reinterpretation of the Jewish law that results in twofold benefits for the people of God:

(a) For Jewish believers, the reinterpretation gives the Mosaic law new life and meaning since the Mosaic law in its custodian role has ceased and since the Jewish believers must live in the power of the Spirit (no longer living under the Mosaic law that manifests and controls sin) as adult heirs of God (thus in freedom and in ownership of God's inheritance).

(b) For the Gentile believers, the reinterpretation of the Mosaic law (via Lev. 19:18) now makes the God of the Jews relevant to them. This reinterpretation opens up to the

Gentiles a new existence in Christ, and one that produces the fruit of the Spirit. To this end the law of Christ is consistent with the intentions of the Mosaic law to grant life.

The controversy concerning which symbol best represents the people of God (the law or Christ) is ultimately determined by the freedom each gives. Yet, Paul's answer is not "either/or," but "both/and." So the answer for Paul is "the law of Christ."

Fourthly, H. D. Betz makes the subtle differentiation between "the Jew who is obliged to *do* the Torah (cf. 3:10, 12; 5:3; also 6:13) ... [and] the Christian *fulfills* the Torah through the act of love, to which he has been freed by Christ" (5:1, 13).[22] By fulfilling the law, one does not have to do every prescription of the law – though doing all the requirements is a noble task – one has to be committed to the essence of the law. Fulfilling the law implies obedience and being true to the spirit of the law. Paul alerts to the fact that in Galatia those who receive circumcision do not themselves keep the law (Gal. 6:13). Paul objects to external laws and ceremonies; he highlights the essence of the law, viz., love. The situation in Confucius' day was similar. A meticulous observance of the Zhou *li* or the *Book of Rites* (*Li Ji*) can protect one from errors, but it can also be an unbearable burden. "Fulfilling the law" as a whole through love is to know the fundamental thrust of the law and be able to live one's life out of the freedom to love. More significantly, fulfilling the law in the eschatological age means God's Spirit is guiding and empowering believers to live a life that bears the fruit of the Spirit, rather than struggling without the Spirit (i.e. flesh).

2.4 Law, freedom, and law of love

Paul's reinterpretation of the Jewish law by means of love seeks to create harmony and grant freedom for all. Dieter Georgi argues that Paul has new understanding of law after his reinterpretation. Georgi articulates that Paul does not see the law as "a demand, a norm, or an authority. It is, rather, an environment of loyalty and solidarity, of fidelity and confidence, of spirit and community. Thus the law becomes a prophetic entity, an expression of creative power and imagination. It establishes neither the past nor the present, binding and limiting the future. It opens the future and is a message of freedom."[23] This idea is consistent with Paul's understanding of the *law of love* as the law of freedom, that is, love makes us free, and as humans we are free to love.

It is clear from the example of the Galatian community that those who do the law without observing Leviticus 19:18 will still end up with divisiveness and self-destruction: "If you bite and tear each other, watch out or you will be destroyed by each other" (Gal. 5:15). Metaphors of animal violence (serpents biting [*daknein*, cf. Num. 21:6], lions devouring [*katesthiein*], wild beasts consuming [*analiskein*]) are used to describe the dangers inherent in community strife. Paul has suggested to the Gentile believers in Galatia that though the law plays no role in their religious identity in the age of Christ, the freedom for which Christ redeemed them necessitates that they reinterpret the whole law in the one commandment of Leviticus 19:18. It is this commandment that guaranteed freedom for the community.

This is what Paul means when he says love your neighbor to fulfill the law, and when in Romans 13:8, he writes, "Let no debt remain outstanding, except the continuing debt to love one another." Here Paul is saying that we can claim completion and perfection in all other religious duties but in the command of loving our neighbor Christians are always debtors. The obligation to love one another is not because others have done, but because of what God has done for all in Christ Jesus – or as Confucius would say, because heaven (*tian*) has imparted in human beings the nature of *ren* (love), heaven has mandated all to love (become *ren ren*).

The paradox of the love commandment is: love cannot be mandated. The law of loving one's neighbor can be practiced by everyone, it is the law of life, the mandate of *tian* (heaven). While Confucius uses the language of "best self" (*jun-zi*) to describe the virtue of a *ren ren* (a person who loves others), Paul uses the language of "serving one another in love" to speak of fulfilling the law.

3. Paul's Cruciform *Ren* and Love One's Enemies

Despite Confucius' ideal notion of *ren ren* and Paul's high command of "loving one's neighbor," they would find it difficult to accept Jesus' imperative to "love your enemies" (Matt. 5:43–48; Luke 6:27–36). Paul's "love your neighbor" in Galatians is still limited to racial, gender, and social differentiation, with a preference to love ("do good") to those in the household of faith (Gal. 6:10). Confucius' understanding of *ren*, comparable to the Stoic ideal of universal brotherhood, is still limited. The extension of self to others often stops short of concern for persons not family members. Familism in Confucianism prohibits strangers from being a part of the family/clan relationship.

Jesus' parable of the "Good Samaritan" (Luke 10) and his command to "love your enemies" are radical. Matthew and Luke suggest that to love one's enemies is a mark of a higher righteousness, because even tax collectors and Gentile sinners love their neighbors (Matt. 5:46). Matthew characterizes the mark of a higher righteousness as being perfect "as your heavenly Father is perfect" (Matt. 5:48); Luke characterizes the mark as being "merciful as your heavenly Father is merciful" (Luke 6:36). Therefore, as children of God, the love command pushes the envelope from loving ourselves to our family, our friends and our neighbors, and ultimately to our enemies. To be human is to embody the law of Life. Jesus said, "Do this and you will live" (Luke 10:28).

The comparison of Paul's and Confucius' understanding of loving others is helpful. However, once we compare their knowledge of the source and content of love, their views depart from each other radically. Such contrast is unfair because Confucius did not know Christ. Thus, Confucius may believe *tian* (heaven) to impart *ren* (love) as part of human nature (*xing*), but he does not know of the love of God as shown on the cross – *cruciform love*. Paul knows love among people, and he traces the source of that love to God, who demonstrates it by sacrificing his only begotten Son on the cross for the salvation of all humanity. Paul's understanding of the passion of Christ as the love of God can supplement Confucius' understanding of *ren* (love). The reflection below seeks to construct for Chinese Christians how the cruciform love challenges and fulfills the already highly idealized *ren* (love) as taught by Confucius. Paul's theology of the cruciform love and Confucius' ethics of love (*ren*) become the core of the theological and moral identity of Chinese Christians.

The cruciform love of God in Christ is the center of Paul's theology. It is radical of Paul to use the cross as the identity symbol by which Jews and Gentiles are united. The cross is a scandal and a stigma. In contrast to Paul's opponents who boast of the mark of circumcision, Paul places his confidence on nothing but the cross of Jesus Christ. "May I never boast except in the cross of our Lord Jesus Christ, through which the world has been crucified to me, and I to the world" (Gal. 6:14). Paul only boasts in the Lord Jesus Christ (cf. 1 Cor. 1:21; 2 Cor. 10:17; Phil. 3:3), that is, he boasts in the sign of the cross. In a culture in which the cross was reserved for criminals and rebels, Paul's statement that he boasts in the cross is absurd, if not shocking.

The reason for boasting in the cross is: "through which [the cross] the world has been crucified to me, and I to the world." In contrast to the opponents' fear of persecution, to their oppressive requirement of circumcising Gentile believers, Paul openly proclaims his confidence in the cross. The dominion of the present evil age (Gal. 1:4; 4:3, 9) was broken and rendered ineffective over Paul ("the world crucified to me"); and Paul dies to the power of evil, sin, and death ("I [am crucified] to the world").

The ethical implications of cruciform love for Chinese Christians are significant. The purpose of our work here is to reinterpret Confucian *ren* to have the content of Pauline cruciform love. Confucian *ren* does have a notion of self-sacrifice, and in that sense, Jesus can be said to be a *ren ren*, whose love for others makes him sacrifice his own life. Confucian *ren*, however, does not have the idea of "loving your enemies." Cruciform love reveals that Christ dies for all, including those who crucified him. This forgiving and self-sacrificing love of God for those who oppose and wound him can supplement the Confucian *ren* which often does not extend mercy beyond one's community. Cruciform love is God stooping down to reach and save sinners, even though they do not deserve grace.

Love, whether *ren* (benevolence toward others) or *agapê* (divine love), is reciprocal, but *agapê* is unconditional. The cruciform love does not demand of the other the satisfaction of one's own needs. *Ren* (love) does understand mutual indebtedness as the basic human condition. Cruciform love, however, does not require reciprocity of reward or repayment. Thus, *cruciform ren* (self-sacrificing love toward one's enemies) does not manipulate the other in order to minimize risk.

To be human is to be bound to God; and to be bound to God is to be bound to loving our neighbor. The test of faith/piety comes when our neighbors are our enemies. While sometimes enemies turn out to be good neighbors, cruciform love (*ren*) will continue even when the neighbor is an enemy. This test is especially important in Confucianist society where family/clan interests often marginalize outsiders. To live a life of the cruciform love is to hear the cry of the forsaken and despised neighbor whom God has created for our care.

God in Christ reveals to humanity how completely God identifies with "the forsaken and despised neighbor." Jesus' cry of dereliction (of God-forsakenness) on the cross ("Why has thou forsaken me?") echoes the cries of humanity in despair and yearning for hope. Christ, the beloved Son, became the God-forsaken one on the cross. He was treated as a victimized other, a rejected neighbor, and a crucified enemy. In this human tragedy (the crucifixion) divine pain is found. Here lie two paradoxes of faith and life that Confucian ethics can find its fulfillment: (1) Cruciform love is *the* way of *life* because Jesus' suffering love becomes God's suffering love for humanity. God is in Jesus *as* the Christ, we can imitate Jesus who shows us what it means to be fully human – in Confucius' language, to be *ren ren*, vis-à-vis, to love sacrificially even our enemies. (2) Divine love risks all – obedience even unto death, yet being totally vulnerable means trusting fully in God, and thus live fully as our "best self" – in Confucius' language, to be *jun-zi* (best self). Jesus was raised from death, proving that God has vindicated and exalted him.

Paul's way of highlighting cruciform love can enrich Confucius' understanding of *ren* in that, the reality of God in Christ informs the ethics of the people of God, vis-à-vis, divine grace is the spiritual force of ethics. Confucius sees morality (*de*) as the expression of heaven, *ren* the essence of being human. The apostle Paul teaches that divine grace is the foundation of ethics, cruciform love the way God redeems the world. Cruciform love for Chinese Christians, who combine Confucian ethics with Pauline theology, is the way to become fully human. Confucius and Paul have granted them resources to be fully human. The cruciform love of Paul's theology and Confucius' ethics of *ren ren* believe that to be human is to reach out in love. Both believe that no human being is alone. The other's welfare is our well-being; Christ's passion is our peace, and divine love the mandate for all to be human.

Notes

1 Yeo Khiok-khng, *What Has Jerusalem to Do with Beijing? Biblical Interpretation from A Chinese Perspective* (Harrisburg: Trinity Press International, 1998). My work, *Chairman Mao Meets the Apostle Paul: Christianity, Communism, and the Hope of China* (Grand Rapids: Brazos, 2002), is an extension of the previous work, with the narrower focus of reading the Thessalonian correspondence in the context of the Cultural Revolution in China. See also Charles H. Cosgrove, Herold Weiss, Yeo Khiok-khng, *Cross-cultural Paul* (Grand Rapids, MI: Eerdmans, forthcoming), and Yeo Khiok-khng, "Culture and Intersubjectivity as Criteria of Negotiating Meanings in Cross-cultural Interpretations," in Charles H. Cosgrove, ed., *The Meanings We Choose* (Edinburgh: T&T Clark, 2004), pp. 81–100.
2 This chapter is a portion of a larger work I am working on regarding the political ethics of Confucius and Paul. The project is partially funded by the Luce Foundation, coordinated though the Association of Theological Schools.
3 Shun Kwong-loi. "The Concepts of Jen and Li in the *Analects*," *Philosophy East and West* 43.3 (1993), p. 453 (457–79).
4 English readers need to be careful that the English transliteration "*ren*" can refer to two different Chinese words, 仁 (*ren*) and 人 (*ren*), meaning "benevolence" and "person" respectively. In this section we are discussing the first word 仁. When the two words

appear together, the order is always 仁 人 (*ren ren*), meaning "benevolent person." Since Chinese does not have articles and the word itself does not indicate singular or plural, *ren ren* can mean a benevolent person or benevolent persons.

5 Fung Yu-lan. *A Short History of Chinese Philosophy*, edited by Derk Bodde (New York: Macmillan, 1948), pp. 69–73, and Chan Wing-tsit, "Chinese and Western Interpretations of *Ren* (Humanity)," *Journal of Chinese Philosophy* 2 (1975), pp. 109–115, at p. 109.

6 Tu Wei-ming says, "Etymologically *ren* consists of two parts, one a simple ideogram of a human figure, meaning the self, and the other with two horizontal strokes, suggesting human relations." See *Confucian Thought: Selfhood as Creative Transformation* (Albany: State University of New York Press, 1985), p. 84.

7 Fung, *A Short History of Chinese Philosophy*, pp. 69–73.

8 Taken from Tu, *Confucian Thought*, p. 84.

9 My translation.

10 My translation.

11 D. C. Lau, translated, *Confucius: The Analects* (Harmondsworth: Penguin Books, 1979), p. 65.

12 Roger T. Ames and Henry Rosemont, Jr., *The Analects of Confucius: A Philosophical Translation* (New York: Random House, 1998), p. 110.

13 This is what Tu Wei-ming means by "the primacy of *ren* over *li* and the inseparability of *li* from *ren*." See his "*Li* as Process of Humanization," *Philosophy East and West* (1972), p. 188.

14 Shun, "Jen and Li in the *Analects*," p. 58.

15 See Shun, "Jen and Li in the *Analects*," pp. 59–61.

16 See Shun's interesting suggestion of bringing the two readings together: "On the instrumentalist interpretation, *ren* is an ideal that is intelligible and can be shown to have a validity independent of *li*; *li* is a means to realize this ideal and is to be evaluated in terms of its efficacy in performing this function. On the definitionalist interpretation, a *ren* person is just someone who generally observes the actually existing *li* practices, and advocacy of the ren ideal is linked to an extreme conservatism toward li. My proposed interpretation lies between the two extremes. On this interpretation, the ideal of ren is shaped by the actually existing li practices in that it is not intelligible and cannot be shown to have a validity independent of *li*. However, it is not totally determined by li because advocacy of the ideal allows room for departing from or revising an existing rule of li" ("Jen and Li in the *Analects*," p. 67).

17 R. Akiba (late first-century A.D.) says "Love is the greatest principle in the law." And Aristeas 229: "piety ... is the pre-eminent form of

beauty and its power lies in love, which the gift of God." But it is Paul who best interprets Jesus' radical reinterpretation of the Jewish law. See James Moffatt, *Love in New Testament* (London: Hodder & Stoughton, 1929); Victor P. Furnish, *The Love Command in the New Testament* (Nashville: Abingdon, 1972); Pheme Perkins, *Love Commands in the New Testament* (New York: Paulist, 1982); Viktor Warnach, *Agape: Die Liebe als Grundmotiv der neutesta-mentlichen Theologie* (Düsseldorf: Patmos-Verlag, 1951); Ceslaus Spicq, *Agapè dans le Nouveau Testament: Analyse des Textes* (Ètudes Bibliques 3 vols.; Paris: Libraire Lecoffre, 1958–1959). *Agape in the New Testament* (3 vols.; English translation; St. Louis: B. Herder Book, 1963–1966); Paul Brett, *Love Your Neighbour: The Bible as Christian Ethics Today* (London: Darton, Longman and Todd, 1992).

The greatest commandment is no doubt the *Shema*, which pious Jews repeat twice daily (Deut 6:4–5: love God with all that you are). However, according to Mark 12:31, Jesus links these two great commandments together ("Love God maximally" and "love your neighbor as yourself"), and adds that they "are more important than all burnt offerings and sacrifices" (Mark 12:33). Jesus is responding to the hostile questions of scribes and Sadducees (v. 28a) regarding the *protê entolê* ("chief commandment"). Jesus does not consider burnt offerings and sacrifices ways of loving God or he is criticizing the false piety of the Sadducees who are devoted to their liturgical and cultic practices while failing to love their neighbor. According to Matthew 22:38–39, Jesus was speaking to Pharisees, the teachers of the law when they ask which commandment is the greatest. Jesus eliminates any possible tension between loving God and loving one's neighbor, by equating the two: "the second is like (*homoia*) it, and the whole Law and Prophets hang on these two command-ments." In Matthew the two commandments are not ranked as first and second but simply listed and equated. This is what Paul does in Romans 13 and Galatians 5 as well.

[18] Romans 13:9 is a summation of ten commandments (v. 10 says "love is the fulfillment of the law"; see also James 2:8 the "royal law" as loving your neighbor).

[19] P. Stuhlmacher, "The Law as a Topic of Biblical Theology," in *Reconciliation, Law, Righteousness: Essays in Biblical Theology* (Philadelphia: Fortress, 1986), p. 126.

[20] Romans 15:1, 2 Corinthians 4:17 and 1 Thessalonians 2:7 suggest this meaning also. The spiritual community has the responsibility to support one another, though Galatians 6:5 will also add that each individual "will have to bear his own load (*phortion*)."

[21] Other New Testament texts define early Christian communities with the word *"nomos,"* connoting a Jewish understanding of their Christian convictions, rather than just meaning "principle" or "norm." E.g., Romans 3:27 refers to the "law of faith" (*nomou pisteôs*); Romans 8:2: "the law of the Spirit of life in Christ Jesus"; James 1:25: the "perfect law" (*nomon teleion*) and the "law of freedom;" and James 2:8: the "royal law" (*nomon basilikon*; 2:8).

[22] H. D. Betz, *Galatians: A Commentary on Paul's Letter to the Churches in Galatia* (Philadelphia: Fortress Press, 1979), p. 275.

[23] Dieter Georgi, "God Turned Upside Down," in *Paul and Empire. Religion and Power in Roman Imperial Society* (ed. Richard A. Horsley; Harrisburg: Trinity Press International, 1997), p. 155.

11

Christianity and Buddhism

Significant Points of Contact and their Missional Implications

Sung Wook Chung

1. Introduction

Buddhism is one of the major religions. It enjoys about 400 million adherents all over the world.[1] According to a recent survey, we have more than one million Buddhists in the USA, and Buddhism is rapidly growing in the West.[2] In this context, we may raise a question: What does Jesus have to do with the Buddha? What kind of attitude should we, as Christians, maintain toward Buddhism and the Buddhists? In relation to these questions, one may put forward three possible options.

The first option is total separation and condemnation. Many conservative Christians maintain implicitly and explicitly the separatist or oppositional attitude toward other religions including Buddhism. They argue that Jesus has nothing to do with the Buddha because Buddhism is a product of demonic power working in the heart and mind of the Buddha. Therefore, according to them, Christians should reject unhesitatingly and unconditionally the truth claims of Buddhism. Engagement with Buddhism may lead Christians to fall into the hands of the Devil's deception. Those who advocate this model believe that Christianity is absolutely contradictory to Buddhism. So, the only possible attitude that Christians can maintain toward Buddhism is separation and condemnation.[3]

The second model is religious pluralism. According to those who espouse the ideology of religious pluralism,[4] Buddhism has equal access to the ultimate truth. Buddhism and Christianity are equal partners on their way to salvation and the truth. Therefore, Buddhism and Christianity are not mutually exclusive or contradictory, but rather complementary. Buddhism expounds one aspect of the truth, and Christianity delves into the other aspect of the truth. Buddhism and Christianity are common seekers of the truth and liberation. Therefore, Christians must not take pride in their having the unique position and privilege in relation to the truth. Christians must accept the Buddhists as equal partners on the path of seeking the ultimate truth and meaning.

I personally believe that both of these two models are problematic. The first model is inadequate. We should never be separated from Buddhism and the Buddhists because we are commanded to love even our enemies and to be witnesses of Christ to the ends of the earth. We should share the good news of Jesus Christ even with the Buddhists. If we separate ourselves from them, we commit the sin of not obeying the great commission and great commandment. We are commanded to be the salt and light of the world. This means that we are commanded to be the salt and light for the Buddhists as well.

The second model is not proper, either. Christians are those who accept our Lord's absolute claim that "I am the way and the truth and the life. No one comes to the Father except through me" (John 14:6). So, Christians are those who affirm the absolute uniqueness of Jesus Christ as the only savior and Lord for all humanity. This affirmation of the uniqueness of Jesus Christ leads Christians to reject the pluralistic option because religious pluralism is squarely opposed to the finality of Jesus Christ.

We have the third model, and I believe that it is the best way. The relevant question is how we can maintain the uniqueness of Christian faith without endorsing religious pluralism and how we can share the gospel of Jesus Christ without separating ourselves from those who are committed to other religions. I would like to call this third model "a missional model."[5] The missional model is a position that allows Christians to explore the possible points of contact between Christianity and other religions and to employ these points of contact to share the gospel with those who are adherents of other religions.[6] This paper is an attempt to apply this missional model to the case of Buddhism.

2. Fundamental Differences Between the Christian Worldview and the Buddhist Worldview

Before we discuss the points of contact between Christianity and Buddhism, we should keep in mind that the Christian worldview is fundamentally different from the Buddhist worldview. First of all, Christianity is a theistic religion, which affirms a personal God as the ultimate reality behind everything. The God of Christians is viewed as the creator, sustainer, and ruler of the entire universe and history. In addition, the God of the Bible is the one who is both transcendent over and immanent in everything. He has his own plan and purpose toward the universe, and works in order to accomplish his own goal throughout the entire human history. The God of Christians desires to have a personal relationship with human beings who have been created in accordance with the *imago Dei* even after they fell from their original and glorious state. Human beings are the essential objects of God's concern and they take a central place in God's economy of salvation.

However, the Buddha did never believe in the existence of a personal God, who is the ultimate reality behind everything and transcendent over the universe. Therefore, Buddhism is a non-theistic religion. Although we can find a savior figure, Amida Buddha,[7] in Pure Land Buddhism, this savior is not the ultimate reality that creates, sustains, and rules over the whole universe.

The second point of difference between Christianity and Buddhism lies in the fact that Christianity affirms that God created the universe and therefore he is distinct from the universe. The absolute and sharp distinction between the creator and the creation is one of major implications of the Christian doctrine of creation. When this distinction is blurred, all kinds of confusions including idolatry and self-glorification can be brought about. The Christian doctrine of creation also implies that the universe has the beginning and the end and thus human history is not identified with a cyclical and endless process, but rather a linear progress, which has the definite starting and ending point.

In contrast, Buddhism does never teach the idea of creation of the universe. The universe has not been created, but rather has ever existed without any beginning point. Besides, the universe will not have any ending point, but exist forever and ever. Therefore, for the Buddhists, human history is not a linear progress from creation to the last judgment, but rather an endless and cyclical process.

It seems to me that these two fundamental differences between Christianity and Buddhism cannot be easily harmonized or dismissed. It is because the doctrine of creation is essential to the identity and authenticity of the Christian faith. The confession that God is not only the creator but also the ruler of the universe has been one of the most essential articles of Christian faith throughout the history of the Christian church. In addition, the affirmation that history has begun with God's creation and will end with the second coming and the last judgment of our Lord Jesus Christ has been one of the most fundamental tenets of Christian faith.

The third point of difference between Christianity and Buddhism lies in the fact that Christianity affirms the absolute uniqueness of Jesus Christ, the Son of God, as the only Lord and savior of humanity. Jesus Christ himself taught this truth by saying, "I am the way and the truth and the life. No one comes to the Father except through me" (John 14:6). This statement confirms that Jesus Christ is the only and absolute way to God the Father and the unique mediator between God and human beings. The apostle Peter also confirms this truth by saying, "salvation is found in no one else, for there is no other name under heaven given to men by which we must be saved" (Acts. 4:12). This statement affirms that it was an apostolic consensus that Christ alone can save sinners and the salvation in Christ alone is the true and genuine salvation.

However, Buddhism does not teach the uniqueness of Christ for salvation. The Christian affirmation of the absolute uniqueness of Christ as the only mediator and savior seems to be a stumbling block against most Buddhists. The Christian idea of the savior itself seems to be scandalous because most Buddhists believe that they are their own saviors and do not need any savior outside of themselves. Of course, as I have already mentioned in the above, Pure Land Buddhism has been teaching that Amida Buddha plays a role as a savior, who helps the Buddhists in their pursuit for liberation and salvation. However, Amida Buddha is neither identified with the only mediator between humanity and the ultimate reality nor with the Son of the ultimate reality.

The differences between Christianity and Buddhism are inevitable and undeniable. It seems that we have not only differences but also contradictions between Christianity and Buddhism. This means that both Christianity and Buddhism cannot be true at the same time. If Christianity is true, then Buddhism must be false. If Buddhism is true, then Christianity must be false. It seems that there may be no way to harmonize these two different belief systems. If you want to harmonize their teachings and beliefs, dismissing their fundamental differences and contradictions, it will inevitably result in either compromising of the truth claims of both religions or a scandalous and monstrous construction of syncretistic systems.

However, it is important to appreciate that this should not prevent Christians from exploring the ways to share the gospel of Jesus Christ with the Buddhists. Is there any way for us to overcome the impasse between the worldviews of Christianity and Buddhism? How can Christians be faithful to their Lord's missional commission in introducing the gospel to the Buddhists? How can Christians obey faithfully their Lord's command to love the Buddhists? Although the Buddhists uphold a belief system different from and contradictory to Christian faith, Christians are under obligation to demonstrate their love toward the Buddhists by sharing the gospel of Jesus Christ, which is the greatest gift available in the world.

3. Significant Points of Contact Between Christianity and Buddhism

In response to the above questions, I would like to argue that there are several significant points of contact between Christianity and Buddhism in spite of their fundamental differences and contradictions. If Christians identify and make the best use of these points of contact in an endeavor to build a bridge to faith for the Buddhists, they can have a meaningful and fruitful dialogue with them. These points of contact can play a role as the point of departure of the dialogue between Christians and the Buddhists. Furthermore, in the process of the dialogue, they can help Christians draw Buddhists' attention to the gospel of Jesus Christ and lead them to rethink and reevaluate the truth claims of Christian faith.

3.1 The first maxim of the Four Noble Truths

One of the major points of contact that we can identify is the Buddhist insight into human reality. Buddhism has a profound insight into the reality of human life and the world. According to the Buddhist tradition, after his Enlightenment, the Buddha began to teach the truth about *duhkha*, suffering. Buddha's teaching about suffering was summarized by the Noble Fourfold Truth or the Four Noble Truths. Although there are many different philosophical traditions within Buddhism, the Four Noble Truths are regarded as the central teaching of the Buddha that determines the very identity of Buddhism.

According to the first maxim of the Four Noble Truths of Buddhism, human life inevitably involves suffering. Human life is bound up with frustration. Concerning the truth of suffering, Buddha said,

> The Noble Truth of Suffering (*duhkha*) is this: birth is suffering; aging is suffering; sickness is suffering; death is suffering; sorrow and lamentation, pain, grief and despair are suffering; association with the unpleasant is suffering; dissociation from the pleasant is suffering; not to get what one wants is suffering – in brief, the five aggregations of attachment are suffering.[8]

Life is filled with grief, unfulfilled desires, sickness, old age, physical pain, mental anguish, and frustration. Human life is characterized by trouble, sorrow, vanity, and meaninglessness. The Buddhist picture of human life is dark and gloomy. According to John M. Koller, "*Duhkha* has a deeper meaning of 'unsatisfactoriness'."[9] For the Buddha, unsatisfactoriness comes not only from ordinary suffering but also from the endless and vicious cycle of birth, death, and rebirth (*samsara*), which conditions and oppresses human life.

In this context, it is important to appreciate that the Christian ideas of the fall, sin, curse, and corruption have something in common with this Buddhist picture of the reality of human life. According to the Christian Scripture, human life itself is filled with vanity, suffering, and frustration. For example, the King Solomon declares, "Meaningless! Meaningless! ... Utterly meaningless! Everything is meaningless"! (Eccl. 1:2) Moses also states, "the length of our days is seventy years – or eighty, if we have the strength; yet their span is but trouble and sorrow, for they quickly pass, and we fly away" (Ps. 90:10). The apostle Paul also makes a significant remark about the reality of the fallen creation, "For the creation was subjected to frustration, not by its own choice, but by the will of the one who subjected it, in hope that the creation itself will be liberated from its bondage to decay and brought into the glorious freedom of the children of God" (Rom. 8:20–21). The Bible clearly teaches that sin has brought human beings the curses of suffering, vanity, and frustration. In addition, according to the Bible, sin will eventually lead human beings to the eternal condemnation and death in hell if their sins are not forgiven.

On the basis of the above discussion, we can conclude that the ideas of frustration, suffering, and the meaninglessness of human life can be significant and substantial points of contact between Christianity and Buddhism. Both religions describe negatively the reality of human life: human beings are enslaved to decay, suffering, and despair. Therefore, when Christians approach the Buddhists to share the gospel of Jesus Christ, we can make the best use of this idea of sufferings in human life. We can tell the Buddhists that the Christian view of human life is similar to their view of human life. Furthermore, we can emphasize that Christianity also teaches the meaninglessness, unsatisfactoriness, frustration, and suffering that are inherent to human life. Probably, most Buddhists will welcome and consent to the Christian idea of the vanity of human life apart from God and Jesus Christ. This consent may lead them to open their hearts to the message of the Christian gospel.

3.2 The second maxim of the Four Noble Truths

There is another significant point of contact between Christianity and Buddhism. According to the second maxim of the Four Noble Truths of Buddhism, suffering and frustration originate in human desires and attachment – desires for sensory pleasures, for fame and fortune, and attachment to impermanent things. Concerning the second maxim of the Four Noble Truths, the Buddha said,

> The Noble Truth of the origin of suffering is this: It is this 'thirst' (craving; *trishna*) which produces re-existence and re-becoming, bound up with passionate greed. It finds fresh delight now here and now there, namely, thirst for sense-pleasures; thirst for existence and becoming; and thirst for nonexistence (self-annihilation).[10]

So, Buddhism condemns human desires and attachment to the world because those desires and attachments bring human beings frustration and sufferings. Buddhism also affirms that the world is impermanent (*anicca*) and passing away. "There is no existence that is either permanent or separate. All existence is of the nature of interdependent arising; all things are constantly changing and interrelated with all other forms of existence."[11] There is nothing permanent and constant in the creation. Everything is in flux and in the process of vanishing. Human life itself is bound up with the meaningless, vicious, and endless cycle of birth, death, and rebirth (*samsara*). On account of their ignorance of the true reality of the world, human beings have craving and thirst for a "separate and permanent self to be attained through attachment to the various processes of existence."[12]

It is important to note here that Christian faith also condemns the evil and selfish desires because they separate us from God. For example, the apostle John declares, "Do not love the world or anything in the world. If anyone loves the world, the love of the Father is not in him. For everything in the world – the cravings of sinful man, the lust of his eyes and the boasting of what he has and does – comes not from the Father but from the world. The world and its desires pass away, but the man who does the will of God lives forever" (1 John 2:15–17). The apostle Paul also affirms that greed is idolatry, which means that when we are greedy about something, we worship it rather than God, who alone deserves our worship and praise. In line with Buddhism, Christian faith condemns the selfish desires of and attachment to the world because the world and its desires inevitably pass away and our love of the world separates us from the love of God the Father. Our selfish desires are a result of our attempt to be independent of God, our creator, sustainer, and ruler although we are ever dependent on Him in reality. Our love of the world demonstrates that we depreciate and dismiss deliberately the fact that we must live under the command of God, the ruler of the universe.

On the basis of the above discussion on the commonality between Christianity and Buddhism, we can conclude that the Buddhist condemnation of selfish desires and attachment can be a significant and substantial point of contact between Christianity and Buddhism. Of course, there must be a significant difference between the Christian understanding of selfish desires and the Buddhist understanding of the selfish craving. For Christians, selfish desires of the world are the product of moral evil within human hearts and they lead human beings to idolatry and self-glorification. In contrast, for the Buddhists, selfish craving is a product of human ignorance of the true reality of the world and leads human beings to frustration and despair.

However, it is still undeniable that both Christianity and Buddhism condemn selfish attachment to the world. Therefore, when we, as Christians, approach the Buddhists with the intention to share the gospel with them, we can make the best use of this point of contact. We can inform the Buddhists that

Christian faith also condemns human attachment to the world and encourages people to remove their selfish desires. We can also let the Buddhists know that Christianity teaches the ultimate impermanence of the world. We can tell the Buddhists that Christians believe the present world is passing away and under God's condemnation. The recognition of the commonality between Christianity and Buddhism may lead the Buddhists to open their mind and heart to the gospel message of Christianity. Although the fundamental reason why Buddhism condemns human selfish craving may be different from the major reason why Christianity condemns human selfish desires, we cannot deny that their condemnation of human selfish craving and desire can be a significant point of contact of which Christians may make the best use in making the Buddhists open their hearts to the gospel of Christ.

3.3 The third maxim of the Four Noble Truths

We have another significant point of contact between Christianity and Buddhism. According to the third maxim of the Four Noble Truths of Buddhism, suffering will cease if all desires cease. Concerning the removal of desires, the Buddha said,

> The Noble Truth of the Cessation of Suffering is this: It is the complete cessation of that very thirst (craving), giving it up, renouncing it, emancipating oneself from it, detaching oneself from it.[13]

When all desires cease, illusion ends and ultimate reality, or nirvana is revealed. Buddhism not only condemns desires, but also attempts to remove desires. Removal and elimination of desires is the way to liberation or nirvana.

We can find here a point of contact between Christianity and Buddhism. Christianity also teaches that we should put off all kinds of evil desires in order to put on the righteousness of Christ. We should remove the old garment of evil and the desires of the flesh in order to put on the new self in Jesus Christ. Augustine was strongly impacted by the apostle Paul's statement, the night is nearly over; the day is almost here. So let us put aside the deeds of darkness and put on the armor of light. Let us behave decently, as in the daytime, not in orgies and drunkenness, not in sexual immorality and debauchery, not in dissension and jealousy. Rather, clothe yourselves with the Lord Jesus Christ, and do not think about how to gratify the desires of the sinful nature. (Rom. 13:12–14)

The Word of God demands that Christians should put aside the desires of the sinful nature and be clothed with the Lord Jesus Christ.

I believe that this can be an excellent point of contact between Christianity and Buddhism. When Christians approach the Buddhists that are struggling with the task of removing their selfish desires, we can sympathize with them and inform them that we are undergoing the same struggle. We can tell them that Christianity is a religion whose main purpose is not to preserve the old life style, but to bring meaningful change and transformation to our life. Most sincere Buddhists will probably respond positively to such a presentation of Christianity. They may realize that Christians are struggling with the same or at least similar problems. This may lead the Buddhists to open their ears to the message of the gospel of Jesus Christ.

3.4 The fourth maxim of the Four Noble Truths

We have another important point of contact between Christianity and Buddhism. According to the fourth maxim of the Four Noble Truths, the way to eliminate *duhkha* is to practice the Noble Eightfold Path. Concerning the way to cessation of suffering, the Buddha said,

> The Noble Truth of the Path leading to the cessation of suffering is this: It is simply the Noble Eightfold Path, namely, right view; right thought; right speech; right action; right livelihood; right effort; right mindfulness; right concentration.[14]

By making this statement, the Buddha insists that the Noble Eightfold Path is the way to remove selfish craving and cease suffering. When the Buddhists practice these eight ways of moral cultivation, they can lead to nirvana or liberation from suffering and frustration.

It is important to appreciate here that Christianity also urges Christians to focus on moral cultivation as the way to sanctification of their souls. The ways to sanctification for Christians are similar to the ways to nirvana for the Buddhists. The Bible also teaches the importance of right intention, right speech, right action, right liveliness, right effort, and so on. According to the Bible, Christians are commanded to speak truthfully to their neighbor (Eph. 4:25) and "not to let any unwholesome talk come out of your mouths, but only what is helpful for building others up according to their needs, that it may benefit those who listen" (Eph. 4:29). Besides, the Bible also teaches about right livelihood: "He who has been stealing must steal no longer, but must work, doing something useful with his own hands, that he may have something to share with those in need" (Eph. 4:28). Furthermore, the Bible is not silent about the importance of right action, right intention, and right effort.

Of course, the reason why the Bible emphasizes the necessity and importance of right speech and right action may be fundamentally different from the reason why Buddhism stresses the essentiality of the Noble Eightfold Path in the Buddhist life. However, it is undeniable that the idea of moral cultivation in Buddhism is deeply similar to that of Christianity.

Therefore, when we, as Christians, approach the Buddhists in order to share the gospel with them, we can make every effort to employ these similarities and commonalities between Christianity and Buddhism. These similarities can play a role as the significant points of contact between the two religions. When we employ them wisely, they can make a significant contribution to removing the Buddhist fear of Christianity and leading the Buddhists to open their hearts to the message of Christianity.

3.5 Bodhisattva

In Mahayana Buddhism, we can find another significant point of contact with Christianity. It is the idea of *Bodhisattva*. A

Bodhisattiva is a Buddhist believer who is dedicated to attaining enlightenment and to helping other people in their pursuit of enlightenment. According to a statement about the compassion of the Bodhisattva,

> A Bodhisattva resolves: I take upon my self the burden of suffering. I am resolved to do so, I will endure it. I do not turn or run away, do not tremble, am not terrified, nor afraid, do not turn back or despond. And why, At all costs, I must bear the burdens of all beings. In that I do not follow my own inclinations. I have made the vow to save all beings. All beings I must set free. The whole world of living beings I must rescue, from the terrors of birth, of old age, of sickness, of death and rebirth, of all kinds of moral offense, of all states of woe ...[15]

Bodhisattvas are usually viewed as mature Buddhists who have accumulated sufficient merits to enter nirvana. They can help other people achieve enlightenment either by transferring them some of their own merit or by taking on themselves the burden of their suffering. In addition to these earthly *Bodhisattvas*, according to the Mahayanan tradition, there are numerous heavenly *Bodhisattvas* who hear the pleas of those who are suffering and worshippers can pray to them for help. Among especially popular *Bodhisattvas* are Avalokiteshvara (the Buddha of mercy) and Maitreya (the messianic Buddha).

The Buddhist idea of heavenly *Bodhisattva* seems to have a commonality with the Christian idea of the mediator between God and humanity. A heavenly *Bodhisattva* can transfer his or her own merit to the seekers of enlightenment and take on himself or herself the burden of their suffering. This reminds Christians of the mediator Jesus Christ who takes on himself the burden of their sin and death. Although we cannot deny that there remain fundamental differences between Buddhism and Christianity in terms of their ideas of God, the world, and humanity, we, as Christians, can make the best use of the Buddhist idea of Bodhisattvahood in order to open the hearts of the Buddhists to the gospel of Jesus Christ, the only and true mediator between God and humanity.

3.6 *The Amida Buddha of Pure Land Buddhism*

In the tradition of Pure Land Buddhism, people worship Amida Buddha, the Buddha of Boundless Light, for their salvation. Amida Buddha is viewed as an ancient prince who vowed to attain enlightenment. It is believed that he created a paradise, called the Pure Land. Everyone who invokes his name even once in faith will be reborn there. When people get to the Pure Land, it will be much easier to reach nirvana from there.[16]

In Pure Land Buddhism, Amida Buddha is a savior figure. It is not moral behavior but faith in Amida Buddha that leads the Pure Land Buddhists to the paradise. It seems clear that the worship of Amida Buddha can be a significant point of contact with Christian faith. Of course, Pure Land Buddhism is not a dominant tradition in Buddhism. However, Christians may try to make the best use of the idea of the savior, Amida Buddha, in sharing the gospel of the unique Savior, Jesus Christ, with people in Pure Land Buddhism.

3.7 *The idea of karma*

The Buddhist idea of *karma* can be another significant point of contact with Christianity. The word *karma* means the consequences of human actions that are accumulated as time passes. In the Buddhist context, the consequences of human beings' negative actions make an impact upon not only this life but also lives to come. *Karma* is understood to be the energy that drives the wheel of *samsara*, the vicious and endless cycle of birth, death, and rebirth. Because human beings accumulate *karma* through their bad conducts, they are enslaved to the cycle of *samsara*. "*Karma* is a natural law of moral cause and effect": *samsara* is the effect of *karma*.[17] In order to achieve nirvana, people must be liberated from *samsara* by removing *karma*.

Christianity also teaches that human sins result in bad consequences. Sin brings us corruption, punishment, and curse; there is a causal relationship between iniquity and its bad effects. It seems undeniable that there is a significant similarity between the Christian idea of sin and the Buddhist idea of *karma*. Therefore, Christians can make the best use of this similarity as a point of contact between Christianity and Buddhism. However, it is important to understand that in order to remove *karma* and its effects, the Buddhists are urged to accumulate merits by performing moral actions. This means that in Buddhism *karma* is never atoned or removed by free grace of forgiveness. Buddhism has no parallel to the Christian idea of free justification of sinners on the basis of free forgiveness of their sins. It seems that the idea of free justification of sinners is strange to Buddhism. The idea of free remission of sins makes Christian faith unique.

However, it is still important to appreciate that when Christians embark on a dialogue with the Buddhists for the sake of evangelism, they can employ the Buddhist idea of *karma* in order to open their hearts to the Christian message. Christians can tell the Buddhists that they are struggling with a similar problem, sin, which enslaves them to do moral evil against the holy God of the universe and brings them condemnation and eternal judgment. Moreover, Christians can tell the Buddhists that although the problem of sin is insurmountable through their own effort, they have the savior, who paid the penalty for their sins by tasting the judgment of God and eternal death on behalf of them. Furthermore, Christians can also inform that on the basis of the sacrificial death of the savior, free forgiveness of sins is available to anybody who receives the savior as his or her Lord. Most sincere Buddhists who agonize over their problem of *karma* and their inability to remove it may feel attracted to this presentation of the gospel of Christ.

4. Merit and Limitation of the Points of Contact

On the basis of the above discussion, we may conclude that there are significant and substantial points of contact between Christianity and Buddhism, and we, as Christians, can identify and employ these points of contact in sharing the gospel with the Buddhists. However, we need to remember an important truth here. The points of contact remain the points of contact; they have both merit and limitation. Although Christians can agree with the Buddhists at many points, we should tell them our solution is fundamentally different from theirs.

The best example would be our Christian response to the fourth maxim of the Four Noble Truths of Buddhism. According to the fourth maxim, there is a way to realize the state of liberation from suffering and frustration or nirvana. It is the way of a life of morality, concentration, and wisdom. This way of moral life is epitomized by the Noble Eightfold Path including right understanding, right thought, right speech, right action, right livelihood, right effort, right mindfulness, and right meditation. So, according to the Buddhist faith, if you seek salvation from suffering by practicing the Noble Eightfold Path, then you can remove your desires and attachment, and realize the state of liberation and nirvana.

At this point, the commonality between Christianity and Buddhism eventually ends. Although Christians can appreciate the sincerity of those Buddhists who are practicing this style of moral life, we cannot endorse it as a way of salvation. It is because Buddhism, in spite of its good intentions and insights, remains a self-salvific scheme, which elevates human power and ability. As a self-salvific scheme, Buddhism remains an impossible human attempt to save themselves from the pit of suffering, vanity, and frustration through their own works, which both Jesus Christ and the apostle Paul reject outright.

Therefore, we need to remember that our endeavor to identify and explore the points of contact between Christianity and Buddhism should never be allowed to prevent us from presenting a solid and clear message of the gospel of Jesus Christ. In particular, in the face of the Buddhist self-salvific scheme, we should be able to present the pure gospel of grace, which promises the free gift of salvation and unconditional forgiveness of our sins. Exploration and employment of the possible points of contact between Christianity and Buddhism can never be incompatible with the clear and distinct presentation of the gospel of pure grace as an endeavor to save lost souls from their predicament.

On the contrary, our endeavor to explore and employ any possible contact points between Christianity and Buddhism will enhance the possibility for leading those Buddhists to pay their attention to the gospel message and to eventually accept the Lord of the gospel. This is because the points of contact may make a great contribution to disarming the enmity against Christianity that the Buddhists may have instinctively. By showing that Christian faith has significant and substantial similarities to Buddhism, we can pave a better way for a successful mission among the Buddhists.

5. Conclusion

When we approach the Buddhists, we should not condemn them first. Rather, we should endeavor to understand their beliefs and thoughts. This endeavor will demonstrate our genuine concern and love for them. Our love and concern must be accompanied by an intelligent analysis of the structure of the Buddhist faith. On the basis of such an analysis, we should explore any possible points of contact between Christianity and Buddhism. We should employ these points of contact wisely in order to open their hearts and to attract them to the gospel message.

Although the points of contact have great merit, they also have limitation. Our exploration and employment of the points of contact can never guarantee automatically success in our missional task. Furthermore it can never replace our task of solid and clear presentation of the gospel of grace in the Lord Jesus Christ. However, there is no doubt that the points of contact between Christianity and Buddhism can be of great service to the essential aim of our missional work among the Buddhists if they are used wisely and in prayer.

Notes

1 *http://www.adherents.com/Religions_By_Adherents.html# Buddhism.*
2 *http://www.adherents.com/rel_USA.html#religions.*
3 Such an attitude is prevalent among Christians with extremely fundamentalist commitment.
4 See John Hick, *A Christian Theology of Religions* (Louisville, KY: Westminster/John Knox, 1995; idem, *God has Many Names* (Louisville, KY: Westminster/John Knox, 1982).

5 The word "missional" comes from Darrell L. Guder's seminal work, *Missional Chruch: A Vision for the Sending of the Church in North America* (Grand Rapids, MI: Eerdmans, 1998).

6 Alister E. McGrath emphasizes the significance of the points of contact between Christian faith and secular religious and philosophical traditions, and urges Christians to use them in their apologetic endeavor. McGrath calls his position the "creative" approach. See, idem, *Intellectuals Don't Need God & Other Modern Myths: Building Bridges to Faith through Apologetics* (Grand Rapids, MI: Zondervan, 1993), pp. 30–47, 56–65.

7 Mary Pat Fisher, *Living Religions* (Upper Saddle River, NJ: Prentice-Hall, 2002), pp. 174–76.

8 John M. Koller and Patricia Koller, *A Sourcebook in Asian Philosophy* (New York: Macmillan, 1991), pp. 195–96.

9 John M. Koller, *Asian Philosophies* (Upper Saddle River, NJ: Prentice-Hall, 2002), p. 156.

10 Koller and Koller, *Sourcebook in Asian Philosophy*, pp. 195–96.

11 Koller, *Asian Philosophies*, p. 157.

12 Koller, *Asian Philosophies*, p. 157.

13 Koller, *Asian Philosophies*, p. 159.

14 Koller and Koller, *Sourcebook in Asian Philosophy*, pp. 195–96.

15 Edward Conze et al., *Buddhist Texts Through the Ages* (trans. Edward Conze; Oxford: Bruno Cassirer, 1954), pp. 131–32.

16 T. Patrick Burke, *The Major Religions: An Introduction with Texts* (Oxford: Blackwell, 2000), pp. 74–75.

17 Joseph A. Adler, *Chinese Religious Traditions* (Upper Saddle River, NJ: Prentice-Hall, 2002), p. 74.

Beyond the Impasse:
Toward a Pneumatological
Theology of Religions

Amos Yong

Christian discussions have often not got beyond the question: 'Can non-Christians be saved?' The task of producing an encompassing theology of religions – a robustly theological account of the nature, role, and purposes of the diversity of religions – remains to be done.

Beyond the Impasse sketches a way forward by suggesting a pneumatological (i.e., Spirit-focused) approach. Yong writes that holding together the claim that the Spirit is present everywhere and the claim that he is still the Spirit of Christ guides us to a distinctively Christian way of understanding and engaging religious 'otherness'. Yong's theology allows for the work of the Spirit in non-Christian religions and the presence of other spirits. It opens the way for inter-religious dialogue in which there can be transformation on both sides through the encounter without surrendering claims about the uniqueness of Christ.

In critical dialogue with others who have begun but never fully developed a pneumatological theology of religions – including Georges Khodr, Stanley Samartha, Jacques Dupuis, and Clark Pinnock – Yong offers a comprehensive framework for such a project from biblical, theological, and philosophical perspectives.

ISBN: 84227-208-X

Alister McGrath and Evangelical Theology

Sung Wook Chung (ed)

Alister E. McGrath has had a tremendous impact on the renaissance of evangelical theology over the last twenty years. Regarded as one of the most influential and significant theologians alive in world Christianity, his theological work and writings have made an immense contribution to the vitality and dynamics of evangelical theology.

This book invites evangelical theologians from various backgrounds to demonstrate the appeal and attraction of evangelical theology. Part One follows the theology of McGrath on justification, redemption, theology and science and post-liberal theology, whilst Part Two encompasses the essence, character, identity, methodology and future of evangelical theology. Evangelical theology is not a theological movement in isolation, but a movement in dialogue with other theological camps such as narrative theology, divine openness and religious pluralism.

With contributions from Graham Tomlin, Gerald Bray, Clark Pinnock, Gabriel Fackre, Andrew Goddard, William Abraham, and a response given by McGrath himself, this collection of groundbreaking essays will encourage evangelical theologians worldwide to think over our legacy, resources and responsibility towards the dynamic and vital future of evangelical theology.

ISBN 1-84227-202-0